D0596985

Father

The Figure and the Force

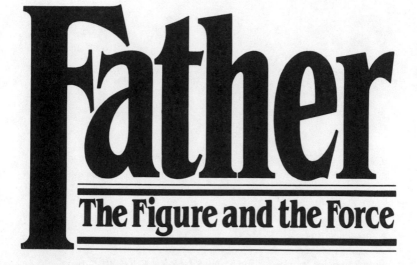

Father

The Figure and the Force

Christopher P. Andersen

WARNER BOOKS

A Warner Communications Company

Copyright © 1983 by Christopher P. Andersen
All rights reserved.
Warner Books, Inc., 666 Fifth Avenue, New York, NY 10103

W A Warner Communications Company

Printed in the United States of America
First printing: September 1983
10 9 8 7 6 5 4 3 2 1

Book design: H. Roberts Design

Library of Congress Cataloging in Publication Data

Andersen, Christopher P.
    Father, the figure and the force.

    Bibliography: p.
    Includes index.
    1. Fathers. 2. Fathers—Family relationships. I. Title.
HQ756.A59 1983   306.8'742   83-42691
ISBN 0-446-51256-7

For my father, Edward Francis Andersen,
and for his granddaughter, Kate

CONTENTS

ACKNOWLEDGMENTS

It happened during my interviews with Katharine Hepburn and Henry Fonda, and again with Dan Rather and Sophia Loren. They were among the many celebrities who went out of their way to tell me about how profoundly they had been influenced by their fathers, and how seldom anyone had bothered to ask about their fathers. How often, I wondered, did most of us dare to ask *ourselves* about our fathers? In recent years, bookstore shelves have bowed under the weight of best sellers decrying the plight of working mothers, housebound wives, middle-aged divorcées, lonely singles, and adolescents suffering every psychological disorder from anorexia nervosa to suicidal depression.

But what about Dad? He is, at the very least, usually the second most important figure in our early lives, and yet we are loath to examine our sometimes turbulent, always powerful feelings toward him. Of all family members, he is the one about whom we know the least—and from whom we often demanded the most. He was invariably the one who fed us, clothed us, scrambled for the mortgage payments, and sent us through school. He was also three times more likely than our mothers to develop heart disease, four times more likely to wind up with an ulcer and, on the average, stood to live seven years less than Mom. Throughout our lives with him, we may never have paused to question whether this was just—not even when our parents divorced and Father, barred then from even the possibility of being granted custody of his children, was nonetheless obliged to pay for their support. This is the way things were and, to a great extent, still are.

Becoming a parent opens a window on the past as well as the future. It was not until my first child was born in September of 1980 that I began to see the truth: In order to truly know myself, I must truly know my father. In all cases, a father's legacy is complex. Much of what is good about us came from him, but so, too, did many of our anxieties, fears, guilts, doubts, and neuroses.

To sort it all out, I interviewed scores of men and women—many famous and many not—about their relationships with their fathers. I also tapped the leading experts in the field for their personal and professional insights. First, however, I owe a particular debt of gratitude to my editor, Nansey Neiman of Warner Books, to Jonathan Lazear, and to my agent, Ellen Levine, for their encouragement, guidance, and support.

My special thanks to Michael Maccoby, director of the Harvard Program for Technology, Public Policy and Human Development at the John F. Kennedy School of Government, faculty member of the Washington School of Psychiatry, and author of *The Gamesman* and *The Leader;* Lionel Tiger, professor of anthropology at Rutgers University and author of *Men in Groups;* Eda LeShan, noted psychologist and author; Dr. T. Berry Brazelton, director of the Child Development Unit of Children's Hospital Medical Center in Boston; John Munder Ross, clinical associate professor of psychology, State University of New York, and assistant professor of psychology in psychiatry, Cornell University Medical College; Dr. Richard Robertiello, senior training consultant at the Long Island Institute of Mental Health and author of *Man in the Making;* Dr. Joyce Brothers; David Halberstam; Susan Brownmiller; Florence Rush; Gay Talese; Erica Jong; and Erma Bombeck.

My wife, Valerie, as always proved an exacting critic and proofreader—not to mention a pillar of patience and understanding. Along with our daughter, Kate, she tried to help me see what it means to be a daughter, and in the process made me understand what it means to be a dad. As for my sister, Valerie, my mother, Jeanette. and my father, Edward Andersen, there can be no ample way of expressing my feelings toward them. *Father: The Figure and the Force* is a first step. This is their story.

Christopher P. Andersen
New York City

The Child is father of the Man.

—William Wordsworth,
"Ode: Intimations of Immortality"

And as I hung up the phone, it occurred to me
He'd grown up just like me.
My boy was just like
Me.

—Harry Chapin,
"Cat's in the Cradle"

Father

The Figure and the Force

CHAPTER I

Fatherhood at the Crossroads

I love my father, yes. But it has taken half a lifetime to explain to myself how that is possible when like nearly everyone else, I barely know the man and, I suspect, vice versa. Whether we admit it to ourselves or not, that sorry state of affairs is common. Dad may be domineering or passive, generous or stingy, garrulous or aloof, mean-spirited or kind-hearted, confident or reticent, calculating or quixotic. He can be the ditchdigger who settles disputes with the wisdom of Solomon and holds his family together with the mortar of his own morality. Or he can be the $200,000-a-year corporate officer who is emotionally capsized by the tiniest domestic swell. He can be as handsome as Gable and as charming as Cary Grant, or have all the appeal and personality of a pet rock. But whatever his characteristics, Father is invariably one thing: alone.

There is an imaginary scene that Nancy Friday describes in her pathfinding account of a daughter's search for identity, *My Mother/My Self*. In the scene, Friday's mother sits her down and confesses that she really is not all that clear that she's cut out for "this mothering business." I cannot even imagine such a scene with my father, and I doubt very much whether many people can. That vignette

1

presupposes some clear definition or at least tacit agreement about what constitutes "fathering business." Society, unfortunately, holds fathers in such low regard that it has not even bothered to define their emotional responsibilities. Whatever uneasiness my father may have felt about his relationship with my younger sister and me, those doubts sprang from within—and not because of any obvious clash with a perceptible norm. Accordingly, he was left to sort out those doubts for himself, to come up with his own answers. For even though a father's legacy profoundly colors the lives of his sons and daughters to a degree that must approximate if not equal (and in some cases transcend) a mother's influence, we are woefully reluctant to acknowledge that fact, much less try to understand it.

Indeed, the father-child bond has always been shrouded in mystery, obscured by the Norman Rockwell image of the benign patriarch at the head of the dinner table. But that was not the case for many of us. And while simple biological closeness to our mothers at least made it possible to come to terms with our feelings toward that parent, fathers are so emotionally estranged, so distant from the onset, that we are never even asked to recognize the inner conflicts arising from that most basic human bond.

"We experience a vague sense of embarrassment when we're asked how we feel about our fathers," says Harvard psychiatrist Michael Maccoby, author of the best-selling *Gamesman*. "Mother represents love; father is the model for the outside world—the prototypical stranger that we as children must prove ourselves to. When we are first toilet-trained, Daddy is the first 'outsider' before whom we proudly display our newfound talent. You can always express love for your mother, but your father represents accomplishment; when we become adults we feel we are not independent if we haven't cut the ties that bind us to Dad." There is another role fathers play that may heighten tensions even long after we have left the nest. "A two-year-old must express anger in a way that is not overtly destructive," says Maccoby. "Wrestling and roughhousing with Dad provide the first healthy outlet for rage and aggression." Dad as stranger. Dad as punching bag. Hardly an auspicious start to one of the most important relationships in our lives.

Noted child psychologist Eda LeShan argues that distance between father and child is not necessarily unhealthy: "We are all much closer to our mother, not just because she bore us, but because that is the way our culture wants it. Until very recently, men had not been given permission to be nurturing, and since they were not available for the child's emotional needs, the mother was left to do the worrying. But," she points out, "this situation merely adds to the sense of awe and respect we have for our fathers—and that can be just as deep." Concurs sociologist Florence Rush, author of *The Best Kept Secret: Sexual Abuse of Children:* "It's not necessarily bad for a father to keep his distance. The more removed he is the more likely we are to have a positive image of him. The trouble comes if these fantasies get out of hand. As we grow up they can darken with reality, and the result is psychological pain and anxiety for both father and adult child."

Annie Hall Oscar-winner Diane Keaton is devoted to her mother, but it is her father about whom she has the fondest memories. "I was not close to my father," she concedes, "but he was very special to me. Whenever I did something as a little girl—learn to swim or act in a school play, for instance—he was fabulous. There would be this certain look in his eyes. It made me feel great." Keaton's father, Jack, a civil engineer in the southern California town of Santa Ana, had been a diving champion at the University of Southern California and instilled a love for the beach in the oldest of his four children (three daughters and a son). Diane, painfully shy as an adolescent, stuck close to home. "I was what you call a late bloomer. All the girls around me were getting breasts! My reaction was to spend more time at home." A strong memory from this period occurred one hot afternoon when the Keatons piled into the family station wagon and headed for the beach. Diane ran up to her father and blurted out, "Hey, Dad, don't you worry about me, I'm not going to grow up. None of that stuff is going to happen to me, I'll just stay the same and everything will be fine." He looked up at her, smiled, and said, "Oh, Diane, no. I think you'll have to grow up." Diane remembers her reaction: "The wind was knocked out of me. It's hard to explain what I felt. Some kind of terrible loneliness."

If Diane's father effectively played the part of Maccoby's "prototypic stranger" and LeShan's awesome authority figure, many years later he would still be lending her moral support. When Keaton was upset about baring her breasts in the steamy *Looking for Mr. Goodbar,* she called Jack for reassurance. "Don't worry," he told her. "They're just a couple of globs of fat on your chest."

Noted anthropologist Lionel Tiger, a professor at Rutgers University Graduate School and author of the landmark *Men in Groups,* is convinced those "globs" are what will always relegate fathers to a second-place position in the family. Tiger insists a father's battle for equality as a parent is lost from the beginning. "All things being equal, the mother is clearly more important. We are mammals and a mammal survives by feeding off its mother. She will always have the edge."

Norman Rockwell's turkey-carving patriarch, William Powell glowering over his newspaper in *Life with Father,* and a pre-Sankafied Robert Young coping valiantly with the kids in TV's *Father Knows Best*—all contributed to the image of Father as flawed autocrat, not an alien but not exactly one of us, either.

"When I was a little kid," says columnist Erma Bombeck, "a father was like the light in the refrigerator. Every house had one, but no one really knew what either of them did once the door was shut." Now in her mid-50s and with grown children of her own, Bombeck told me that more than ever she is haunted by the memory of her father, who died in 1936. "It surprises me," she says, "but it still hurts a lot." Writing a Father's Day column about that pain was one way of sorting out her ambivalent feelings:

> My Dad left the house every morning and always seemed glad to see everyone at night.
>
> He opened the jar of pickles when no one else could.
>
> He was the only one in the house who wasn't afraid to go into the basement by himself.
>
> He cut himself shaving, but no one kissed it or got excited about it.
>
> He signed all my report cards. He put me to bed early. He took lots of pictures, but was never in them.
>
> I was afraid of everyone else's father, but not my own. Once I made him tea. It was only sugar water, but he sat on a small chair and said it was delicious. He looked very uncomfortable.
>
> Whenever I played house, the mother doll had a lot to do. I never knew what to do with the daddy doll, so I had him say, "I'm going off to work now" and threw him under the bed.
>
> When I was 9 years old, my father didn't get up one morning and go to work. He went to the hospital and died the next day.
>
> I went to my room and felt under the bed for the father doll. When I found him, I dusted him off and put him on my bed.
>
> He never did anything. I didn't know his leaving would hurt so much.
>
> I still don't know why.

However unrealistic the perceptions of fatherhood have been in the past, however little we understood his role or comprehended this impact on our lives, he was at least generally acknowledged to exist. In one popular television commercial of the 1980s a boy and a girl—presumably brother and sister—are being treated to a grand time, eating ice cream cones, swimming, going to an amusement park. "Who else takes such good care of you?" asks the announcer. "If it's not your mother," answers the jingle, "it must be Howard Johnson." Howard Johnson! Infinitely preferable are the traditional commercials that have always depicted Dad as a benign moron who must be told by his ever-patient wife and kids which dishwasher detergent or peanut butter to pick up at the supermarket. And any student of the tube will be quick to point out that it is more often than not Father who suffers from ring around the collar, bad breath, dandruff, or body odor—a clear indication of how demographically minded Madison Avenue, with its hand on the consumers' collective pulse, gauges our opinion of Dear Old Dad.

It is, in fact, one of the great myths that fathers don't mind being resented, neglected, or ignored. In looking back on theirs, many adults think of Dad as satisfied with being a person apart. When she first talked to me, Linda was 32 and had already carved out a lucrative career for herself as a corporate tax consultant. Born in a small Pennsylvania town where her father owned the only mortuary and the only ambulance service, Linda was the sole daughter in a houseful of boys. She relocated to Los Angeles as soon as she graduated from college. A strikingly beautiful brunette and an engaging personality, Linda nonetheless describes her personal life as "a shambles." She blames it all on Dad:

> Yes, he was busier than all my friends' fathers. But even when my dad was there, he wasn't there. You couldn't talk to him. There were times I would come home from school crying about what the other kids would say about what he did for a living. But he just coldly sat there in the living room reading his

afternoon paper. He'd always say, "Go ask your mother," and she would do her best to explain to me that being a mortician was an important job, and that we should be proud of Dad. Then at night I would hear my mother pleading with my father to talk to me. He never did.

Not surprisingly, Linda's resentment of her father's apparent disinterest in her state of mind grew unabated.

We lived in a small community, small enough so that my father knew many of the people whose crumpled bodies he pried out of wrecked automobiles. Many of the people he embalmed and buried had been friends of his for years. What kind of cold bastard could do that?

Linda hated even more the fact that she found herself attracted to the same sort of man:

I came to realize after several disastrous affairs that all the men I fall in love with are just like my dad physically; they are tall, athletic, handsome. Emotionally, they are close-mouthed, unfeeling, *cold*.

At about the same time she resolved to seek out lovers who were more "open and giving," Linda learned that her father had become an alcoholic. Not long after, he suffered a heart attack. She visited him at the hospital, and for the first time they talked, he lying with tubes running in and out of his body, she curled up at the foot of his bed listening to the answers she thought she would never hear.

He told me that he had been drinking ever since I was a child—something he had managed to conceal from everyone but my mother. He said that he knew if he ever started to talk to me about his life, if he ever tried to explain the way he felt, he would start crying and not be able to stop. Then he cried, and it finally dawned on me that the emotional hurt I had felt was nothing compared to his feeling of isolation. All that time I thought he didn't care, he was suffering in a hell all his own. At last I can say I love my dad, and mean it.

Remarkably similar was the experience of advertising executive Anne Holton, whose father, James, was fighting in Korea when she was a toddler and battling up the corporate ladder as soon as he returned. "I was always talking about my father the executive," Anne said, "but it was like talking about Kennedy. He was not a presence, there was no emotion, no communication. My father doesn't know how to show his feelings; he withdraws. I'm like that, too. Rather than be rejected, I rejected him first." But when she split from her lover in 1978, Anne recognized the parallels between him and her father. "I knew I could not have a relationship with others unless I dealt with my father. So I phoned my mother and cried, 'I'm twenty-eight years old, and I need my father. He has never given me anything.' Half an hour later he called Anne home for the weekend. They avoided each other all weekend, until he drove her to the airport. "I wish you liked me a little more," she told him, "because I would like to talk to you."

For the next several months they exchanged affection and anger. Now, says Anne, "I feel I've connected with a whole part of me that until now I've completely denied— as if by making friends with my father I've finally been able to make friends with myself."

Linda and Anne's long-delayed realization that their fathers were indeed human came about because they cared to pursue the matter. Not all of us, it is sad to say, do. Elton John has been estranged from his father for years, and that is apparently the way the rock star wants things to remain. A pudgy only child, Elton was born Reginald

Kenneth Dwight. He was 4 years old before he first saw his Royal Air Force squadron leader father, and foreign tours of duty kept father away from son for three of the next five years. "I made good grades and was well behaved," recalls Elton, "but I never could please my father." John vividly remembers being sent away from the dinner table by his disciplinarian dad because he made noise eating celery. "Stanley," Mrs. Dwight recalls of her husband, "wanted a girl." Hence their son, she concedes, "grew up a bundle of nerves." So much so, in fact, that in the late 1960s he stuck his head in a gas oven and even in 1977—when his personal income was estimated at $7 million—John swallowed eighty-three sleeping pills. Although he has rebounded from both suicide attempts, John traces much of his continued unhappiness to his tense relationship with his father. Unlike Linda, the rock idol emeritus shows no signs of pursuing a reconciliation.

Sometimes it is the father who seeks out the child in an effort to explain his absence—physical or otherwise—when the child thought he or she most needed him. To be sure, the answer is by no means always satisfactory. Former President Gerald R. Ford, christened Leslie L. King, Jr., took his stepfather's name after his natural parents divorced and his mother remarried. In his autobiography, *A Time to Heal,* Ford remembers receiving "the first major shock" of his life while working at Bill Skougis' luncheonette in Grand Rapids, Michigan. He was 17.

> One day at noon, I was behind the counter in my regular spot near the register when I noticed a man standing by the candy display case. He'd been there fifteen or twenty minutes without saying a word and he was staring at me. Finally he came over. "I'm Leslie King, your father," he said. "Can I take you to lunch?"
>
> I was stunned and didn't know what to say. When I

was 12 or 13, Mother had told me that Gerald R. Ford, Sr., was not my real father, but we hadn't really discussed the situation at home. I knew that the court in Omaha had ordered my father to pay her between fifty and seventy-five dollars per month child support. He hadn't paid what he owed. Until now, my father had made no attempt to get in touch with us.

I looked him in the eye. "I'm working," I said. "Ask your boss if you can get off," he persisted. Bill Skougis told me it was all right. My father took me outside to a new Lincoln. A woman was sitting inside; he introduced her as his wife.

Our talk over lunch was superficial. My father knew I was an athlete and he wanted to know how good my high school team was. Leaving the restaurant, we drove back to school, where my father handed me twenty-five dollars. "Now, you buy yourself something, something you want that you can't afford otherwise," he said. Then, with a wave, he and his wife were gone.

That night was one of the most difficult in my life. I don't recall the words I used to tell my mother and stepfather what had happened, but I do remember that the conversation was a loving and consoling one. Nothing could erase the image I gained of my real father that day: a carefree, well-to-do man who didn't really give a damn about the hopes and dreams of his firstborn son. When I went to bed that night, I broke down and cried.

It is no small quirk of fate that, having been abandoned by his own father, Ford would himself prove to be an essentially absentee father, spending an average of two hundred days on the road each year while his wife, Betty, raised their three sons and one daughter. To compound the irony, Betty Bloomer, the daughter of a traveling salesman, vowed she would never marry a man who stayed away from home for long stretches. Her first husband, Bill Warren, was constantly on the move, first as an insurance salesman, then as a salesman for Continental Can, and finally as a salesman for a furniture company. "I wonder what Dr. Freud might have had to say about it," says the former First Lady. "I loved my father, who'd gone away and left us, and here I was married to another good-looking traveling salesman." That marriage ended after five years, leaving her to wed a consummate politician whose schedule as congressman, congressional leader, vice-president, and finally president made both her father and husband number one look like shut-ins by comparison. "I love my father, but I didn't know I had a father until I was 10 or 12 years old," says Ford's daughter, Susan. "Everybody was supposed to be home for dinner Sunday night because Daddy always made a point of being home for Sunday night dinner. Well, it meant nothing to me. Just a man sitting there at the table."

Even in those instances where we are convinced that our father was a cipher, that he just wasn't there because he didn't care, both father and child are left to carry some heavy psychological luggage. Peter is a respected Manhattan urologist. He is 47, married, with a 14-year-old son— and though he would never admit it, he is clearly obsessed about his relationship (he would say nonrelationship) with his father, a wealthy dress manufacturer.

> He was a fabulously accomplished complainer, and he had a need to show off to his friends. He would give expensive presents to neighbors to impress them, but he ignored my younger brother and me. We were not allowed to listen to music because it bothered him. We never talked, and the only time he had anything to do with me was when he needed a chess partner. We played in total silence, and he always had to win. I was

afraid of my father, and in the end I just did my best to stay out of his way.

Peter's father hated doctors, and his son achieved some revenge in becoming one. But what Peter cannot explain is the fact that his father unhesitatingly paid his son's way through Harvard Medical School, and as a graduation present he made good his promise to reward Peter with a gleaming new Mercedes. "No matter. The few times I tried to reach out to my father," says Peter, "his answer was unequivocally 'No.' So I've tuned the guy out of my life as much as possible." In 1982, shortly after his eighty-first birthday, Peter's father nearly succumbed to kidney failure. "I was wishing he would die," says Peter candidly. "I was disappointed when he didn't."

It is easier for us to paint our fathers with broad brushstrokes—to see them either as demons or dieties—than it is to view them as moral and emotional equals. Item: A study released by Johns Hopkins in the winter of 1981 indicated that, while the death of a spouse does not decrease the life expectancy of a woman, a man's remaining years are cut in half by the death of his wife. The reason given by the researchers who conducted the study: Males are, contrary to popular belief, *more* dependent psychologically (and hence physiologically) on family ties.

And yet, as I intend to make clear in ensuing chapters, Daddy Dearest is traditionally given emotional short shrift by the American family and society as a whole—a fact that has led in many cases to anger, despair, guilt, and bewilderment. In a very real sense, I am calling for Father's Liberation.

The time has arrived for all of us—men *and* women—to analyze the psychological legacy bequeathed by our fathers, to understand what role father love played in shaping us as adults, and ultimately to redefine what we want from this fundamental human tie in the future. Toward that end we must listen to the experts, but also to the sons and daughters—the famous and the anonymous—in search of the elusive truth about our fathers and ourselves.

Sex is the core of our muddled notions of fatherhood—the riddle wrapped inside the enigma. Once a woman bears a daughter, her own sexual life becomes carefully circumscribed. Apprehensions she had once conquered are resurrected. She not only must care for and guard her daughter against those who would take advantage of her sexually, she must also set an example. That means retrenching, reverting to the cherished role of mother protector, giving up whatever sexual ground the mother may have gained so that her female child is not imperiled. To ensure that the daughter grows up properly, Mother will shield her from improper language, too-tight jeans, and R-rated movies. And though it may cost her dearly in terms of her sexual fulfillment, Mom will go to great lengths to make sure that she is, in the eyes of her little girl, essentially an asexual being. Given this common set of mother-daughter ground rules, the American mother is not far from the Virgin Mary. We all discover eventually that she did it with Dad, but no daughter is willing to believe that she derived any pleasure in the process.

The trouble with this is twofold: First, mothers do not harbor the same fears for the sons. Their little boy is certainly no more willing to accept the thought of his parents engaging in sexual intercourse, but the unspoken messages transmitted to him by both mother and father make it clear that, unlike his sister, he is not to regard sex as a danger. "I know it doesn't sound terribly enlightening or liberated of me," acknowledged the mother of a 7-year-old son and a 4-year-old daughter, "but I'm afraid that Jennifer is a natural target for somebody out there. She is so vulnerable, and I know I'll always have to be there to make sure she doesn't become a victim. Jason? No. I don't worry about him half as much. Once he's 12 or 13, he'll be able to take care of himself in that department."

Oedipal considerations aside for the moment, we are

left with the second half of a mother's message to her children. If she spends most of her time portraying herself as the eternal virgin to both male and female children, but makes it clear that sex is a threat to her daughter while it is not a threat to her son, then she opens a Pandora's Box of fears and anxieties regarding Dad. What sinister forces did Father unleash in the night? What was the threat to our mother's purity, and why was she forced by our father to submit to it? And why do all male children, while apparently exempt from any such harm themselves, presumably appear destined to inflict similar humiliation on the women of their own generation?

These apprehensions, rooted in childhood ignorance, are seldom dispelled with age. The alleged liberation of recent years notwithstanding, even college-age men and women who have supposedly sampled a sexual smorgasbord reject out of hand the very idea that their parents sweated and moaned as they became what Shakespeare's Othello wryly called "the beast with two backs." The unthinkable is no less so for those who have distinct recollections of creaking beds and peculiar night sounds emanating from the master bedroom, or from the startlingly large percentage of us who, stumbling from our rooms in search of a midnight glass of water or tiptoeing in to wake them up, caught our progenitors in the act.

If we deny our mother's sexuality, then we mystify our father's sexuality. In doing so, we distance ourselves even further from Dad. Mothers and daughters are permitted to suffer from loneliness. In fact, they are exhorted by books, magazines, movies, works of fiction and nonfiction, to face up to the notion that without a man they are expected to feel incomplete. They are then exhorted to dispell this notion, invariably to blame their unjustified feelings of worthlessness either on some unthinking, callous male, or on male-dominated society as a whole. That there is an epidemic of loneliness across the nation there is no doubt.

Suicides have nearly doubled over the past five years, and for males and females under the age of 21 the rate has tripled over the past decade—to thirty per day. To hang responsibility for what appears to be our profoundly depressed state of mind on those men who run the households and the country is patently unfair. Nevertheless, that is precisely what we are doing. Mom is invariably the victim. Don't worry about Dad: he can cope.

A lie, of course. Perhaps one of the greatest tricks we as children play on ourselves. And in a peculiar way it makes victims of both parents. In *Child and Society,* Dr. Erik Erikson contends that underneath his proud sense of autonomy and his exuberance for life, the troubled American male (who often looks the least troubled) "blames his mother for having let him down. His father, so he claims, had not much to do with it—except in those rare cases where the father was an extraordinarily stern man on the surface, an old-fashioned individualist, a foreign paternalist or a native 'boss.' In the psychoanalysis of an American it usually takes considerable time to break through to the insight that there was a period early in life when the father did seem bigger and threatening. Even then, there is at first little sense of that specific rivalry for the mother as stereotyped in the Oedipus complex."

In placing the burden of guilt squarely on Mother's shoulders, Freudian theory panders to these sublimated fears concerning father. We prefer that he remain a stolid nonentity on the conscious level, where we can deal with him. Whatever psychological distress we as adults now experience must derive, we tell ourselves, from the one parent who is essentially familiar to us as a mirror of ourselves. If we are happy in our grown-up lives, we thank Mom first, Dad second if at all. If we are unhappy, it is overscrutinized, overanalyzed Mom who is to blame. "I am sick to death of the 'Guilty Mother Syndrome' that has dominated our thinking over the past twenty years," complains

Eda LeShan. "Every time I would go to a symposium, the papers were titled 'Asthma and the Rejecting Mother' or 'Migraines and the Rejecting Mother.' It wasn't so much that most people in the psychiatric profession were men, or that fathers themselves were copping out. It was that we were just never willing to delve into that mystery called the American Father. He never got the credit, but he never got the blame, either."

Those papers linking our subconscious resentment of Mother with everything from nail biting to impotence have not ceased altogether, though psychiatrists and psychologists are discernibly more reluctant to fly in the face of feminism and the working mom. More significantly, we are beginning to see the subtle shift in the way fathers are portrayed in the popular media. Joan Crawford has come to symbolize America's love-hate relationship with Mother both as a character on the screen (the sainted restaurant owner with a conniving daughter in *Mildred Pierce*) and in real life as the wire coat hanger–hating villainess of her adopted daughter Christina's best-selling memoir, *Mommie Dearest.*

In recent years, however, Hollywood has apparently taken note of a new interest in exploring Pop. Portraying the young father in *Kramer vs. Kramer,* which won one Academy Award as best picture of 1979 and another for him as best actor, Dustin Hoffman had teary-eyed audiences cheering when he proved to the court that he—and not the erstwhile mother (Meryl Streep)—deserved custody of their 8-year-old son. *Ordinary People,* which copped the top Oscar the following year, went *Kramer vs. Kramer* one better; it not only laid bare a father's anguish over the suicidal tendencies of his teenage son, but it also depicted the man's futile attempt to hold his marriage and his family together in the face of his wife's own emotional intransigence. Both films are rare in that they eschew easy answers and stereotypes in an effort to show us that Father is like the rest of us, an all too human bundle of contradictions.

The public had to wait for Katharine Hepburn and Henry and Jane Fonda to take to the screen in Ernest Thompson's *On Golden Pond* before they were treated to a glimpse of a daughter trying to come to terms with her feelings for her estranged father. Arrogant, self-absorbed Norman Thayer, a retired professor, had always been a bastard to his daughter Chelsea. When Norman, played by Hank Fonda, and his adoring wife Ethel (Hepburn) are joined by Chelsea (Jane) at their summer cabin in the Maine woods on his eightieth birthday, old wounds are opened.

There are striking parallels between Norman and Chelsea and the actors who played them on the screen. Although Henry and Jane had experienced several periods of genuine hostility over the years, they were reconciled well before the filming of *On Golden Pond* actually began in New England. "The grouchiness is real," conceded Jane. "The difficulty is seeing that one causes suffering for someone else—that's true of my dad. But he doesn't always know when he's hurt somebody." Jane recalls one scene in which Ethel, Norman, and Chelsea's fiancé, Bill (Dabney Coleman), play Parcheesi while Chelsea sulks. "Chelsea doesn't like to play," Henry observes as Norman, "because she's afraid of losing." Chelsea shoots back, "Why does he like to beat people so much?" Jane remembers that it was a moment of "real hostility, and I felt I really had to look him in the eye."

When it came time for close-ups, she asked her father if he could see her. "I don't need to see you," he snapped. "I'm not one of those method actors." Jane was stunned. "It hurt me deeply," she admits. "I was mortified and furious—I felt like crying. I'm 44 years old, I have my life and my family, and still he can reduce me to feeling abject helplessness." Chelsea, move over.

My father was a mustang. That is a military term to describe an enlisted man who works his way up through the ranks to become a career officer. At the time Dad joined the navy at 17 in the fall of 1937, this was still a rare breed. The officer corps of both the army and the navy was derived almost entirely from West Point and Annapolis; during that period practically anyone who attended either military academy was only able to do so because his family had financial or political clout—invariably both. Dad had neither, but when he exhibited a talent for flying and for leadership as the United States poised on the brink of World War II, he was given a commission. The events that ensued in my father's life—fighting in the Pacific, starting a family, pursuing a career as a naval officer that would take us around the country and the world— were the events that I assumed shaped his outlook. It was not until I became a teenager that I began to realize the powerful impact his father had had on his life and, consequently, on ours.

My grandfather, Edward Albert Andersen, was the son of a sailor who allegedly deserted the Norwegian navy to settle in the then-booming textile center of Fall River, Massachusetts. The deserter, Peter Andersen, married a local Irish Catholic girl with the unforgettable name of Mary Fitzpatrick. Their oldest son became a physician, journeyed to China as a missionary, and returned to die from a disease he acquired there. Their youngest boy, my grandfather, was born with a handicap: the thumb and forefinger of his left hand were fused together, giving it a clawlike appearance. By way of overcoming his deformity, he developed a quick wit, a nose for local business opportunities, and a sense of people. He started a candy store, then a drugstore, then a carpet-cleaning business. To do business with the various ethnic groups that had flocked to Fall River to work the mills in the early 1920s, he learned Portuguese, Yiddish, and the Quebecois of the French Canadian immigrants.

The bantam with the crumpled fedora, neatly trimmed mustache, and crisp blue eyes became something of a fixture in town, and he would later relish regaling anyone who would listen with stories about Fall River's stranger characters. For instance, Grandfather told of sitting in the back of a packed courtroom day after day listening to witnesses give grizzly testimony as the defendant, Lizzie Borden, sat weeping. Then he would gleefully recite the famous verse just as he heard it back in 1892:

> Lizzie Borden took an ax
> and gave her mother forty whacks.
> And when she saw what she had done
> she gave her father forty-one.

She was acquitted, but did he think she did it? "Of course," snapped Grandpa, more than a little exasperated. Being a merchant, however, he most loved talking about Hetty Green, the Witch of Wall Street, who was born in nearby New Bedford and walked around town with millions of dollars sewn into the lining of her black Victorian dress. Reputedly worth more than a $100 million at the time, Hetty was so miserly that she delayed taking her son to a doctor when he developed blood poisoning. As a direct result, the boy's leg had to be amputated. "Can you imagine?" Grandpa marveled.

His business acumen aside, my grandfather was no match for the Depression. For the first time in his life he was a failure. His three children were then dispatched to search through slag heaps for chunks of coal that would be suitable for burning in the family furnace. In the fall of 1934, anticipating another harsh New England winter, the Andersens packed all their belongings in the back of a Model A and headed south. Once in Macon, Georgia, they hooked up with Ringling Brothers. My grandfather sold peanuts and popcorn while his daughter and two sons peddled balloons. Things got so bad that at one point it was suggested that my grandfather could himself become a sideshow attraction. They even had a poster made up depicting the Lobster Man but reneged in the end. The family moved on to California, where by the mid-thirties he managed to bounce back with a floor-polishing service.

Nearly three decades later, when I was 13, we visited my dying grandfather at a tile-roofed, white-walled country hospital in Oakland. He was 72, and this was only the last, most depressing in a series of human warehouses where he had spent his final years. The nurses there all behaved as if they had trained at Auschwitz. I had been enlisted to smuggle in a tiny, heart-shaped bottle of Paul Masson cream sherry. Once the nurses had turned their backs or left the room, I pulled the bottle out of my jacket pocket, unscrewed the cap, and handed it to my father. Grandpa was too weak to hold the bottle himself, so my father held it up to his lips. We repeated this ritual on each of our thrice-weekly visits. It was the only time during those closing days of his life that anyone saw Grandpa smile. Probably not so much because he loved the taste of the booze but because he loved defying the hospital rules.

With the exception of that little good-natured conspiracy, my grandfather did not seem to share much with his son. There was plenty of the usual hail-fellow-well-met back-slapping stuff, but any direct exchange of affection was to be avoided at all costs. When my grandfather finally died, no tears were shed. I asked Dad if he was upset, and he did not hesitate to respond with the usual "It's all for the best" and "He had a good, long life" lines that we so often use to disguise our own confused feelings about the death of a parent. After all they had been through together, my father and his father were, for all intents and purposes, still strangers.

We never get over Father.
"I have always thought that the initial trouble between me and my father," Laurence Olivier told me over lunch

at London's Savoy Grill, "was that he couldn't see the slightest purpose in my existence. There, in splendid relief, was his beautiful daughter, his eldest child, and three years younger was his son and heir—my older brother—the only one he needed, thank you very much. Everything about me irritated him. I was an entirely unnecessary extra burden on the exchequer; he would describe how the enormous amount of porridge I consumed at breakfast put him in a bad temper for the whole day; he found himself staring in disagreeable fascination at the seeming distension of my stomach gaining such an increase in dimension that it would force my chair farther away from the table....One must add that the undisguisedly frank favoritism of my mother for her baby could not have been a helpful influence in soothing and smoothing my father's shredded patience."

Whenever he discusses his father, Olivier has a difficult time trying to disguise his lingering bitterness. "My father used to describe how he was frying sausages for Dr. Rawlings and himself when the doctor appeared in the kitchen doorway bearing a tiny, healthy-looking infant in his arms, as yet unwashed and smeared with blood. My father's telling of this always indicated a sense of slight disgust as Dr. Rawlings placed me in his arms. After a decent enough pause, he handed me back and returned his attention to the sausages."

The senior Olivier's chief failing seems to have been parsimony. "For my father," says his son, "saving was craving." That including sharing the bathwater, with little Larry the last one in the tub. On one of these occasions, while he was lowering himself into the water, he dared to ask his father when he would be following his older brother to serve in India. "My father's answer was so astonishing that it gave me a deep shock: 'Don't be such a fool; you're not going to India, you're going on the stage.' 'Am I?' I stammered lamely. 'Well, of course you are,' he said; and as he went on I realized not only that he had been thinking of me quite deeply, which was something I had long before decided he never did, but that he had been following these thoughts in pleasingly creative and caring ways."

Like most sons, Laurence Olivier never even tried to untangle the Gordian knot of contradictions in his father's behavior. "Never once in my life," he admits with some remorse, "did I dare venture to ask my father about his own life, let alone question his motives or conduct." When his father died early in 1939, Sir Larry was playing in a pre-Broadway tryout of *No Time for Comedy* in Indianapolis. He did not attend the funeral. "I am sure that to anyone fortunate enough to be brought up in a close and loving family, the death of one's old man feels something like a blunt biff to the nose," allows Lord Olivier with typical stiff-upper-lip understatement. But Olivier went on to confess that it was impossible to avoid "intense fits of recalling the past. Such bouts are mercilessly penetrating in their self-questioning; when did I ever have the guts to confront my father about anything, to tell him his attitudes were stupid, childish, wrong, and sometimes close to being wicked in their dangerous prejudices and ignorance?" When indeed. The price for such universal moral cowardice when it comes to our fathers is always the same: eternal, soul-wrenching speculation.

Dr. T. Berry Brazelton, Director of the Child Development Unit at Children's Hospital Medical Center in Boston, is a pioneer in the study of family interaction. "I hardly knew him as a child," Brazelton says of his own father, a businessman who spent most of his free time on the golf course. "He died when I was 21, and I felt cheated. I felt that I *never* knew him." Many of us—perhaps most of us— never bridge the chasm between our father and ourselves, if for no other reason than our failure to recognize that a chasm exists. All too often we have ourselves reached beyond middle age before realizing too late that we never sang for our fathers.

I do not intend to make that mistake. My father and I are probably closer than most, but in all the years we shared the same roof, we never really openly shared our fears, frustrations, disillusionments, and apprehensions. He was willing to keep an emotional arm's length, and I was willing to let him. Not anymore. Exactly when do we expect this friendship to begin? Now.

Becoming a father is easy enough,
But being one can be rough.

—Wilhelm Busch

I am stronger, I am more intelligent,
and I think I am better than he is.
I don't want to be a pal, I want to be
a father.

—Clifton Fadiman

CHAPTER II _____

Beginning Apart: Dad as Resident Alien

"I love my parents equally, of course." It is at once the common claim—and the great lie. For like it or not, most of us were emotionally ostracized from our fathers beginning at birth, when they paced the waiting room guzzling black coffee from paper cups and chain smoking until the nurse popped through those swinging doors to announce our arrival. It was that event, our fathers will confess to us often painfully, that set them apart from the rest of the family, making them feel like resident aliens in their own homes. "Fathers have traditionally felt left out," says Michael Maccoby, "starting with the birth of the child." Observes Wellesley College researcher James A. Levine:

> Our whole society has had the notion that a biological bond between mother and child made fathers less able, less interested, and less important than mothers in caring for children. Courts have based decisions on that notion, therapists have treated patients on the basis of it, and men and women have made life choices because of it.

Fathers have not, in fact, been a favorite research subject. Whenever behaviorists wanted to look at fathers, they did not want to observe his impact but the impact of his *absence*—through divorce or death—on the family. "When I started out seventeen years ago, there just wasn't much data," admits University of Rhode Island psychology professor Henry Biller. There still isn't, but clinical psychiatrists and psychologists have at least begun to look at the important "other person" in every child's life.

The greatest scarcity, according to San Diego psychiatrist Martin Greenberg, is "most glaring in the area of the early father-newborn relationship, particularly in the first week." That should come as no surprise. If society had intended to isolate the father from the rest of his family, it could not have found a more forbidding way. Like nearly every other father of his generation, mine knew only that his wife would get bigger and bigger until the time came for him to drive her to the hospital. In my particular case, it was the hospital at the U.S. Naval Air Base in Pensacola, Florida, where Dad was then a flight instructor. He would often tell me that he saw no reason why fathers should not be present at the birth of their children, but that did not make him any more eager to buck convention eleven years later when my sister was born on the Tachikawa Air Force Base outside Tokyo. I vividly recall being rousted out of bed to accompany my parents to the hospital, then waiting three hours before the obstetrician popped his head into the lounge around two a.m. to tell us to go home. At seven we got the call: Mom had just given birth to a 7-pound 2-ounce girl, my sister, Valerie. My father had been totally excluded from the event, as if his mere presence would somehow contaminate the proceedings. The look of loneliness—*aloneness*—on his face and the faces of the other expectant fathers in that space capsule known as a hospital waiting room is one I have not been able to forget.

What has it meant for most of us that our fathers were absent at the arrival? Sophia Loren told me that aside from her overriding love for her mother, the single driving force in her life was overcoming the rejection she suffered at the hands of her father. That rejection began when he refused to marry her mother, but showed up nonetheless at the hospital where Sophia was born to acknowledge for the record that she was his issue. "I saw my father only six times in my life," Sophia told me. "He was a great source of pain and humiliation for my mother, whom he seduced and abandoned, for my sister, Maria, who suffered terribly because he would not give her his name, and for myself. Growing up in a small Neapolitan town, it was the dream of my life to have a father. That is why I sought him everywhere—I made my best films with actors and directors like him and I married an older man like him. Despite all the bitterness, when my father died in 1975 I felt only pity and love."

Carrie, a 37-year-old art director with a top Madison Avenue advertising agency, is devoted to her 70-year-old father, whom she always considered a buffer between her and her abrasive mother. When she gave birth to a boy, she noted that her husband was not only willing to be present for the event, but eager to witness it. Since her dad had always been attentive to her, even as a very small child, she wondered how he felt about being denied entrance to the delivery room. He had always told her that the family doctor would not allow it—such things just weren't done—but she discovered from her own obstetrician that the physician who delivered her was famous for encouraging a new father's presence even back then. Carrie pressed her father for the truth. Tearfully, he confessed that he had been with his mistress when Carrie's mother went into labor two weeks early. With that one revelation, Carrie learned the source of her mother's long-harbored bitterness toward both her husband and her daughter.

Dr. Brazelton, long one of the leading advocates of allowing fathers in the delivery room, is loath to admit that he did not witness the birth of his own children. "It just wasn't an option that was open to fathers in the 1950s and '60s," he explains. "And if you were a doctor, there was another taboo: It was a little like operating on a relative if you showed up to peer over another physician's shoulder."

Nor is there any overriding proof that all men are capable of looking upon the birth of their own child as anything more than just another biological act. One San Francisco physician coolly admitted to his son that after delivering some 450 infants, observing the birth of yet another, albeit his own, did not particularly appeal to him at the time.

Many women get their first inkling of what kind of fathers their husbands will make rather late in the game. One wife remembers her spouse's reaction when she told him she was pregnant with their first child: "How in the hell did you let that happen?" he demanded to know. "From that time on," she now freely admits, "I knew he was going to be a lousy parent—and it turned out he was."

Many fathers of past generations admit that they just don't have the stomach for it. In most cases this probably stems from the understandable fear of seeing someone we love in not inconsiderable pain. But there are, of course, many weak-stomached males for whom the identity of the sufferer is of secondary importance, or no importance at all. As a 17-year-old newspaper reporter starting out in northern California, I recall covering a Rotary Club luncheon at which the guest of honor was the chief obstetrician at the local hospital. The highlight of the doctor's presentation was a short and very graphic film on childbirth. The film ended and the lights went up, but the projector just kept on running; its operator was sprawled on the floor, out cold.

It is too early to tell whether a father's presence at the birth of his child will have any impact on the long-term relationship. After all, it has only been in the last decade that fathers have been offered a ringside seat. But common sense dictates that if a father has a desire not only to be as close to his wife as humanly possible at this critical time, but also to be an equal partner in the rearing of his children, he will gladly grab the chance. Still, some would suggest that a father's motive in wanting to witness his child's birth may not be altogether wholesome.

One of those is William Reynolds, author of *The American Father:*

> Some Fathers, rather passionately linked to their women, will take the course so that they can be present during labor and the actual birth. Part of their motivation is that Father is near suffocation with terror about anything happening to her, but another part of it seems to be a bit more on the interpersonal side. The intellectual, natural-living crowd finds this inspiring. Father boldly challenges the male stereotypes, thereby showing himself to be a caring, sharing guy. The thought that Father might be enjoying Mother's pain when she, in turn, shows off the ultimate human capability is quickly dismissed as insensitive and perverse.

In fact, recent studies show that a father's presence actually eases stress on the mother during delivery. What is undeniably "insensitive and perverse" is the social taboo that has inexplicably barred men from witnessing one of the great dramas of human life. Granted, it remains to be seen whether the so-called new breed of father thinks his responsibilities have been fulfilled once he has gone through six weeks of Lamaze courses and helped his wife through her Moment of Truth. There is disturbing evidence that, given the rise in the number of two-income families, more and more children are being raised by nannies and baby-sitters in the absence of both parents. For all his intimacy with his child at birth, the New Father may in the long run turn out to be even less involved in the day-to-day rearing of his own children. Ideally, however, a father's emotional involvement begins at the very beginning and follows through to the very end.

Early paternal involvement cuts both ways. If we cannot yet document its impact on the children, there is plenty of testimony from dads about how it has affected them. For starters, there is a measurable difference even between fathers who actually saw the child's birth and fathers who did not see the birth but held the child only minutes after its arrival. In a London study, members of the first group were not only more comfortable holding the baby, they frequently shared the observation that "when you see your child born, you know it's yours." This "knowing it's yours" notion was not a reaction shared by fathers who were not present at delivery.

For both groups the critical factor seems to be that they first laid eyes on their newborn within one hour of its birth. "This may be the most significant period for both the father and the mother to have contact with the newborn," state Martin Greenberg and Norman Morris, professor and chairman of the Department of Obstetrics and Gynecology at London's Charing Cross Hospital and Medical School. Reason: An infant tends to have its eyes open, cries more, and has stronger sucking motions during its first sixty minutes on the planet than in the subsequent hours, when it seems for all intents and purposes to be resting up, recuperating from the experience.

Greenberg and Morris found in their research that the father-infant bond is cemented with the first encounter. Several fathers in their study felt that the baby was acknowledging their presence in the room simply by opening its eyes. "He was sleeping yesterday and his eyes were closed," observed one, "and as I looked over he opened his eyes and I moved away and he closed them and I moved back again—and he opened them. Now, I don't know what that is, maybe some kind of telepathy or something, but I just think that he knew I was standing over him and he opened his eyes...it felt wonderful." Another new dad marveled that his daughter "seem[ed] to try and seek out the sound" when he talked to her. "And when you wave your hand at her, she seems to try and follow you with her eyes.... I don't know if she sees or not, but she's got really dark blue eyes, really dark, and beautiful, really beautiful."

A publicist friend of mine prided himself on being able to get by on five hours of sleep a day, a talent that allowed him to work twelve-hour days and spend the balance of his time bar hopping. That changed little when he married. It took the birth of his son to dramatically alter his view of himself and his approach to life—and it all happened, he insists, in a matter of minutes. "After those six weeks of Lamaze courses I was just so damned ready to get the whole thing over with," he confessed to me. "It was all pretty boring, and I couldn't wait to have the kid born and turn it over to Janice and get back to the way things were. But when I held Matt and he grabbed my thumb with his tiny fist and the grip was so damned tight, well, I've got to admit that for the first time it dawned on me that this was a real little human being—a part of me. I wasn't about to blow it on late nights at the office or partying with friends. Everything else seemed to pale in comparison to being with Matt."

Matt's dad was surprised by his reaction to parenthood, and he had good reason for surprise. His own father, a wealthy liquor distributer in the Midwest, was so totally engrossed in his career that he did not even interrupt his business travels for the birth of either of his two boys. Although Matt's dad had intended from the beginning to go through with Lamaze and participate in the delivery, he admits that to him it was little more than a charade. "I never really liked to be around kids much, and I guess I thought I was just like my father," he says. "It never occurred to me that there would be something magical between Matt and me."

How does that make him feel about his relationship with his own father? "I'm a grown-up guy and I guess I'm supposed to say that I forgive my father for never being around, for not even being around when I was born. But

I don't forgive him. I resented him before, but I sort of thought it was a genetic thing; he had never been close to my grandfather, either. Now that I know that it isn't some family curse or something in our makeup, I am mad as hell at my father." Not that Matt's dad intends to make his feelings known to Matt's grandfather. "Why," he asks, "should I give him the final satisfaction of knowing how much he hurt me?" Does that mean Matt won't have the opportunity to get to know his grandad? "That," says Matt's dad matter-of-factly, is "up to him." So far, Matt's dad seems to be every bit as loving a grandpa as he was a father: By the time he turned two, Matt had yet to lay eyes on the old gentleman.

A father is a man that moves around the home with a big stick in one hand, and love in the other.

—Rayna, age 12

CHAPTER III _____

Wait Till Daddy Gets Home: The Great Santini Syndrome

Nearly every adult American alive today has been raised in his or her father's absence. That is an economic as well as a social fact. Dad went to the office or the factory or the store or the hospital or, as in my case, the air base sometime before we got up in the morning, and if he came home at all that day, it was just in time for dinner, an hour or two of television, and bed. Mom sometimes worked, too, though even if she did she somehow managed to sneak home for lunch or get out of the office early enough to meet us when we got home from school.

   Not being there is a problem in itself. For a new generation of working women, this is new; for fathers, it has always gone with the territory. It has also been up to the entire family, particularly Mom, to decide how Dad's image will be shaped as a result of his daily hours away from home. In *Discovering Daddy: The Mother's Role,* Dr. Richard N. Atkins, assistant professor of psychiatry at the State University of New York, offers clinical proof that Mom plays perhaps the most important part in defining how her children will come to regard their father. In the case of 2-year-old Pete, for example, "Mommy often invokes Daddy as a subject of conversation. If Pete asks Mommy, 'Daddy at work?' Mother constructs an elaborate playful escapade around 'Daddy at work.' She picks up a crayon and paper, starts drawing, and says, 'Daddy writes at work.' She then runs a wooden car across the floor, explaining, 'Daddy drives to work, and then he drives home to see Pete!'" Atkins then goes on to describe how Pete joins in the game, squealing with laughter. The boy's concepts of Dad "appear to blossom," observes Atkins, "even in the absence of Father."

Conversely, Atkins cites the case of 23-month-old Charlotte, "grossly overweight, as is her mother." Charlotte is depicted as sitting in her mother's lap at a play group that serves as Mommy's main social outlet, vacuously asking "Daddy?" If it was one of the infrequent times that Mommy seemed to be paying attention to Charlotte, she would snap, "Daddy is at work!" and return to chatter with the other mothers. Atkins' conclusion:

> We may do well to remember that psychological birth can never appropriately be equated to the birth of evocative representations, although our current tendency in psychoanalysis seems to force this representational world to become a system of psychic microorganization. The subtle nuances in human relatedness may ultimately find their developmental origins in that vast and relatively unexplored territory of human life before ideas take hold, when the warmth of a mother and her alliance with the father create a milieu in which all subsequent representations are based.

The fantasies we spin about Father do not end when we become adults. David Halberstam, who won a Pulitzer prize for his coverage in Vietnam when he was a correspondent for *The New York Times* and has since written several best-selling nonfiction books (*The Best and the Bright-*

est, The Powers That Be, Breaks of the Game), confesses that as he enters his 50s he maintains the same feelings for his father that he had when he was a child. "My father was a mythic figure," explains Halberstam, "made even larger by his absence and his early death. He was a wonderful, beloved man. He was enormously handsome; there was a touch of Gregory Peck in his face. There was always a sense of his kindness and gentleness, a feeling that nothing negative or bad would happen to me when I was around him. He used to take me to Yankee Stadium to see DiMaggio, and he introduced me to one of the great loves of my life—fishing. My father was one of seven children born to Russian immigrants in a tiny town in Pennsylvania, and after service as a medic in France and Germany during World War I, he returned to Penn State and eventually got his M.D. from Tufts. His family had all been sort of failed peddlers, so there was a genuine sense of pride that he was the first to actually become a professional man, a surgeon."

The day after Pearl Harbor, Charles Halberstam signed up with the U.S. Army Medical Corps and shipped out. He was 44, his son 7. "I saw almost none of my father from then until the war ended five years later. But World War II was an heroic, patriotic war, and even though we were terribly strapped financially in Dad's absence, there was a sense of obligation and pride that never allowed us to think badly of him." Shortly after the war ended, Charles Halberstam resigned his commission as Lieutenant Colonel and returned to private practice. Three years later, at the age of 52, he died unexpectedly of a heart attack. David was 15. "When you haven't had much of someone as important as your father and he suddenly dies just when you need him the most—you don't even know how deep the loss is until much later. I remember crying that first day he died, but then my brother and I were told that we had to be strong for our mother's sake, so we adjusted quickly to his death. Eventually I came to understand what a terrible toll my father's death took on my life. It's something I've been struggling with for thirty-five years."

A key to Halberstam's unrequited respect for his father is in all probability his mother, who never complained about her husband's absences and at every available opportunity talked about "where he was, what he was doing, and how proud we all should feel about him." Mrs. Halberstam never remarried. "The terribly difficult task most people have to perform when they grow up is the *demythologizing* of their parents," observes Halberstam. "The adult sees his parents getting older, starting perhaps to become more dependent on others, and our view of them naturally changes. But none of this happened in my case. My father was still a strong, powerful man when he died. I never saw him old-aged or tired. So the myth, the love, the respect for him, are all frozen."

So much so, in fact, that Halberstam still finds himself using his father as his ethical and professional model. Charles Halberstam was a charter subscriber to *Commentary* magazine, so when David sold his first major piece to *Commentary* at the age of 22—seven years after his father's death—he thought only of how proud his father would have been. "And when I won the Pulitzer prize in 1964, part of me wished desperately that he could have known." In fact, what disturbs David most now is simply that, although he would go on to distinguish himself at Harvard, he was a rather poor student at the time of his father's death. "I only wish he knew that I did not turn out to be the great fuck-up it seemed I would. I wanted him to know I turned out okay."

Then, too, there were the doubts about how his patriotic father would have viewed his criticism of the United States' involvement in Vietnam. But even more disturbing to David Halberstam was the period between his first and second marriages when he was being linked with a number of women in the gossip columns. "When the papers started mentioning who I was going out with, I was physically sickened," he recalls. "My father would have said, 'Is this what he's come to?' I did not like myself then."

To be sure, trying to live up to a ghost of the past constitutes a crushing psychological burden. "Your real father is something you're always in search of," confesses Halberstam. But, he continues, "there is also a real reluctance to destroy our fantasies. Nobody really wants to break the crockery about their father's image. The trouble comes when you're caught between the myth you've created and reality."

Charles Halberstam was an absent father by nearly every definition. Yet his wife's enduring love and respect, obviously transmitted to her children, ensured that he would remain a powerful force in their lives long after his death. Mrs. Halberstam also showed admirable restraint by refraining from using her husband—as too many mothers have always done—as the Ultimate Weapon in her disciplinary arsenal. The threat of punishment from Daddy is one that nearly all of us have been subjected to at one time or another. But even on the one occasion David Halberstam remembers fearing punishment from his father, Dad responded with characteristic understanding. "It was just a few months before my father died, and I really screwed up a report card," says Halberstam. "I expected a tongue-lashing, but he just looked at it and said, 'Well, I guess we should do better next time.' It was totally the way to handle it. I respected my father enormously, but I never feared him. How could you fear a man like that?"

More often than not, however, fear—even hatred—is part of the father-child equation. In the moving film *The Great Santini,* based on the novel of the same name by Pat Conroy, Marine Corps fighter pilot Bull Meechum is both hero and villain to his children. During his long absences Meechum could not hope for a better P.R. person than his loyal wife. She does far more than keep the home fires burning; she fans the flame of Bull's flamboyant reputation as the most macho, derring-do sky jockey in Air Corps history. On those increasingly rare occasions when he spends more than a week with his family, Bull does his best to live up to their expectations. He is every inch the mean marine, the molder and shaper of raw recruits. Only in this case the recruits are his children.

Since long absences of men in the military provide a sustained source of subjects for study, it is not at all surprising that psychiatrist Erik Erikson found one such case history worthy of special attention. During World War II a neighbor of Erikson's underwent a dramatic and seemingly inexplicable personality change from mama's boy to a violent, rebellious brat with a disquieting penchant for pyromania. "The boy's parents had separated just before the outbreak of war," writes Erikson in *Childhood and Society*. "The mother and the boy had moved in with some women cousins, and when war began the father had joined the air force. The women cousins frequently expressed their disrespect for the father and cultivated babyish traits in the boy. Thus, to be a mother's boy threatened to be a stronger influence than to be a father's son."

War and the father's unexpected talent for it changed all that. Father became a hero, and the mother dropped her plans to divorce the man whom she and her cousins had spoken so negatively about in the past. The father was eventually lost in Germany, but the damage had already been done to his son's psyche. "After the father's departure and death, the affectionate and dependent boy developed more and more disquieting symptoms of destructiveness and defiance, culminating in fire setting," observes Erikson. "He gave the key to the change himself when, protesting against his mother's whipping, he pointed to a pile of wood he had set afire and exclaimed (in childish words), 'If this were a German city, you would have liked me for it.'" Clearly, the boy fantasized about following in Father's footsteps as a bombardier.

Erikson sees in the story of the pilot's son all the classic

oedipal conflicts that arise when a child is given contra-
dictory images of the absent father and then expected to
assimilate them. "The father, at first successfully replaced
by the 'good' little boy, suddenly becomes both a revitalized
ideal and a concrete threat for the mother's love." The
result: the child radically devaluates his feminine identi-
fications in an attempt to regain his own sexual equilibrium. Before he can forge a strong link with his father,
the father dies and he is left not only confused but with a
palpable sense of guilt because subconsciously, he may have
wished this new competitor for Mom's affections out of
the way.

Erikson stresses that this set of circumstances need not
result in disaster. If, say, our little would-be bombardier
were to be taken aside by his mother and made to understand in no uncertain terms that his confusion about his
father is not only understandable but natural given the
situation, he might incorporate his father's best qualities
(courage, healthy aggressiveness, a sense of duty and responsibility) into his development without jettisoning those
positive feminine attributes communicated to him in a
household dominated by women. "Where such a synthesis
succeeds, a most surprising coagulation of constitutional,
temperamental, and learned reactions may product exuberance of growth and unexpected accomplishment. Where
it fails, it must lead to severe conflict often expressed in
unexpected naughtiness or delinquency." And if not resolved before adulthood, Erikson warns, such deprivation
of identity "can lead to murder."

One thing is certain: Much confusion and even anguish stem from the conflicting demands made on the
American father. He is generally excluded from the raising
of his children, and then, when they reach maturity and
become too much for Mom to handle, he is expected to
take over. Adolescent problems revolving around drugs,
sex, and school are thrust upon Dad and he is ill-equipped
to cope. Mom must take a large share of the blame for this

dilemma. In most households until relatively recently in our history, her principal responsibility was the management of the home. Understandably, her operation ran more efficiently without interference from amateurs like Dad. If his name was mentioned to the children at all during the day, it was generally to put the fear of God into them. "Wait until your father gets home" was the standard threat used by mothers to get ornery kids back in line, and it usually worked. "Father," says Dr. Joyce Brothers, "is the one Mother went to when she reached the end of her rope." Or wanted to avoid responsibility for making a decision—particularly an unpopular one. Dad is no less to blame for his peculiar position, however. He was perfectly content to be allowed to pursue his ambitions outside the household while at the same time experiencing the genuine comforts and joys afforded the family man.

Father's conventional role as provider is unquestionably the reason that he is regarded as an outsider not only by members of his own family but also by experts who have long since dismissed the possibility of his making any significant personal contribution to family life. For most of us who grew up in the 1940s and 1950s, Dad could be defined in terms of one thing: money. He was the breadwinner, the signer of the checks. Our expectations of him were almost strictly material. It was up to his abilities as a provider whether we had a room all to ourselves or shared one with a sibling, whether we had new clothes or hand-me-downs, whether we had two cars or made do with one, whether we took vacations to faraway places or spent the sweltering summer months trying to amuse ourselves at home. As a result of the average man's all-consuming involvement in pursuing his career, an involvement that has been traditionally encouraged in our society, he has little or no time left over for anything else—particularly something so trivial as Danny's adjustment problems or Jennifer's math homework.

Conversely, there are millions of mothers and children

who would gladly trade places with those affluent suburban families in which the most important thing about Dad is his credit rating. Fatherless families not only have an infinitely harder row to hoe financially, they are far less stable in nearly every measurable way. The fatherless child continues to be less well fed, well housed, well clothed, and well educated than the child with the father who is around taking at least a material interest in his family. Those children must also contend with seeing less of Mother, since the business of survival falls squarely on her shoulders. "So monotonously do the fatherless turn up in the poverty and social-deprivation statistics," observes Maureen Green in her book *Fathering,* "that psychologists and social workers attempting to come to grips with and define the specific characteristics of fatherlessness find themselves bogged down among the basic questions of survival that the poor have always had to face."

Short of losing both parents, in this century there has been no greater blow to the welfare of a child than to be deprived of a wage-earning father. To further complicate matters, today's divorce and separation—not death—are the chief causes of a father's removal from the scene. Financially, at least, arrangements can be made to cushion the family unit in the event of a father's death. There is no way to effectively insure against divorce.

We have come to regard the patriarchal role of Father in the last century, where Dad exerted moral leadership in the household commensurate with his provider role, as some sort of ideal. And there is little doubt that Father exerted far more authority then than he does now. Yet Michael Maccoby stresses that the Victorian patriarch was a European invention that should never have taken hold in America. "The difference between us and other societies is that we have always had an ideal of equality of the sexes," says Maccoby. "From the beginning, we needed strong women on the frontier, and that meant an essentially equal division of labors and responsibilities. The rise of the patriarchal society in the late nineteenth century was a complete aberration. It got us far away from those frontier ideals of men and women caring and sharing equally. Today we are closer than ever to de Tocqueville's America in that women have more political and economic power than ever." But for sacrificing some of that power, men have gotten nothing in exchange emotionally. They remain strangers to their children at a time when they are most needed to fill the void being left by Mother as she enters the work force.

As children ourselves, we fell somewhere between the aberrant patriarchy of our great-grandfathers and Maccoby's newly "democratized" American family. World War II accelerated the transition. During this period American families became accustomed to the extended absences of their menfolk, and millions of middle-class women were thrust into war-related industries. The birth of Rosie the Riveter gave mothers an exhilarating but decidedly short-lived taste of competence and independence. As soon as Dad came home from the war, he picked up where he left off on the assembly line or in the office, and Mom turned in her hod for a pie pan. Whatever frustration Mother experienced at the time—and it must have been considerable—she sublimated. By way of a trade-off, she settled for reigning as mistress of her own carefully circumscribed domain. Dad, no longer absolute ruler inside and outside the home, as his father had been, would at least be allowed to keep a firm grasp on the family purse strings.

One might assume that because Dad remained essential to his family's material well-being, he remained center stage in the family drama. Not so. It is precisely because he cast such a giant shadow as a provider that he cast such a small one as a human being. Father financed the production, but it was Mother who was now directing the kids in the starring roles. In the past decade, the billing has changed somewhat, as more than half the mothers in America have taken jobs outside the home—partly out of

heightened expectations inspired by the women's liberation movement but mostly out of economic necessity. But
if 50 percent of us now live in families where both parents
bring home a paycheck, we are pathfinders. Our mothers,
for the most part, turned the age-old observation that "the
hand that rocks the cradle rules the empire" into twentieth-
century reality. While Father spent more and more time
at the office and in the bar car of a commuter train, his
wife was unconsciously creating the "generation of vipers"
Philip Wylie described in his best seller of the same name.
"Momism" flourished, and despite the trends of recent
years that have reduced Mom's influence in the family, we
are not about to see her matriarchy replaced with anything
resembling "Dadism."

No one met the qualification of the absent father more
completely than my own. As a navy pilot, he was gone six or
eight weeks at a time, usually ferrying personnel to and from
such exotic locales as Saudi Arabia, Japan, Hong Kong,
Thailand, the Philippines, and India. After each journey he
returned laden with gifts, and gradually my room began to
look like Teddy Roosevelt's den. Where other kids' walls were
covered with posters and pennants, mine were hung with
python skins, bamboo blowguns from a tribe of pygmies in
the Philippines (I would practice my blowgun technique on
a conventional dartboard and became quite good at it), an
elaborately carved ebony spear from Malaysia, a sinister-
looking, curved-bladed Siamese dagger called a kris, wood-
block prints of samurai on horseback, and Japanese No
masks. The neighbors were impressed.

Aside from my periodic target practice using the
blowguns, there was only one time when any of the weapons were ever used for anything but decoration. When we
were living in a suburb of San Francisco, a mouse had
somehow managed to find its way into the house, and in
that one brief moment that it emerged from its hole and
skittered across the floor, my father, by then well into his
40s, almost instinctively grabbed the ebony-handled spear

from my wall and hurled it across the room at the scurrying rodent. No one was more stunned—and instantly remorseful—than my father when the spear struck its mark. The incident, not without its comic aspects, says much about the way in which we see our fathers and they see themselves almost as primitive protectors.

Yet Dad was then, as he is now, the antithesis of Bull Meechum—gentlemanly, soft-spoken almost to the point of being self-effacing, and grateful as hell to have spent most of his career as a warrior *without* a war to fight. Dad was, in truth, a bewildering tangle of incongruities: He was ambitious but not overtly competitive. In his macho military world, where reeling off football and baseball statistics was de rigueur, he made it clear to all that he not only had no interest in such matters, but he thought the win-at-all-costs mentality that made monsters of Little League mothers and fathers was unseemly (an attitude for which I was grateful, since when it came to Little League baseball I made a terrific lacrosse player). Politically, he was something of a liberal; when General Douglas MacArthur disobeyed presidential orders in Korea, my father praised Harry Truman for "firing the bastard." He spoke passionately about the rights of minorities and talked of his own revulsion at seeing how blacks were treated in the South during the 1940s and '50s. That sense of social justice seemed strangely out of place on a U.S. military base in Occupied Japan long before the dawn of the civil rights movement, and even though I was only 11 when we ended our four-year stint there, I remember admiring him immensely for his maverick stance.

How did he remain a dominant force in our lives even though he was gone one-third of the time? To be sure, Dad did not make an issue of being the boss of our tight little family; he just was. My mother made it easy for him. An attractive, high-cheekboned woman whose friends often compared her to the actress Frances Farmer (though I think she has more of a Kate Hepburn look about her),

Mom was torn between her own desire to be a journalist and the need to be a traditional housewife and mother. Once she had made up her mind to choose the domestic route, she also made a conscious decision not to vie with my father for control of the family.

Clearly, this desire for a firm male hand at the helm stemmed from her difficult relationship with her own father. He was a hard-drinking Swedish-Irish painting contractor who managed to keep his four sons and two daughters clothed and fed during the Depression, but was not about to win any awards as Father of the Year. When he was sober, the handsome redhead was stolid and reasonably responsible. When he was imbibing—and he could be counted on to go on a bender a couple of times a month—Grandpa transmogrified into a bona fide bully. He routinely picked fights with his boys (two of whom became boxers—one amateur and one professional—in self-defense). He humiliated his daughters with drunken displays in front of their guests, and his frequent rampages through the neighborhood bars became legendary. The ways in which his daughters handled this dicey situation differed greatly. My aunt, profoundly resentful and ashamed of her father, did everything she could to pretend he didn't exist. No one ever visited her at home. Dates were met at movie theaters or malt shops, or they picked her up on the sidewalk in front of the family's gabled white clapboard house on Oakland's Forty-second Avenue.

My mother took a radically different tack. All of her dates picked her up at home, and if they chose to make an issue of her father's state, she gladly showed them the door. It was a matter of pride with her; she was not about to apologize for any member of her family, and that included Grandpa. Despite her quickness to draw the wagons in a circle whenever the family was confronted with outsiders, my mother had whatever it is that makes cookies tough when dealing one-on-one with her cantankerous father. As the oldest girl ("Sis" is what her brothers always

called her), Mom was often the only thing standing between the other kids and physical abuse at the hands of
their dad. She was also her mother's main line of defense.
Grandpa's charming habits included sitting in the living
room and methodically cutting his wife out of every photograph in the family album. And when he turned truly
violent, that rage was often directed at his wife. It was my
mother, armed with a flatiron, who came to her mother's
defense.

Growing up in this environment left its indelible mark
on my mother. When it was her turn to start a family, she
made the conscious effort to reinforce Dad's stature as a
person. That meant keeping track of where he was at any
given point on an overseas trip, bringing him up a hundred
times in the course of a day's routine events, and making
elaborate plans for his return. Once he was back, we did
everything together. My most vivid memories of my childhood are of these excursions. In New York, we hit Times
Square and Radio City Music Hall, Grand Central and the
Statue of Liberty. In Japan, we often sampled the nightlife
of Tokyo's Ginza (for some reason the Japanese did not
seem to mind the presence of a child in their nightclubs)
and made side trips to places like Hiroshima, Fuji, and the
magnificent Shinto shrines on the island of Miyajima and
at Kamakura, where I crawled inside the hollow back of
the Great Buddha. My father looms large in those recollections; I would say larger than many fathers who actually
spent more time with their children. A nifty trick, and one
that was as much my mother's doing as Dad's.

A mother's cooperation was, in fact, essential if Dad
was ever to be regarded by the children as less than a full
member of the family. Ronald Reagan's mother, Nellie,
made sure Ronald and his older brother, Neil, took the
best of what their father, Jack, had to offer and forgave
him his fatal weakness. "I was 11 years old the first time
I came home to find my father flat on his back on the
front porch and no one there to lend a hand but me,"

recalls Reagan. "He was drunk, dead to the world. I stood over him for a minute or two. I wanted to let myself in the house and go to bed and pretend he wasn't there.... I felt myself fill with grief for my father at the same time I was feeling sorry for myself. Seeing his arms spread out as if he were crucified—as indeed he was—his hair soaked with melting snow, snoring as he breathed, I could feel no resentment against him. That was Nell's doing. With all the tragedy that was hers because of his occasional bouts with the dark demon in the bottle, she told Neil and myself over and over that alcoholism was a sickness—that we should love and help our father and never condemn him for something that was beyond his control."

Carol Burnett's parents, both alcoholics, abandoned Carol to be raised by Mae, her powerhouse of a Christian Scientist grandmother, in a one-room Los Angeles apartment. Mae repeatedly told Carol that her parents, like Ronald Reagan's father, were the victims of an illness, that they could not help themselves. Burnett remembers that her parents were not affected by booze in the same way. Her mother would get "mean" after she had had a few belts, but, Carol recalls, "My father became kind of nice, sweet." Still, Carol is quick to admit that she was as resentful of her father as she was of her mother for simply not being there when she needed him. "Of course, I carried that with me for years, but you can't let bitterness eat away at you. You have to grow up sometime. My parents had an illness, and they weren't responsible for their behavior. It was very sad." It seems strangely appropriate that Burnett's father would give his comedienne daughter a brilliantly succinct definition of comedy: "Comedy is tragedy, plus time."

The degree to which we assume or reject our father's neuroses varies dramatically. In many instances we develop serious neurotic tendencies of our own in an effort to exorcise Father's negative influence on our lives. One friend, a working mother in her 30s, is a cleanaholic. The minute a cigarette ash hits an ashtray, she runs to the kitchen to empty it out. Her dishwasher and clotheswasher hum constantly. She vacuums the entire house twice a day, scrubs the kitchen and bathroom floors at least once every twenty-four hours. Every surface is spotless, gleaming. Her home looks like a furniture showroom—immaculate and sterile.

The friend's husband has complained bitterly for years, but to no avail. Besides, he has never been the problem. The woman's father was a truckdriver whose sloppiness and personal habits would have sent Emily Post into cardiac arrest. Her father has been dead for years, but she is still subconsciously cleaning up after him.

Katharine Hepburn is the first to acknowledge that she is what her parents—most specifically her father, Dr. Thomas Norval Hepburn—made her. "My parents. Now, they were two *damned* fascinating people," Kate told me. "I am absolutely *dull* compared to them." Kate's mother, Katharine Houghton Hepburn, was an early feminist—a crusading suffragette and (though she bore six children) an outspoken supporter of birth control pioneer Margaret Sanger; in fact, Mrs. Hepburn frequently dragged Kate and the other kids along to carry placards at demonstrations on behalf of both causes. But the Hepburn clan was essentially a patriarchy. Dr. Hepburn was a Virginia-bred graduate of Johns Hopkins and a surgeon on the staff of the Hartford Hospital in Connecticut, specializing in urology. He was also an accomplished tennis player, swimmer, and golfer, a canny investor who made millions playing the stock market, and something of a social maverick himself. He shared his wife's political views and encouraged all members of the family to express themselves openly on every imaginable subject. No one was permitted to leave the room until Dr. Hepburn decided all arguments had been resolved.

Freedom of speech was one thing, but the Hepburn offspring came to realize that ultimately the opinion that counted most was Father's. Along with that went a Yankee upbringing that included household chores, freezing showers, and frequent spankings. Kate still takes several cold showers a day. "Those baths were responsible for my later perversity," said Kate. "They left me thinking the more bitter the medicine, the better it was for you." As for those spankings: "I deserved them. Back in those days, I was something of a second-story man. I used to like to break into neighbors' houses when they weren't home and just poke around." And then there was the matter of the now-legendary Hepburn temper: "I can still hear my mother saying, 'Kathy, you will have to do something about that temper of yours.' They called me Kathy back then."

Kate never doubted whose approval she would have to secure before embarking on a stage career. She remembers telling Dr. Hepburn of her decision to join Edwin H. Knopf's stock company in Baltimore as she was driving home to Hartford with her father from Bryn Mawr, where she was a student. "I'm going to be an actress, Daddy," she blurted without warning. Daddy was not amused. "You just want to show off—and get paid for it!"

"But, Daddy," Kate protested, "you let Mother make speeches for the suffragettes."

"That was for a political purpose," Dr. Hepburn shot back. "This is just stupid vanity."

They continued arguing for nearly an hour before Daddy relented. "All right. Here's fifty dollars. If you don't make it to first base, that's the end." Kate agreed to the terms. During her bumpy beginning years in the theater— Hepburn was almost routinely fired from plays because of her willful temperament—Kate could always rely on her father's brutally frank opinions concerning her acting. She was always grateful for the firm masculine hand in her life, so much so that she sought it out again years later in the person of Spencer Tracy. These were to be the only two men—Tracy and Dr. Hepburn—that Kate would ever love and trust completely. When I asked her what kind of parent she might have made, Kate replied without hesitation, "A lousy one. The first time a child of mine didn't do what I wanted, I'd kill him."

Cleveland Amory's lifelong concern for the welfare of animals stems from his disciplinarian dad. When he was 10 years old, Amory experienced his first encounter with cruelty to animals—his own. "I shot a bird with a BB gun," he recalls. Amory's father, a wealthy Massachusetts textile manufacturer, looked at Cleveland with disgust as the little bird flopped around on the family porch. "You shot it," the elder Amory told his son, "now you kill it." Remembers Cleveland: "I had to stomp on that bird until it was dead." Cruel? Certainly. Amory senior had driven home an important point to young Cleveland in a way the boy would never forget.

Janet is a 39-year-old mother of two teenage daughters who credits her strict father with keeping her from going off the deep end during her adolescence. "It was the mid-1960s, and the kids I had grown up with had suddenly stopped studying and started doing drugs—speed, downers, acid," Janet recalls. "I was a fair student in high school, and I was always a follower—much more interested in being liked by the rest of the crowd than getting good grades. I started with the drugs, too. My mother was aware of what was going on, but we both knew that she didn't have the strength to do anything about it. One day my dad came home from work early—he managed the local Safeway—and found me stoned in my room. It was only four p.m. He dragged me screaming out into the living room, threw me into a chair, and demanded an explanation. I told him I didn't know what he was talking about. He said that what I was doing was not only illegal but dangerous to my health, and I, of course, just laughed. Then he grabbed me by the shoulders and shook me hard; I had bruises for a week—but I knew I mattered to him. People don't straighten out overnight; I didn't. But he was as persistent as I was, and if I ever started to doubt that my folks cared, all I had to do was remember the way Dad looked into my eyes that first time he shook me."

It would be years before Janet let her father know how grateful she was that he had assumed the role of disciplinarian. "Back in those days when I was a real handful," she says, "I always did my best to make him feel rotten. And when I finally told him not that long ago how sorry I was, he admitted to me how much it had hurt him. I was so selfish at the time. I never noticed that he felt isolated enough from my mother and me that he was on the verge of leaving for good. Thank God he didn't, or I'd probably be dead today."

Diana is more than a decade younger than Janet, and like Janet, she credits her dad with saving her life. But where Janet experienced a few emotional skirmishes with her father, Diana seemed to be waging an all-out war at times during her turbulent teens. Her mother, unlike Janet's, acknowledged Diana's drug problem the first time she was sent home from school under the influence of Quaaludes. "Mom kept asking what I was taking, and I just kept yelling that she was a typical suspicious parent." When her father left work in the middle of the day to come home and deal with the problem, Diana reacted to his concern with unbridled hostility. "I told him to go fuck himself," she says, "and when he slapped me hard across the face, I tried to hit him back. We were so much alike— we *are* so much alike—that even though he and my mother were saying exactly the same things, I only hated him for it. It's difficult to explain, but the similarities in our personalities made everything he said seem so much more painful to me. It was like me seeing the bad in myself."

Diana continued to test her parents' patience. When her father was at last pushed to locking Diana in her room to prevent her from seeing her drug-using friends, she climbed out her second-story window at two a.m., slipped, and fell fifteen feet to the cement driveway, fracturing her left leg in two places. "It sounds rotten, but it was probably the best thing that could have happened," Diana's father now says. "She was not able to physically leave her bed. She was taking painkillers for the broken leg, but still, for the first time she was thinking straight for a long stretch of time, without being influenced either by her friends or the stuff—pills, mostly—that they kept pushing at her. I won't pretend that before the accident we hadn't considered going into her room and breaking her leg with a baseball bat just so we could keep her away from the drugs and get her straight again."

Diana admits that her involuntary confinement marked a turning point in her life, but she also contends that it precipitated a change in her father—a difference without which there would have been no lasting change in her. "Dad didn't take advantage of the situation in the way he could have," she recalls. "He didn't preach to me; he didn't ever say 'I told you so' or ever made me feel like an ass. He knew how I was feeling anyway, I guess. He just seemed genuinely concerned, and sorry about the pain I was in. It was as if he was sharing responsibility for everything that had led up to that point, instead of pretending to be the perfect parent above it all." Why did Dad change? "I just got tired," he shrugs, "of playing the heavy."

Margaret Trudeau's father also played the heavy during his daughter's formative years. According to Maggie, "The unmistakable stamp of his authority was on everything we did. The childhood friends, the fads and passions of my early years, pale into a shadowy insignificance beside his towering presence. He had the dour outlook of a Presbyterian Scot. An excessively strict upbringing had left its mark on him." Trudeau recalls that her father, at one time Canada's fisheries minister, did not even allow radios or record players to be played at home: "'Turn off that din,' he would yell upon entering the house, guided by some sixth sense to an almost inaudibly distant tune in the attic." Margaret's father would brook not even the slightest trace of insolence from any of his five daughters. "He never actually beat me, though, until I was 14," remembers Maggie. "I was supposed to be cleaning up after a party. I was being lazy and clearly somewhat insolent and on being told to hurry up, shouted a careless 'I hate you' in his direction. That was enough. He was out of his chair in a second, chased me all over the house, and when he finally caught me, he spanked me. The one thing you can't do if you're a Scot is hate your family."

Margaret Trudeau's recollections of her father are tinged with resentment, but they also convey implicit warmth and appreciation. Can we take for granted the fact that, however consumed by his career Father may have been during the day, he was involved enough in our lives to assume the wholly unpleasant (but utterly indispensable) role of disciplinarian once he walked in the front door? Wouldn't it have been preferable, given how little time he spent with us during the week, for Dad to have spared himself this enormous responsibility? Shouldn't we have just left it up to Mom, the parent with whom most of us had the familiar (if not always warmer) relationship?

It may be that Dad is the disciplinarian merely because he is so well equipped for it. Not only is he physically better suited to the task—he is bigger, stronger; his voice is deeper, his hand heavier—but, once again, he brought to the family the rules of the outside world. If Dad meant play, Eda LeShan observed, then he also meant pain. We sought our father's approval; that meant testing the limits of his tolerance, looking for him to either confirm (as he was invariably apt to do) or contradict the system of order set down by Mother.

There are excesses, and none are more evident than in the way the poet W. S. Merwin was treated by his father, an exceptionally dour minister in Union City, New Jersey. "At home," Merwin recalls, "our lives were surrounded by injunctions. On visits there were more of them." The family motto might have been "Don't touch," as young Merwin was constantly cautioned to keep his hands to himself. When the boy asked why his father treated him so harshly, the reply was that all too familiar refrain. "He always answered that he treated me that way," says Merwin, "only because of love, and that he was afraid I might get hurt."

Merwin senior occasionally made clumsy attempts to appear more benevolent to his son, though they had quite the opposite effect. "I could stand in front of his desk, uncomfortable, hot, wondering what I had done wrong now, and he would tell me to shut the door behind me. Then he would fish in the lower recesses of his desk for a moment, shut a drawer and sigh, and tell me we just were not spending enough time together, he and I, and that he was sorry it was happening but he could not help it right now because he was so busy and had so much on his mind. But these were precious years that would not come again. He would tell me how hard things had been for him as a boy, and how fortunate we were, we children, and how much easier life was for us with our yard to play in. And he said how important it was for me to study hard and do well in school. Then he would start telling me about insurance, how I would come to realize its importance when I was older. And he might give me some things, such as cards printed with the Ten Commandments, and pat me and say he would try to find more time to be together and we would be pals, and I would nod, and go, feeling grief inextricably tangled with my own unexpected and unconvincing goodness, and shutting the door behind me." The roots of Merwin's problems reach at least as far back as Merwin senior's peculiar attitude toward *his* father. Merwin senior never spoke of him and allowed the boy to meet his grandfather only once, the day the old man was being committed to a convalescent hospital.

Where despair is the legacy left by Merwin's father, it is also a large part of Aram Saroyan's emotional inheritance from his celebrated dad. For a time during the spring of 1981, Aram kept a journal recording the last days of William Saroyan. At the time, the father was 72, the son 37.

"What am I describing here, after all," Aram says in the preface to the resulting book, *Last Rites*, "but the continuing skirmish of my very life itself, with my father in front of me, the great writer, bigger than I, or more famous, and no matter where I go, no matter how I struggle to get past him, he is still there in front of me?"

Aram's memories are damning, apparently unleashed in print by the same sort of posthumous pettiness—both Aram and his sister, Lucy, were cut out of their father's will—that prompted Christina Crawford to write *Mommie Dearest*. Aram claims his father, who married Aram's mother twice and divorced her twice, was "an emotional miser, adored by people all over the world, but not yet loved by and not yet loving one person truly."

Can this be William Saroyan, the fabled conjurer of whimsical tales that sent the spirit soaring? "He wanted me to die," Aram says almost matter-of-factly. "He wanted me to be a disgrace and a failure, to be a blot on his good name—the hopeless son of a great man. Someone who kills innocent people driving down the wrong isle of the highway. Someone who shoots heroin and dies of an overdose because he can't face the world. Somebody who drives off a cliff and kills himself the way his mother's brother, his uncle Aram's son Chesley, killed himself after he failed to become a writer. He wanted me to be a failure like Chesley, so he could stand at my funeral, the big, wonderful, disappointed father.

"My father never liked me or my sister, and he never liked our mother either, after an initial infatuation, and in fact, he never liked anyone at all after an hour or two, no one except a stooge, someone he could depend on to be a lackey, a nitwit he could make fun of behind his back, someone he could control completely by whatever means he could make work—fear, intimidation, or, because he was a famous and admired man, blind worshipfulness."

Aram Saroyan sees even his father's trademark mustache as a work of calculated deception. "My sad beleaguered father had grown the large walrus mustache of an old-country patriarch, as if, having in reality failed to become a family man, he would henceforth become a sort of walking advertisement for the condition at its outmoded extreme—the proud, quixotic, old-country peasant looking directly out into a world gone mad. This would be a stance my father henceforth would refine, along with the mustache itself, for the rest of his life."

For all the bitter feelings he understandably harbored toward his father, Aram Saroyan knew that it was up to him to seek a deathbed rapprochement. Aram's sister Lucy was the first to try, driving from Los Angeles to visit her father at the hospital in Fresno where he spent his final weeks. William Saroyan had not seen his daughter for a full decade, and when she arrived with tears in her eyes and a basketful of food, Saroyan exploded, throwing her peace offering to the floor and screaming for her to get out. Aram, who had not communicated with his father in four years and was told in no uncertain terms not to attempt to visit him now, tried a different approach. Aram's daughter, then 7 years old, walked ahead into her grandfather's hospital room carrying a bouquet of fresh flowers. Aram followed behind, bearing a collection of Boris Pasternak's poems. The ploy appeared to work; at least the pair managed to enter the old man's hospital room without provoking a violent rage. But for the first few moments, Saroyan ignored his son. The nurse, totally confused, proffered an awkward introduction: "You know your son...." At this point William Saroyan turned to his son, and for the first time after so many years their eyes met. "I'll never," the father responded enigmatically, "forget him."

The lesson Aram Saroyan seems to have learned from this bittersweet reunion with his father is that if there is any chance for immortality at all, it rests with the family. Since William Saroyan never knew his own father—the elder Saroyan died in 1911 when William was three, leaving his son to be raised in a series of orphanages—William did not have a role model to either accept or reject. Ultimately, the buoyancy of his prose was born of sentiment rather than experience. In knowing his own father for what he was, Aram was more fortunate than the great William Saroyan. The son discovered that if perhaps he did not become a great writer, there was much virtue in being a responsible father.

The conflict between public image and private reality is common among fathers. One suburban Maryland housewife remembers that her father, a high-powered insurance executive, was called the Iron Chancellor by his intimidated co-workers. At home, he was unconcerned about how his children behaved. Dad left the messy job of keeping the kids in line to his wife, and when she wasn't around they were allowed to get away with just about anything. The Iron Chancellor's daughter concluded that her father gave greater priority to whipping his salesmen into shape than to disciplining his own children. The executive's staff may have resented him for his toughness in the office, but not half so much as his family resented him for his lack of backbone at home.

At the other end of the spectrum was the kind of father who stayed the model of calmness and sanity in the turbulence of the workplace, then was transformed into the Incredible Hulk once he stepped through the front door. From the standpoint of job security this would appear to be a perfectly logical way to proceed through life. Ted Pearson has worked for the same auto parts business in Memphis for thirty years, and throughout that time he not only was the employee deemed most capable to handle a crisis, but also the one fellow whom workers turned to for personal advice. Women did not get their hair cut or undergo minor surgery, men did not buy a new car, ask the boss for a raise, or change their golf swing, without first consulting Ted. The price for such commodious public behavior, Ted's grown son will now tell you, was paid at home. Ted virtually forbade conversation at the dinner table and laid down a Draconian set of rules for both his son and his daughter (including morning "inspections" when they were examined for clean fingernails, spiffily shined shoes, and straight creases and pleats in their clothes). "We spent practically every weekend doing chores," recalls Ted's son. "Of course, we cleaned up the house, mowed the lawn, and that sort of thing. But we also did all the grocery shopping, washed the car every weekend—we were like Dad's little army. If we ever had any personal problems, we went to our mother. But she was just as scared of him as we were."

When one of Ted's "soldiers" got out of line, punishment generally consisted of being beaten with a wide leather belt Ted kept tucked away in his closet expressly for that purpose. "The really frustrating thing was that nobody else knew it, and when you told your friends what he was really like, they wouldn't believe you. He was so nice to everybody else's kids, and their parents were always telling them what a nice person Mr. Pearson was. As soon as my sister and I were both in college, Mom filed for divorce, moved 1,600 miles away, and married a dentist. In a funny way, I think it was easier for her than it was for us—you can't divorce your father." Today Ted, who has not remarried, is still the most popular employee at the auto parts store.

Susan Strasberg was another child confused by the contradictions in her father, acting guru Lee Strasberg. "In his drama classes my father spent hours cajoling actors to contact their innermost feelings and express themselves without fear. 'Are you a human being?' he would demand. 'Then just get up and act like a human being, don't complicate things. Look at her, touch her, be aware what's happening to you, to her.' But with me he would often sit totally uncommunicative. It was difficult to make myself heard over the thunder of Beethoven, and catching my father's eye was impossible because he was constantly reading. Years before, he had begun to collect books that related in any way to theater—art, psychology, painting, music, great literature. Eventually, this collection became the finest artistic and theater library in the country. But to me his books and music were like a fortress wall, a barrier too high to scale. Since he rarely touched me, the absence of words reinforced my feeling that I had done something terribly wrong to cause him to withdraw."

Even Henry Fonda, who rode with his children on an emotional roller coaster for over forty years, choked back tears as he told me of "the most important memory" of his life. Fonda's father, a stolid Midwesterner, viewed his son's interest in acting with disdain, just as Kate Hepburn's father had. Fonda senior grudgingly went along with the rest of the family to watch his son's first performance on stage, and when Henry came home he found his father glowering behind the newspaper while his mother and sister were involved in a heated discussion about flaws in the production. Finally a voice erupted from behind the newspaper. "Shut up," commanded Hank's father. "He was perfect."

It is touching that in telling that story, Fonda seemed to be confiding that this was the one true moment of candor between father and son. It is also sad. Those of us on this side of the newspaper came to view it as an impenetrable barrier. We were intimidated by it, in awe of the man sitting in our midst but willfully separating himself from us. What we failed to see, however, was that the newspaper (or book or television or job or hobby) was essentially a defensive mechanism. How many fathers felt they could connect with, much less confide in, their growing children? Again, there arises this profound sense of isolation. When Berkeley sociologist Claude Fischer asked adults whom they talked with about personal matters and whose opinions they considered in making important decisions, he discovered that women, whether married or not, were more likely to have several confidants. Many unmarried men also indicated that they had several people with whom to share personal matters. The greatest difference was that most married men questioned by Claude Fischer—nearly all fathers—usually named only their wives as confidants. *Not one father felt close enough to his adult children to consider them confidants.*

The office was always presumed to be the place where Dad found companionship, male or female, to compensate for the lack of it at home. And to a substantial extent for most of us over the age of 25, that presumption was not far off the mark. Our fathers formed friendships and alliances at work that extended to weekend golf or bowling tournaments, long liquid lunches, happy-hour antics. And they may have found a mistress. All perfectly standard, and all perfectly designed to further distance a man from his children. But even this outlet was not as available to everyone as we might have thought. A Houston man eventually told his two daughters that he was so desperate during one point in his shaky marriage to their mother (he eventually divorced her, after twenty-four turbulent years) that he dialed the operator three times before he decided the voice on the other end sounded sympathetic enough to listen to his problem. The woman on the other end suggested he talk to someone at work. There was a moment of silence. "There's nobody at work for me to talk to. There's nobody there who cares about me. I just sit there taking orders on the phone all day."

Stanford Business School lecturer Thomas J. Peters is well aware of the misconceptions surrounding the American corporate "family." Companies, says Peters, create a sense of family "with hokey stuff, Mickey Mouse things like company picnics."

The sort of corporate paternalism that took root after World War II turned out not to be merely "hokey," but cruelly manipulative. The employee was no longer tied to the company store, perhaps, but he was now dependent emotionally as well as economically on his "family" of coworkers. In lieu of being forced to try to bridge the gap that often separated him from his own flesh and blood, Dad was expected to express filial affection for the next person on the assembly line or at the neighboring desk. In many cases, our fathers chose this easy, artificial intimacy in the workplace rather than suffer through the far more complex and soul-wrenching process of puzzling out his feelings toward his own family.

This was often just as convenient for the rest of the family; they were generally no more equipped emotionally to come to terms with Dad than he was with them. Besides, Mom could do without the distraction and the competition from Father around the house, and the kids were happy to be free of his interference.

How many times my father would come home and revoke a privilege my mother had unhesitatingly granted me, or tell me I'd done a lousy job of mowing the lawn when Mom had already praised me for it. He was gone for weeks at a time, and when he wasn't off on a trip, he was still out of the house practically all day at work, like every other dad. Why did he have to change the rules? He did, of course, have every right. But when he retreated, as he inevitably did to his newspapers or bills, he was just as riven with self-doubt and perhaps even a measure of self-loathing as we were full of disappointment and resentment. For those of us who never broke through that seemingly impenetrable wall he erected around himself— or, more accurately, we helped him to construct—now is the time to start chipping away. Only then can we as sons and daughters begin to dispel the ghosts that still haunt us.

The gods
Visit the sins of the fathers upon the children.

—Euripides

CHAPTER IV _____

Body Image and Sexual Identity: Dad Walks the Tightrope

For his daughter, he is the model of what to expect of men. For his son, Dad is far more—he is the first model of what to *be*. Even as adults it is agonizingly difficult for us to separate the fathering role from the sexual one and then to concede the truth—that, to a very large extent, our sexual anxieties as adults are, one way or another, inherited from Father.

Father also provides our first object lesson in dealing with the opposite sex. "Girls first learn how men are likely to treat them from watching the way Dad treated Mother," says Joyce Brothers. Boys also take their cue from Father. If Dad respects Mom, is understanding, honest, reasoned in his approach to her, a son is more likely to emulate those qualities when he grows to manhood. If Dad is highhanded or overbearing (or conversely, timid and submissive) toward his wife, if it is obvious that a mutual respect is not there, a son may carry these qualities into adulthood as well. Or he may rebel against them.

A woman's anxieties about men, as well as her positive expectations concerning them, are often rooted in these childhood observations. Were Mother and Father a warm, loving couple whose occasional tiffs never jeopardized their relationship, or were they forever battling to the death? Did one side abuse the other physically or mentally while the other suffered in saintly silence? (Remember Freud's assertion that there can be no sadism without masochism.) Were deceit and duplicity the order of the day for Mother or Father—or both?

Two adult New Yorkers—a brother and sister separated by two years—grew up knowing that their dentist dad was one of the city's great womanizers. Throughout his thirty-year-marriage he routinely humiliated his wife by showing up at parties and in restaurants with his mistress-of-the-moment. Even when the marriage finally ended in divorce, it was he who brought the action, not his long-suffering wife. The pain inflicted on their mother left an indelible imprint on both children. Vowing never to repeat his father's cruelty, the son has been married for five years and has three daughters of his own. His wife unhesitatingly calls him "the most decent man I've ever known." The dentist's daughter has fared differently. In her late 20s, she admits she has never been able to sustain a relationship because she is suspicious and afraid of men. "If you had a father like mine," she tells anyone who will listen, "you'd be suspicious too."

"Children of both sexes need a strong relationship with their father," says Florence Rush. "They need to have a definite sense of what he represents for them. If they don't have that relationship, children can be destroyed." One has only to look as far as Marilyn Monroe for a classic example of how the absence of such a paternal touchstone can contribute to a woman's psychological downfall. There were, to be sure, many other factors leading to the star's tragic death from an overdose of barbiturates in 1962 at the age of 36. Born Norma Jean Baker, Monroe was never quite sure who her father was. She was barely three when her mother was committed to a mental institution, and she grew up in a series of foster homes where she was often beaten and sexually abused. There were countless other humiliations along the way. One family, for example, made little Norma Jean bathe in a tub after their six natural children had already used the water. Nevertheless, Monroe's biographers are in general agreement that at the very core of her fatal neuroses was the fact that she never knew her father—or any lasting father figure, for that matter.

A Hollywood contemporary of Monroe's, Nancy Davis (later Nancy Reagan), was luckier. Although she, too, grew up despising her natural father because he had essentially abandoned her mother, Nancy transferred all her love and loyalty to her adoptive father, noted surgeon Loyal Davis. In fact, Nancy has apparently never come to admit to herself the degree to which she still resents her natural father. "I was told as a child that my father wasn't at the hospital when I was born," Nancy wrote in her autobiography, *Nancy*. "It must have hurt Mother as much as it did me when I heard about it. I have no idea how old I was before he saw me for the first time, but I visited him only a few times over the years before he died in the 1960s. He was my father, but I somehow never could think of him that way because there had never been any relationship of any kind."

After her car salesman father, Kenneth Robbins, remarried, Nancy recalled that he "tried to please me, but too many years had gone by and we were really strangers to each other. As I look back, I am sure he was unhappy about it. Since Kenneth Robbins was such a small part of my life, it is impossible for me to think of him as my father." Still, she well remembers her last visit to her father's apartment in New Jersey. "He said something about Mother I didn't like and it made me angry. I said I was going to call my mother and go home. He got upset and locked me in the bathroom. I was terrified, and it seemed suddenly as if I were with strangers. Recalling the incident brings back a flood of memories I would rather forget. To this day, I dislike locked doors and feel trapped behind them."

Nancy was 6 years old when her mother married Dr. Davis. At first she was jealous of having to share her mother with Davis—"a man I really did not know." Eventually, however, she came to regard him as "a man of more strength and integrity than any I have known other than Ronnie. He was strict but fair, the way a father should be." Whether it was because Davis was so good or Kenneth Robbins so bad, Ronald Reagan hardly felt that he could measure up to the vaunted standards of character and achievement set by Nancy. Even after he was elected to the presidency and Nancy was firmly ensconced in the White House as First Lady, Reagan admitted that he still found Dr. Davis a hard act to follow.

Aristotle Onassis' daughter, Christina, is another one of those classic cases: the woman who started out seeking a replica of her father to marry. Ari so worshipped his only daughter, and she him, that he called her Chryso Mou ("My Golden One"). Her first husband, Joseph Bolker, was a high-powered Los Angeles real estate mogul twenty-seven years her senior. Once that marriage dissolved, Christina richocheted off several romances before marrying Alexander Andreadis, a young banker who, though from a wealthy Greek family, lacked Ari's ruthless cunning in business and personal affairs. That interlude was brief indeed; fickle Christina dumped Andreadis after only two years.

Her third and most bizarre union represented Christina's final attempt at severing the ties that bound her to her strong-willed father. In 1978, three years after she inherited the $500-million Onassis shipping empire on Ari's death, Christina wed Soviet citizen Sergei Danyelovich Kauzov, a shy, balding, one-eyed shipping clerk. Not only was he the antithesis of Onassis physically and temperamentally, but as a product of a Communist society represented all that Ari, one of the century's greatest capitalists, despised. After Christina made her point she dumped Kauzov in 1979, paying him off with a tanker of his very own. After going to such lengths to exorcise her father, it is sadly ironic that Christina appears to be lonelier and unhappier than ever.

Although not one to wallow in her personal misfortune, Elizabeth Taylor can chalk up much of her man trouble (and her penchant for wedlock) to her peculiar relationship with her father. Clearly, Francis Taylor took a back seat to his wife's boundless ambitions for their daughter. Elizabeth's mother even urged her to consider studio bosses her substituted "daddies," and since Francis was something of a willing nonentity in the Taylor family, the young actress did so without reluctance.

The first man Elizabeth married—Conrad Hilton's playboy son Nicky—was, like Francis Taylor, a well-bred pushover. Daddy did not approve; perhaps he saw too much of himself in Mr. Elizabeth Taylor No.1. For all their surface differences, actor Michael Wilding, singer Eddie Fisher, and Virginia Senator John Warner (husbands 2, 4, and 6, respectively) all exhibited similarly soft qualities. Ironically, the only two with whom Elizabeth seemed capable of forging a lasting bond were diametric opposites of Francis Taylor—headstrong, dynamic Mike Todd (who died in a plane crash leaving his widow to raise their daughter, Lisa), and the mercurial Richard Burton. After two trips to the altar, it was Burton who finally closed the Burton-Taylor chapter by leaving Liz to marry the considerably younger Suzie Hunt.

If Aristotle Onassis was such an omnipotent figure that he continued to cast a giant shadow on his daughter's relationships long after his death, Francis Taylor had much the same impact by virtue of his apparent indifference. The two men, as different as two fathers could possibly be, provided two extreme examples for their daughters of what to expect from men. For Christina, Elizabeth, and most women, fathers who are either overbearing or emotionally impotent lead to wildly distorted notions of the opposite sex.

According to Dr. John Money, sex roles are fixed by 18 months. By then a little girl has curls, is wearing a dress, and is already Daddy's budding coquette. Women asked to search their minds for their earliest childhood memories invariably dredge up recollections of rubbing their baby-smooth skin against Daddy's rough beard, or the crisp smell of his after-shave. The images conjured up are not always so pleasant; the memories are sometimes of Dad's angry voice, of doors slamming and Mom crying. Susan Strasberg's father was in the same quandary that most parents found themselves in during the 1940s and early 1950s, and she suffered for it. "He was caught in the seesawing philosophy about what was the correct behavior in raising a child," she explains. "This was pre-Spock, post-Freud. One year you were absolutely forbidden to pick up your child when it cried; the next it was necessary to soothe the baby at the first sign of tears. Some well-meaning friend told my father that to touch a daughter often after the age of three had sexual overtones. In his vulnerability as a new father, my father accepted this and drew away from me. I was an outgoing child, and this sudden withdrawal of energy made me contract, shrink imperceptibly inside myself. When I climbed on Daddy's lap, he seemed uncomfortable; if I rushed to hug him, he tensed his muscles or became passive, and as the time passed I knew surely it must be that I was unlovable, not a good little girl."

I come from a family where, after not seeing each other for a year, my father and I greet each other with nothing more than a formal handshake. My mother and sister fare little better; only recently have any of us warmed up enough to hug one another without feeling awkward. This "Scandinavian cold-bloodedness," as my mother is fond of calling it, must have developed only as we children reached maturity. I clearly remember my parents being very tactile with both of us as children. My father cuddled, pinched, squeezed, hugged, bounced, and tickled us un-selfconsciously, and the resulting sense of security remains to this day—regardless of the current fact that nowadays we Andersens sometimes appear to have chilled Lysol coursing through our veins.

Marilyn Monroe once said, "I was never told I was pretty when I was a little girl. Every little girl should be told she is pretty." And not just by anyone. Clearly, the opinion any girl values most is her father's. For most little girls, Father was not only the first human being after Mother to contend with, but the first outsider. Mother's devotion was to some extent to be expected, but Father's was more to be earned. One friend in her late 30s stands 5 feet 10 inches and weighs only 130 pounds, but she is convinced to this day that she is fat. Her father took some sort of sadistic pleasure in calling his daughter Chubby. When she tries to justify the nickname with childhood snapshots, the photos showed she was never even slightly overweight. Whatever her father's reasons for taunting her, the woman still bears the scars into middle age and appears unlikely to erase them. Similarly, a 27-year-old schoolteacher never wears short-sleeved blouses or dresses because of a disparaging comment made by her father when she was 14 about the freckles on her arms. "If it had been anyone else," she allows, "I probably would have forgotten about it the next day."

Men can cart around similar anxieties. Like the skinny woman whose father convinced her that she was overweight, one young writer was chided by his father for being chunky. And like the woman, family photos showed that, as his mother still contends, the son was not even remotely chunky as a little boy. The father apparently saw it all as an elaborate joke, but his son didn't. Rather than spend the rest of his life proving his father wrong, the writer has done quite the opposite. He is an unrepentant glutton who has made no effort to control his eating despite doctors' warnings that at 5 feet 8 inches and 250 pounds, he is dangerously obese.

Such hurtful comments from a father about his child's appearance can and often do have a lifelong effect. Frequently they are rooted in the father's own insecurities. As a boy, Bing Crosby was described by friends as "towheaded and pudgy." Because of the ribbing he received during childhood, Bing would have something of a weight fixation for the rest of his life. But that didn't stop him from mercilessly ribbing his son Gary when Gary turned out to have a similarly chunky physique as a youngster. Bing criticized his son in front of family, friends, and even in the press. In the 1940s, he told one reporter that his other children were beginning to show some musical talent, but that Gary was "just getting fat." Bing claimed that no matter what he and Gary's mother, Dixie Lee Crosby, did, they couldn't "keep him away from the refrigerator." Not surprisingly, Gary was crushed. Eventually, like his father, he overcame his weight problem, and, also like his father, he sought solace in the bottle.

Dads can also shatter our fragile sense of self-confidence by zinging not only our looks but our actions. How many of us go through life never challenging our father's early slurs? Once I had made the grievous error of spilling a glass of milk in a restaurant, my father convinced himself that I was terminally clumsy—destined to stumble through life like Gerald Ford, tripping down stairs, dropping Waterford crystal goblets, knocking over Tiffany lamps. Fortunately, I have proven to be only an average klutz; as an adult I seldom spill a cup of hot coffee in my lap more than once every few days. Yet whenever I do, and have the ill fortune to be in the presence of my father at the same time, he seldom fails to allude to my chronic clumsiness. My response is generally a stream-of-consciousness tantrum that, of course, has absolutely no impact on his opinion but at least leaves me feeling I have fought the Good Fight.

For all of us, but in all honesty particularly for women, it is important to grow up with a sense of pride in our physical appearance. Of the scores of women I have interviewed on this topic, nearly all either credit their father for boosting their self-image, or blame him for undermining it.

"Daddy always called me Dollface," one woman remembers, "and even when I went through that fat period so many people do around 10 or so, he never made me feel like anything but the prettiest little girl who ever lived. But I had friends whose fathers weren't so nice to their children. Nina looked so much like me—blonde hair, brown eyes; we both even had freckles. People thought we were sisters. We both loved Malomars and milkshakes, so we both got chubby at the same time, too. But Nina's father used to criticize her brutally—always apologizing to his adult neighbors and friends for this 'tubby' little girl, telling her in this nagging voice that she should stop slouching, or comb her hair, making her feel rotten about herself every chance he got." Nina's mother made a concerted effort to undo her husband's damage. "She would compliment Nina on the way she looked, and I often heard her telling Nina's dad to let up. But he never did, and no matter what reassuring words Nina got from her mother, there really was no way of offsetting her father's cruel words. My mother was always full of praise for me, but I've got to admit Dad was the one I really wanted to hear it from. Isn't that the way it is with all girls?" Whatever happened to Nina? "She's my age now—29—single, and living in Los Angeles. Nina's quite beautiful, really, though I don't think she will ever know it. Her whole attitude about herself has really screwed up her relationships with men. Funny thing, she still sees her father a lot—and he stills tells her to straighten up and comb her hair."

For any child unlucky enough to be born to neurotic parents—and, as Joyce Brothers points out, "a child who is neurotic is not likely to have an unneurotic father"—there is little hope of emerging without some psychological damage. The father who emotionally tortured his child the way Bing Crosby and Nina's father did was undoubtedly carting around some pretty heavy doubts of his own. But how much of Father's own often inexcusable behavior stemmed from the essentially neurotic nature of the institution of fatherhood itself? Being a father has meant, and to a great extent still means, being in a state of disorientation and doubt. "I guess I could have been a little more encouraging," concedes one man with grown children. "But I was pretty damn unhappy then for a number of reasons. There weren't many ways I could vent that frustration, so the kids suffered. If they were still talking to me, I'd apologize. But I don't think they'd understand."

Father had a right to be bewildered, but he was certainly not encouraged to express that sense of bewilderment. If he was the absentee enforcer, the family's resident second-class citizen, why then was he expected to be the bolsterer of his children's sense of self? How could he nurture others emotionally when he himself was often the odd man out? Behaviorists tell us that in the most fundamental way, Father makes us aware of our gender by giving us the first alternative to Mom as a sexual model. A girl learns she is female by learning that Daddy is male. We began exploring Mother's body from birth (before, actually) but Father was exciting new territory. Long after Mother had swallowed her pride and allowed us to witness her sitting on the commode as part of her toilet-training campaign, we pushed our way into the bathroom behind Dad to see what he was up to. More significantly, it was Mother who took it upon herself to push our hands away when we explored our bodies, not Father. As self-appointed inhibitor of our natural curiosity, she left us only one other sexual model to turn to: Father.

A little girl's earliest impressions of her father may exert a profound influence on the physical characteristics she seeks out in a mate. "For a girl, father is the first quasi-sexual figure," says Lionel Tiger. "Until relatively recently in society, Father and other male relatives were a female child's *only* real standard for judging the opposite sex. Girls saw their fathers far more than any other man, right up to the time they were ready to get married themselves. Now, we have pop figures—movie and TV stars, rock stars and the like—that permit even very young girls to externalize some of these feelings. A seven-year-old might fantasize about the teen idol of the moment, for example, but if she has what is perceived as a normal relationship with Father, he will always eclipse the others."

This sort of imprinting can surface twenty years later in seemingly inconsequential ways. "A woman may wonder why she finds men with hair on the backs of their hands attractive," suggests Dr. Brothers, "until she remembers that her father had hair on the backs of his hands." Accordingly, women whose fathers smoked are more likely to marry smokers; women whose fathers were husky may be attracted to heavyset men. Not out of any conscious desire to marry Father, but because deep in their psyches their notion of maleness is inexorably linked to those first sights, sounds, and smells.

Contrary to popular belief, this doesn't mean that women always seek to marry facsimiles of their fathers. Quite the reverse. They often seek to *become* their fathers. Daddy may have provided the model for what to expect of men, but he was also a symbol of power and authority in the outside world. For the most part, he dominated Mother, and the rest of the family—girls included—envied him for it. "The idea that women want to find a guy like Dear Old Dad is specious," insists Maccoby. "In my practice, I find most people—men and women—wanting to marry their *mothers*. Neurotic women particularly are forever looking for their mother in men. She represents unquestioning love to them, and Father, well, he is threatening. You may want to be like him, but you wouldn't want to marry him." Concurs Dr. Brothers: "The old saw that a man should look at his mother-in-law and that is what his wife will be like in twenty years is all wrong. The husband should look at his *father*-in-law. *That is the type of person his wife is likely to resemble in twenty years.*"

At 23, my own sister, Valerie, is a prime example. Since I was 10 when Valerie was born, and had essentially been brought up as an only child until then, I had a prime vantage point from which to watch her personality take shape. For a time, I was not so much a brother as a third parent, a special responsibility that began when she was 6 weeks old and we boarded the U.S.S. *Sultan* in Yokohama, heading for home. During the two-week voyage across a stormy Pacific, I would often baby-sit Val in our cabin while our parents dined topside. Throughout her childhood in the San Francisco suburbs, I watched Valerie evolve into an adult who more closely resembles our father than our mother. Like Dad (and unlike Mom, who has long suffered from asthma), Val smokes. Both father and daughter are given to long, pensive silences, dislike what they consider pointless chatter (like the trivia games in which Mom and I delight), and are given to Vesuvian flare-ups. Yet, curiously, both are more outgoing. As far back as I can remember, my father and sister made friends easily.

My father was attentive, caring, but by no means did Val become the classic "Daddy's Girl." Yet those women who started in that category will most likely live out their lives in Father's shadow. "I was my father's daughter," wrote Paula Weideger, author of *Menstruation and Menopause,* in *Ms.* "He is dead now and I am a grown woman and still I am my father's daughter. This fact is embarrassing to report. But only a little. The first great love of my life was my pa as is the case for every daddy's girl, and that is not some 'stage' out of which a child grows. It is a life-giving, problem-creating, personality-molding tug-of-war and celebration. I am many things besides, but I am daddy's girl too and so I will remain—all the way to the old folks' home."

The process starts early. "From the beginning," remembers freelance writer Linda Heller, "he treated me like a porcelain doll—afraid I'd crack at the slightest jarring. I was not allowed to play with jacks or marbles—he was afraid I might swallow one. Years later, when my friends were learning how to drive, I would be afraid to try, and he would refuse to teach me. I've never learned.

"His attitude toward me changed little over the years. In his wallet he kept only one photograph of me, as an eight-year-old ballerina posing in a pink tutu. Every year, I would try to give him an older, 'more distinguished' picture, but every year he would insist on keeping the first one. I had won him over simply by being his daughter." After her father's death, Linda launched a writing career of her own, and, like most women who have been pampered by their fathers, she discovered that she had the confidence in herself to carry it off.

One of the obvious drawbacks to being the apple of Daddy's eye is sibling jealousy. In extreme situations father and daughter may focus on each other to the exclusion of Mom as well as brothers and sisters. One woman remembers that she was considered the only person capable of calming Father when he flew into his periodic rages. "Go to your father," her mother would plead. "You know you're the only one he'll listen to when he's like this."

In another family, two brothers grew up intensely envious of the attention Sis received. "At Christmas," one of the sons recalls, "it didn't really matter that the rest of us were there. Dad would politely accept the gifts we'd made for him, but he'd go ape over his present from Donna. My mother made sure we were treated even-handedly—maybe *too* even-handedly—when it came to the presents Santa brought for us. But the gifts my brother and I got didn't mean half as much as the love Donna got from Dad on a daily basis. I have two girls of my own and do everything I can possibly do to treat them equally. I'd never do to them what my father did to my brother and me."

This bitterness is not lost on the Daddy's Girl. She knows all too well that she is resented; the mere fact that Daddy loves her more makes her feel as if she has done something wrong, not right—something that took away from the other people she loved and led to bitterness. It is not enough, however, to ever make her relinquish her cherished position.

Daddy's Girls are, it would appear, more successful in pursuing career ambitions. According to Dr. Francis Symonds, associate clinical professor of psychiatry at the New York University School of Medicine, studies show that "the highest percentage of women that aspire to careers have been encouraged or influenced by a man. Their fathers, usually." But in order to succeed in the workplace, self-confessed Daddy's Girl Paula Weideger explains, "There has to be some smoothing over, temperamentally speaking. And this is no easy thing. A girl who has been extravagantly loved by Pop is liable to grow into a woman who cannot bear it when she does not get her own way. A woman who has made professional success has learned to restrain, and maybe even forget about these temperamental reactions to frustration." Having accomplished this, she may well be on her way to becoming the superwoman Daddy ("My little girl can do anything") envisioned she would become. She may, in fact, live out his unrealized ambitions in much the same way a son might be expected to.

Being a Daddy's Girl may help one's work life, but it is a definite liability where sex and love are concerned. Not that a Daddy's Girl lacks the desire. Says Dr. Symonds: Daddy's Girls "feel sure of their femininity." That stems from Father bolstering their self-esteem and body image from infancy. "These women usually feel more attractive and lovable. And children who grow up that way usually are lovable and attractive later on." Concurs Weideger: "I know that I only feel my normal self when there is a man somewhere around. A man whom I might love, I mean to say. And a man who might love me. Early training gives skills along with the creation of a certain need. Daddy's girls are usually flirtatious, for example, and familiar with one or another mode of seduction." Indeed, a 3-year-old girl's frankly seductive behavior toward her father is apparent to all. She becomes accustomed to dealing with Father in all his various moods and frames of mind. Deprived of this experience, she may never figure who men are and what they are for. But she does figure it out, and the dichotomy between fathers and mothers becomes painfully real.

Dad is in a unique position to serve as the focus of his daughter's fantasies. Often, that is just what they are—fantasies. "My father and I were far closer than I was with my mother," says one woman. "He was the disciplinarian, yes, but he was never *at* us all the time the way she was."

No, the "petty" tasks of nagging us to make our beds, set the table, wash behind our ears, and eat our vegetables had been handed over to Mom. We were often at the end of our tether with her by the time Daddy came home with a warm hug and words of praise. Daughters didn't particularly protest when Daddy asked them to do something they didn't want to, because they were not embroiled in a long-running battle with him. Daddy was fun. Daddy was dessert. Daddy was also distant, mysterious, sexual.

Yet Daddy's Girls may never have been as close to him as they thought they were. Dr. Richard Robertiello notes that these women have "created the illusion of being closer to father than mother." They will even insist that they married men who looked like their fathers. "But inside," Robertiello continues, "you find the man she married is actually more like her *mother*. If a woman's mother was whiny, that woman has often built up enough of a tolerance of these unpleasant characteristics to tolerate them in her husband while telling herself all the time that she married a man just like her dad." The same fantasies of Mother caring for Dad are transferred to her husband. Echoing Maccoby, Robertiello contends that "man or woman, our first marriage is often to someone with the personality of our mother. If your mother wasn't a nice person, you're in trouble."

Terry Dixon is an orthopedic surgeon in Fort Lauderdale. She is also divorced and the mother of two teenage sons. Terry's father, a prosperous contractor, doted on his only daughter from the start; her first recollection of pride in her appearance is the day over forty years ago when he commented that her eyes were "as pretty as Mommy's." Terry's Dad nurtured her emotionally as well as intellectually. He urged her not to marry until she completed medical school and established her career, but Terry dropped out after her first year at Johns Hopkins to marry a classmate. "My father was telling me one thing," she says, "but the rest of the world—my mother, peers, books, TV—was telling me the opposite. To be a happy woman, they said, I had to put my own ambitions on the back burner and make a man my first priority. It took me ten years, but I found out that Dad was right. I was shaken for a while, but the belief he instilled in me that I could be a great doctor survived. All along I knew it was my father I really wanted to be like, not my mother."

Paula Weideger wonders, as all Daddy's Girls must wonder, "if my sureness in myself, which is often buffeted and bruised when I do not have a man around, wouldn't have been steadier and tougher if my father had not been so exclusively the subject of my love and dependence—if he had not been my only example of life lived outside the house. I do not know the answer, of course. But I do know that as a Daddy's Girl I had many emotional advantages, and among them was a built-in acceptance of emotional greed. A little girl—and a grown-up woman—cannot have too much love or too many possibilities."

Like father, like son? There is no escaping the fact that each of us who has somehow survived to adulthood owes his sexual sense of self to Pop. Curiously, this crucial process of "father identification" that took place when we were toddlers has less to do with anatomy than with learning and conforming to what society deems "masculine" behavior. Not that Dad didn't give us some perspective early on when it came to body image. As little boys, we were all impressed by what seemed to us to be Dad's awesome apparatus—though at the time, of course, we had no idea that it might be used for something other than peeing. One friend of mine now nearing 50 told me that the first time he saw his father's penis it reminded him of a "bell-ringer's rope." My friend also remembers the paddling he received when he reached up and gave his father's "rope" a yank.

If we are to follow Freud, the human personality is essentially divided into three parts: the destructive id, the ego, and the conscience, or superego, which really serves as the basis for civilized behavior. Father has traditionally been responsible, Freud postulates, for the nurturing of that third, most "human" level of subconscious development. He was the figure from the world outside who first gave us the idea that there might be objective notions of good and evil, that there were generally accepted values that transcended even what Mother was teaching us, and that feelings of blame and guilt would follow if we did not live up to those larger values and expectations. This may rub more strident feminists the wrong way, but there is plenty of clinical (not to mention commonsense) evidence to support Freud's theory. "Mother's love is unconditional," reiterates Maccoby. "She loves a child just because he or she is her child, not because that child has done anything to earn that love." Erich Fromm, Maccoby's mentor, went on to note that "fatherly love is conditional love. Its principle is 'I love you because you fulfill my expectations, because you do your duty, because you are like me.'"

For boys especially, that final phrase—"because you are like me"—was what we most wanted to hear. Whether or not we managed to live up to those expectations is academic; Father's mere presence provided us with a glimpse of our own future, a walking, talking, and, ideally, a loving prototype of the man we would become.

It is all but impossible to quantify what Father's impact was on our self-image. It is considerably easier to gauge the deleterious effects on a boy's self-image when Dad is not a permanent fixture in the home. That a wildly disproportional number of homosexuals and men suffering from a variety of serious sexual dysfunctions come from fatherless homes is well documented. But what of the fatherless boy with a documented healthy case of heterosexuality? In many instances, he grew up not knowing how men cope with women, what their demands might be, how resolutions are reached between mates. "My father left Mom before I was born," says Danny, a nursery owner and garden supply dealer in northern California. "My grandfathers had both died, and there were no other guys around when I was growing up, either. So the only time I ever really saw men in a family situation as a very young kid was when I saw my friend's fathers. That wasn't enough. It only occurred to me much later, during my first marriage, that I didn't know how to deal with any woman on a day-to-day level. I didn't know how to assert myself when it was necessary, or when to give in." The predictable result: two failed marriages, and two sons now perpetuating their father's sad predicament by growing up themselves in fatherless households.

One study indicated that those new husbands facing the most trouble in their marriages were those whose fathers had died before their sons had reached the age of 12.

They were described as having rather lackluster sex lives and not capable of exhibiting much warmth or affection. "Cold" was the word most often used to characterize this group.

The impact of a father's departure from the scene can be even more basic, leading to confusion about one's own gender. Stephen Bernstein, Betty Steiner and Joseph T. D. Glaister, all researchers at the Gender Identity Clinic of Toronto's prestigious Clark Institute of Psychiatry, studied 163 male patients over a two-year period and discovered that an astounding 55 had lost a parent early in childhood—almost all fathers. "The psychological literature up until now has given minimal importance to the father," says Bernstein. "All of the importance has historically been given to the mother-child relationship. We're not saying fathers are more important than mothers, but we are saying fathers are very important, especially in gender identity formation."

Such confusion may not manifest itself in a sexual way at all. Instead, the boy not imprinted with a clear sense of his sexual self often lashes out in violent, antisocial ways. Having never had a clear picture of himself, having never learned how to deal with his father, he may rebel against male authority figures like the school principal, the boss, or the policeman. Our jails and mental hospitals are crammed with these products of fatherless homes.

Does that mean even a lousy father is preferable to none at all? Though the average boy growing up without an older male around is at greater risk when it comes to sexual difficulties, neuroses, and even psychotic and criminal behavior as an adult, the greatest damage of all seems to be done by a bad father. Once invested with all the power that goes with being the family's predominant authority figure, Dad had better not turn out to be a monster. Mark David Chapman, sitting in jail for the murder of John Lennon, is one of many troubled men who may have mixed feelings about Mother but place the blame for their fouled-up lives squarely on the shoulders of a father they perceive to be uncaring or even overtly destructive. Mom may have had her faults, but Dad, they truly believe, was an SOB.

Tennessee Williams managed to channel some of his frustrations into a handful of the greatest plays any American has ever produced, but his own father's cruelty toward his effeminate son (the elder Williams gloried in taunting the boy, calling him Miss Nancy) certainly contributed to Tennessee's homosexuality, his bouts of depression and lifelong battles with drugs and booze. Paul Lynde, the least-loved son of a small-town sheriff, ranked in the popularity polls as one of America's most popular funnymen during the late 1970s, but in the long run his sense of personal disorientation stemming from the strained relationship with his father led to a chaotic personal life that included an alcohol problem and at least two arrests for disorderly conduct at the height of his career.

Most people, fortunately, grow up in families where Father occupies some tolerable middle ground. If Dad is neither overbearing nor invisible, then his daughter probably has a better chance of forming a more realistic view of the male sex. This, in turn, presumably gives her a cleaner shot at a successful sex life. "An open-minded and loving relationship with her father," contends Maureen Green, "can lay the foundations for many a girl's later sexual attitudes, and consequently for her success with men for the rest of her life. Girls who get on well with their fathers find marriage easier."

That first love spanning the sexes is of such importance in our later lives, many experts feel, that a woman's ability to achieve orgasm may be greatly influenced by her initial feelings toward her father. If a girl is rebuffed by him, or if, say, an unhappy mother sabotages her daughter's natural affection for him, there will be far-reaching consequences. One study of seven thousand women working in topless joints and strip clubs showed that the majority came from fatherless homes. Most of these women conceded that in baring their bodies to strangers, they were probably looking for the male attention that they had never gotten during their childhood. Lacking that foundation, many of these women also admitted that they did not rely on men for intimacy. Of the seven thousand women interviewed for the study, half turned out to be lesbians.

A more common reaction to the absence of father love is the kind of woman who craves affection from men but can never come to conceive of men as full-blown people. Instead, men become inanimate things, often desirable, exciting, mysterious things—but things, nonetheless. The woman suffering from this handicap may wind up treating men as they are so often accused of treating women, like sex objects. Unable to see beyond a male's sexuality, she merely flits from bed to bed without achieving any genuine satisfaction physically or otherwise. Or she may become miserly with her affection, rarely if ever daring to seduce or be seduced.

Karen's father was on the road selling panty hose within a week after she was born, and visited his wife and daughter only twice before taking off for good when Karen was four. After three disastrous marriages, numerous affairs, two abortions, and a bout with Valium addiction, Karen had withdrawn to a sort of self-imposed celibacy. "It's not that I am any less sexual than I always was," she explains, "but one day my father came to visit me. We hadn't seen each other for thirty years, and I was enraged that now he was trying to make amends. There he left this little girl sitting on the front porch, crying every day until I realized he really wasn't coming home. And now he expected me to forgive all just because he was old and alone and probably didn't have that much longer to live. It wasn't fair. We met in this diner not far from the shopping mall where I worked, and I was ready to tell this guy off when he walked in and slid into the booth across from me, as if there was not the slightest doubt that I was his daughter.

I sat and politely listened to him while he said straight out that he had no apologies, that he didn't come expecting forgiveness, that he just wanted to start fresh. It took him about five minutes to deliver his little speech and when it was over I just stood up and dumped a pitcher of scalding coffee right into his lap."

Karen had discovered that this was life, not a segment of *The Love Boat* or *Fantasy Island*. The rage she felt was genuine; it could not be dispelled in a single afternoon, if ever. For Karen, the return of her Prodigal Papa did focus her attention on a true source of her trouble with men. "My father was a grade-A bastard, and his sudden reappearance cleared away any doubts I might have had," she says. "He abandoned me, and because no one was ever there to replace him, I grew up fearing men but wanting their attention. I still want that, but not until I can have it without the fear."

It is that fear, Karen now acknowledges, that prevented her from ever being totally comfortable sexually. For all her husbands, long-term lovers, and one-night stands, Karen claims she has never experienced an orgasm. Sexologist Dr. Alex Comfort, author of the best-selling *Joy of Sex*, lays the responsibility for Karen's dilemma on her father's doorstep. "The greater a woman's conviction that love objects are not dependable, and must be held on to," he has pointed out, "the poorer her capacity for full response. This may come about through the loss of a father, or childhood deprivation of the father's role. Some degree of parental seduction at the unconscious level seems to be necessary for human females to establish full function. Deprived of a stable father figure, the non-orgasmic seem to be unable to face the blurring of personal boundaries which goes with full physiological orgasm. It looks as though a sexual response in women is based on presexual learning, and of a specific kind. Fathers are there to imprint girls for sexual adequacy."

Karen should count her blessings. A disturbingly large

number of women go from one futile relationship to another, never knowing precisely who put them in this curious state of mind and why. During her golf-playing days in California in the 1930s, Joan Fontaine always had the same response when asked "What is your handicap?" Her quick reply: "Men." Four unhappy marriages later the Oscar-winning actress is well into her 60s and still operating under that handicap. She has a sneaking suspicion, she told me, that her ambivalent feelings toward her father, Walter de Havilland, must have laid the groundwork for her lifelong male trouble.

De Havilland, whose other daughter, Olivia, constituted the other half of Hollywood's most famous battling sister act, split from Joan and Olivia's mother when Joan was barely two. Joan, who was born in Japan but raised with her sister in northern California, vividly remembers visiting her father there after he married the Japanese woman who had been the family's upstairs maid. Joan was ensconced in one room of Tokyo's Imperial Hotel, her father and stepmother in adjacent quarters. Joan was enthralled with the exotic street sounds—"the clatter of wooden getas on sidewalks, the plaintive notes of a distant samisen"—but her reverie was abruptly interrupted. "From the adjoining room arose noises too," she recalled. "Odd ones. They got odder and odder. I was thoroughly bewildered. Nothing I'd read in the romance of Milady and D'Artagnan in *The Three Musketeers* ... prepared me for this onslaught of animal noises emanating from my father's bedroom." During the same visit, Joan's father at last began to pay attention to her, but for the wrong reasons. "Father now found his stranger daughter growing attractive to him, especially in her bathing suit. Often he would walk along the beach with me, usually berating Mother, but always requesting that I appear in my one-piece blue 'bathing costume.' I was on guard." The breaking point came when he announced that his wife "was ill, possibly pregnant," recalls Joan, "and that he would have his bed moved into my room. I rejected his proposal with some degree of coolness. His masculine pride was wounded. Soon we were enemies."

Joan did not fare much better with her stepfather. George Milan Fontaine, the man who provided Joan with her professional surname when she decided to enter show business on Olivia's heels, "was of medium height, pink-cheeked, a salt-of-the-earth American; he smelled of castile soap, Harris tweed, and soda mints, and was hypochondriacal." He was also a stern disciplinarian, but what Joan remembers most vividly was that before they reached puberty, both she and her sister would be bathed by their stepfather each night. "The washcloth would tarry too long in intimate places," she recounted. "Olivia and I, never given to confidences, did agree that something was odd. We were to have the same discussion eight years later, this time joined by Mother, with more serious consequences. Fathers and daughters, stepfathers and stepdaughters. The story is not new." Michael Maccoby has encountered this numerous times among his own patients. "Many fathers don't put the time in with their daughters when they are young, then they see an attractive, pubescent girl and they are interested. The result can be catastrophic if Father is not around and attentive from the very start."

Presuming, however, that Dad was there to give us some healthy and what might be perceived as normal concepts of our identities as men, were we any more likely to be happy? Well, we were at least given the foundation that enabled us to devote less of our time to worrying about our own self-image and more to coping with the feelings of others.

Lionel Tiger understates that we "learn our sex roles very early." Michael Maccoby's father was an English-born rabbi, a very formal man who never hugged or even rough-housed with his son. "There really has to be some open affection between father and son in those early years," says Maccoby, "so with my own son I've always made a point of wrestling with him on the living room floor, hugging him whenever the spirit moved me. My son and I are outnumbered by his mother and two sisters, so it was that much more important that he make that physical connection with me that he be able to identify with Daddy."

My own father, though nonathletic, was extremely physical. Standing all of 5 feet 6 inches and tipping the scales at no more than 140 pounds, he was nevertheless a colossus from my perspective as a child. Actually, there were reasons for the perception that had nothing to do with the fact that I was a little boy. His hands were indeed large for a man of his size, and he had a sturdy, square-shouldered build that compensated for his short stature and made him look every inch the career military man.

Dad was always *doing*—building a fourteen-foot powerboat in our garage, zipping around the Japanese countryside on his motorcycle, with me holding on to him for dear life as we straddled the narrow dikes that crisscrossed the ubiquitous rice paddies like the stitching on a patchwork quilt. During the early 1950s he built a two-bedroom split-level of his own design on three acres he had purchased in Castro Valley, some twenty miles east of San Francisco, and when his days of wandering on behalf of the navy seemed to be behind him, that is where we settled for a time on our return from Japan. Meantime, he also built a log cabin for us to use on weekends eight thousand feet above sea level in the High Sierras. And when he was darting about the globe for the navy (as it turned out, we stayed in one place while he kept flying military aircraft to places like Bangkok, Karachi, and Dhahran), Dad constantly adding what real estate types call "improvements" to his properties. During our three years in California, Dad was in a state of perpetual motion, his body a blur as he hammered, sawed, dug, and hauled. The results at home:

a new wing complete with huge master bedroom, a bathroom, an expanded two-car garage, a winding concrete driveway, a corral and barn (to accommodate the two horses he bought me), a toolshed, a huge enclosed patio, three acres of landscaping and fruit trees, etc. He was considerably more laid-back about the cabin. Working on the rare summer weekend, he only managed to add central heating, indoor plumbing, an upstairs sleep area, a wraparound deck, another toolshed, new flooring, and a new septic system.

As far back as I am capable of remembering, my father set this example of male as moving object. Later, I would be pressed into his service. As a 3-, 4-, and 5-year-old, I imitated with glee. Home movies show me in the narrow driveway of our cement-and-brick Philadelphia house, looking like a pint-sized Nehru in my white paper "car-washer's hat" as I go about the serious business of helping Dad scrub down our red-and-white 1954 Ford station wagon. But as I got older, my enthusiasm was dampened considerably by Father's daunting energies and irrepressible perfectionism. It was not enough that, at age 10, I managed to carry a dozen heavy cement slabs for a footpath leading to our front door. Once he saw the results, Dad commented only that the slabs were not perfectly straight and without a word set out to redo the job his way—"the right way." Similarly, now if I took it upon myself to wash the family cars (by this time, like every other California family of the period, we had two), my cuteness was no longer a factor; the cars were never sparkling enough, our three acres of lawn were never mowed straight enough, the horses' stalls were never clean enough.

The situation only worsened with adolescence. When we left our Castro Valley house for a larger place ten miles farther east in tiny Dublin, California, tensions between us reached the point of near-violence. While my father and I were trying to maneuver his rosewood gun cabinet up the spiral staircase and into the master bedroom of our new house, he lapsed into his rather unpleasant practice of barking orders and firing off insults. "Over to the left—no, no, not that much. Up a little higher. Look out! No, dummy, *higher*..." As I neared the top of the staircase, with my mother looking on, for one instant I seriously considered letting go of my end of the heavy cabinet and watching the expression on his face when it carried him to the tiled hallway floor twelve feet below. I didn't let go, mostly because I feared his vengeful wrath, not because I worried what damage the giant rosewood gun cabinet might do as it tumbled over him.

Times were rare when it seemed I had Dad's whole-hearted approval for performing one of these "manly" tasks. He did not criticize the job I was doing, for example, when I crawled up behind the eaves in our cabin and installed all the fiberglass insulation myself. He really had no choice. At 13, I was the only person on hand small enough to crawl into the tiny spaces, rolls of insulation and staple gun in hand.

That was only half of our gender identity equation as Dad formulated it. If a boy was to grow into a man by physical labor of some sort, he also had to have a clear notion of what men did not do. Like most fathers of his generation, he shied from grocery shopping, rarely cooked (and then only bachelor staples like bacon and eggs and his own special fried bologna sandwiches), and never did housework. Like most mothers of her generation, mine accepted this—and still accepts it—as part of the measure of a true man.

Given this male imprinting, made all the more indelible by the rigidly masculine military family in which our little clan existed, there seemed little opportunity for confusion. For the unconscious task of providing his son with a clear gender model, Dad could not have asked for more accommodating surroundings. Of course, there was confusion anyway. I had a pretty unfuzzy idea that, as much as anything, my father's seemingly insatiable appetite for hard physical work was a particularly male trait. I still feel that. Yet as an adult I am just as passionately opposed to doing anything of that nature.

Beyond the simple act of taking out the garbage and doing an occasional chore, I bluntly refuse to do any of those things in which my father obviously still takes such tremendous pleasure. A handyman I'm not, nor do I aspire to be. I know that my father's concept of masculine behavior is not right; I'm convinced it is not altogether wrong, either. Now that he is in his early 60s, he sees no reason to abandon the age-old ritual of pulling up at the gas station, popping out as soon as the ignition is off, and doing what amounts to a tribal dance around the car. This routine, performed even in a driving hailstorm, serves no observable purpose in terms of the maintenance of the car. He may kick a tire or two, or look under the hood for show, but the real message is: "Look at me, the Man and Protector." This is reinforced by the females of the family, who wait behind or make a beeline for the washroom. When I was a little boy, I was eager to leap out of the car with Dad. Now, in my 30s, I sit motionless behind the wheel and expect to be waited on. The most exercise I get is searching through my wallet for the modest fortune it takes nowadays to fill a tank with regular unleaded.

Strangely, Dad, with his uncertainties born of growing up during the Depression and fighting in World War II, was always the first to sing the praises of leisure. When it came to whatever career I might pursue, there was no question in my father's mind that the only way to earn enough money to achieve the ultimate dream of "paying someone else to do it for you" was to become a professional. He had been a superb student, particularly in math and physics. And when the navy paid for him to attend classes in contract law in New York, he got the highest grades.

He loved then, as now, to play the piano, and though he ranked second to my mother when it came to fiction, he was a voracious reader of nonfiction, newspapers, and magazines.

He discussed all his various interests from the beginning, but all that paled in comparison to his actions. Yet for all the planes and ships and guns that surrounded me in my daily life as a military brat, there was one lesson my father unwittingly taught me about masculinity that would have remained indelible regardless of our particular environment.

Not long after our arrival in Japan, my mother developed bronchial pneumonia and, at the age of 31, lay near death at the base hospital. Dad never told me that she might not recover; I learned that only when my cub scout den mother broke down sobbing as she had my fellow scouts and I make get-well cards for Mom as our project for the week. All officers were expected to employ at least one maid, and ours, a kind of Japanese Hazel by the name of Suako, moved into the house and took on the added responsibilities of cooking my meals and seeing me off to school. She leaped at the opportunity. Already married and divorced four times, Suako, a survivor of Hiroshima, had been deserted by each of her husbands when they discovered she was sterile.

Aside from his grim demeanor and palatable sense of detachment, Dad did not express any overt feelings of sadness. He struggled to stay in control as his young wife fought for her life. Another officer's wife, a neighbor and sometime golf partner of my mother's, told me during this crisis that Dad had cried once during Mom's painful ordeal (among other forms of medically prescribed torture, long needles were inserted through my mother's back each day to drain her lungs—all without benefit of anesthesia). I never witnessed any overtly emotional displays on my father's part, and though the woman who told me of his weeping was certainly well-intentioned, Dad would surely have unleashed a volley of sailor's expletives in her direction had he found out, and I would have understood why.

Mom did pull through, and by concealing his feelings, Dad had shown me at the age of seven that inner strength and stoicism were two hallmarks of manhood. Women were to be worried about, protected, and allowed to run the gamut of emotions that we were never to vent. For all the current hair-pulling about a set of values that has discouraged little boys from crying, we cannot fall into the trap of assuming that our fathers were emotional cripples. If they were more dignified in their suffering, they never felt the fear or the hurt any less.

These fundamental notions we learned from Father were greatly expanded upon as we reached puberty. Here, we sons seemed to have a clear advantage over daughters. "Adolescent boys have an easier time finding sexual models than we do," writes Nancy Friday. "They may not think of their fathers as Don Juans, but at least they see them responding to women, turning to look at a pretty girl in the street, talking about sex. We may not like this, it may be done in bad taste, but it gives the boy a sense it is OK to be sexual. But when did you last hear a mother remind her daughter about the sex appeal of a good looking man? Oh, we may talk about his hands, his eyes, the cut of his suit, but what about the seductive line of his hip or shoulder? How does mother react to an off-color joke? No wonder women have no background, no role models for response to blue movies. We have no sexual camaraderie."

Friday goes on to recount her "first trip to the beach when nobody talked about those fascinating bulges in men's bathing suits. I sat with my little shovel, staring at my first man in a latex Jantzen, and learned women's silence." The author overstates her case, certainly; for the most part, our fathers were furtive in their attentions paid to that "pretty girl in the street" and seldom if ever traded dirty jokes with their sons. Quite the contrary. Our fathers were as "silent" as their wives.

I also remember one of my earlier trips to the beach. My father had been asked by local officials in the Japanese town where we lived to serve as the sole American judge in a beauty pageant. He was embarrassed but did not want to insult his Japanese hosts. We were, after all, military occupiers of a conquered but still proud nation. The Japanese were rapidly adopting many Western customs, but the most difficult of these to assimilate were those that entailed abandoning ancient attitudes toward women. Geishas were the only females in Japanese society to be depicted in any sexually suggestive way. Something as seemingly benign as a beauty pageant in the mid-1950s constituted a minor cultural breakthrough for Japanese eager to copy their conquerers. In retrospect, they may well have been better off without this particular American custom, but at the time Japanese women as well as Japanese men were eager to get on with it. So there I sat on the beach one afternoon, watching my dad up on the hastily erected platform squirming and smiling that frozen smile of his as young Japanese women of every imaginable size and shape paraded before him.

In fairness to Nancy Friday, it must be conceded that there are fathers who are frank with their sons in matters of sex. The father who takes his son to a whorehouse to lose his virginity is essentially a creature of fiction. Not so the father who brags openly and continuously of his exploits, daring his sons to outdo him. "It was okay for me to go home and tell my dad I just balled three broads," claims actor James Caan, "and he'd say, 'That's my boy!'" Caan even guesses that, had his father known that his 13-year-old son was making love to a neighborhood girl amid the rooftop pigeon coops of their tenements, "Dad probably would have wanted to jump her himself."

Caan, now well into his 40s, seems to be all the more

determined to live up to his father's grand sexual expectations. The actor remembers one night in the mid-1970s when he and his brother Ronnie were "half bombed in Vegas, and we had a girl with us, and we were all sitting around having a good time. And Ronnie says, 'Come on, let's call Dad and wake his ass up.' It was five o'clock in the morning and we put the girl up to saying, 'Hello, Mr. Caan? I've just been fucked by your sons, and I want to thank you, 'cause they're really great!' And the old man says, 'You ain't been fucked till you been fucked by the old man....Of course, I need two guys to help me on and off.'" After two failed marriages, Caan's own level of sexual maturity can be measured by the following statement: "Everybody makes me out to be some kind of macho pig, humping women in the gutter. I do, but I put a pillow under 'em first."

We have been told that it was Mommie Dearest who sexually programmed us from infancy. If she was overbearing, we would surely suffer the consequences. Daughters ran the risk of becoming hectoring harpies, sons winding up homosexuals, misogynists, or worse. We neglected to see that it was Dad who, in matters of gender, had the upper hand. He provided his children with their first specific example of what it is to be a man—of how a man is to look, smell, walk, talk, act, and react. Of how he is to treat others (particularly Mom), and how they are to behave toward him. In the far broader context Dad, as our first emissary from the outside world, carried home with him all the values and prejudices of that world. If Father bolstered our self-image, then it was all the more important because, we believed, he knew what he was talking about. If he declared little Joanie to be fat and unattractive and Jimmy a sissy, then that opinion carried with it the weight of society as a whole. He may well have been wrong. He was probably unaware of how deep his words cut, but the damage was done.

On a far more subtle and sometimes insidious level, Father could condemn both sons and daughters to search for mates not so much to ensure their own happiness, but to perpetuate their emotional dependence on him. A woman may think she is marrying a man diametrically opposed to her father, when in fact he embodies many of the same characteristics. A man may tell himself that he would never treat his lovers the way his father treated his mother, when in fact he is so much like Dad that he drives away the women he cares for.

Even in consciously rejecting Father, we can never shake his influence on our subconscious. He was the other part of the sexual equation—the larger part, since most of our mothers were relegated to a comparatively passive role. Even in those instances where, as with Lee and Susan Strasberg, Father is so afraid of sending sexual messages to his young daughter that he refrains from embracing her or bouncing her on his knee, he cannot help being her sexual programmer. More than anyone in our lives, it is Father who gives his children their first glimpse of themselves. However distorted that reflection, it will affect our physical and sexual self-image for the rest of our lives.

It is the fate of all of us, perhaps,
to direct our first sexual impulse towards
our mother and our first hatred and our first
murderous wish against our father.

—Sigmund Freud,
   The Interpretation
   of Dreams

CHAPTER V _____

Father/Love,
Father/Hate:
Oedipus and Electra

He was a navy man for over twenty years, but Dad had little tolerance for the kind of language that now seems absolutely essential to get me through the frustrations of an average business day. Not that he didn't swear. He did, but each obscenity was carefully measured to correspond to any given set of circumstances. Being caught in a rush-hour traffic snarl generally warranted a "damn," "god-damn," or "hell," and the degree of frustration determined whether he merely muttered the word under his breath or hissed it through clenched teeth. A white shirt that managed to come back from the laundry even grayer than when we sent it in might have called for a "Jesus," a "Christ," or a combination of the two. Dad, as I think was true of most of his generation, considered the excremental expletives to be the heavy weapons in his verbal arsenal. It usually took something of a catastrophe—smashing his finger with a hammer, say—before Dad yelled "shit" within earshot of his children. (It was not until I married into a Catholic family that I came to learn the bizarre fact that some churchgoing folk are less offended by "shit," "crap," "bullshit," and the like than they are by the uttering of Christ's name in vain.)

"Fuck," needless to say, was a word never permitted to be uttered under our roof during my childhood. The penalty, it was impressed upon my sister Valerie and me, would be unspeakably awful. It was not until I picked up and moved to New York to join the writing staff of *Time* magazine in 1971 that I learned the term was much used around the office by fresh-faced researchers straight from Bryn Mawr and Vassar.

Naturally, the day came—not long after my ninth birthday, as I recall it—when I had one of those "Why can't I stay over at Billy's house?" tiffs with Mom that ended with my using *that* word. My father leaped out of his red Barcalounger, the kind of reclining monstrosity that was so popular in the 1950s, and headed straight for me. Grabbing me by the scruff of the neck, the veins in his forehead turning purple with rage, he practically spit the words at me: "Don't ever talk to *my wife* that way again."

My wife? What happened to "your mother" or "your parents" or just "Mom"? At that moment he didn't seem to mind hearing his 9-year-old utter the forbidden "fuck" half as much as he minded that the word was being heard by his wife. It seemed more than just odd to me then, strange and disquieting enough that I can still see my father's angry face frozen in time as he leaped out of his chair. Like all sons, I would be afforded several looks at Oedipus over the ensuing years, but this was my first frightening glimpse of him.

As defined by Freud, the Oedipus complex begins with the sexual feelings of 4-, 5-, and 6-year-olds for the parent of the opposite sex, accompanied by competitive feelings toward the parent of the same sex. Yet the literature and the folklore are written entirely from the standpoint of the child. *Nowhere does it say how the father is supposed to feel.* His role as provider and protector allows only for storybook feelings. There is no reason for the jealousy of a young boy—a child whom he in all probability deeply loves—who nonetheless may be undercutting him at a time when he cannot afford to be undercut in the eyes of his wife. My father, I would discover many years after that first episode, was going through a crisis of his own at the time, unhappy with the tasks he was being handed by one of his superiors. And though I could not have been aware of it then, perhaps I did occasionally try to pull the rug out from my father when he would return home from his long absences. After all, Mom and I seemed to get along without any major difficulties when he wasn't around, and the last thing I needed was a bossy father barking orders at me.

So what of Dad's feelings? Freud's immense contributions to the understanding of tumultuous psychological goings-on between parent and child are undeniable. He proved rather convincingly that every little boy subconsciously fears castration at the hands of an angry father if he provokes Dad by being too close to warm and wonderful Mommy. It is harder to buy the other half of Freud's theory—that the kid correspondingly harbors incestuous longings for Mom. Attention and approval, yes, and that is sufficient to fan the flames of oedipal rivalry between father and son. So the boy pushes Father away when Daddy seems to be intruding on his private playtime with Mommy, and we are duly admonished to be patient. The child will, we hope, grow out of it.

Again, what of Dad's feelings? The myth of Oedipus, the son, is just as much the tale of Laius, the father. Dr. John Munder Ross, an assistant professor of psychology in psychiatry at Cornell Medical College, sees Laius' story as "a psychological parable of the darker dealings between fathers and sons. Laius," he continues, "is destiny's cruel and indeed capricious human agent."

Freud preferred to all but ignore Laius and his motivations when he hit upon Sophocles' myth of *Oedipus Rex* as his perfect metaphor for father-son rivalry. In a letter written within one week of the anniversary of his own father's death in 1896, Freud excitedly outlined his discovery:

> I have found love of the mother and jealousy of the father in my own case, too, and now believe it to be a general phenomenon of early childhood...the gripping power of *Oedipus Rex*, in spite of all the rational objections to the inexorable fate that the story presupposes, becomes intelligible.... Every member of the audience viewing it was once a budding Oedipus in fantasy...

Two years later, in *The Interpretation of Dreams*, Freud formalized his theory. After outlining the Greek tragedy in which Oedipus unknowingly kills his father, marries his mother, and thus brings down the wrath of the gods on himself and his kingdom, Freud suggested that Oedipus' desires were in fact universal:

> Like Oedipus, we live in ignorance of these wishes, repugnant to morality, which have been forced upon us by Nature, and after their revelation may all of us well seek to close our eyes to the scenes of our childhood.

"And to the sins of our fathers," adds Ross. "The veracity of Freud's formulations has been attested to repeatedly in clinical practice over the more than eighty years which have been followed. Children, sons especially, harbor murder in their hearts, however benign their fathers in actual fact. And, as adults, they suffer anxiety, guilt, and conflict as a consequence of their hidden sensuality and malevolence. Much of the drama's power to move its audience to pity and terror resides in its resonance with the onlooker's own unwanted and repressed childhood wishes and his identification with the hero."

Amazingly, Freud chose not to incorporate the active role of Laius in the Oedipus myth, an omission that casts Father not as a human being bringing his own inherited anxieties to bear on the story, but as a static, inanimate agent in Freud's explosive formula. In 1982 Dr. Ross sought brilliantly to redress this mistake by formulating the "Laius complex." Explains Ross in *The Psychoanalytic Study of the Child:*

> As a baby, Laius himself had been subjected to abandonment and persecution...what happened after this, in Laius's adulthood, was well known...While visiting Pisa, Laius kidnapped and sodomized Chrysippus, the beautiful illegitimate son of his host, King Pelops. The eroticism of the act...was not a crime in the Hellenic scheme of things; but the overbearingness and violence were; Laius's kidnapping and rape were *bona fide* transgressions.
>
> They infuriated the father, Pelops. He cursed Laius and, together with the Olympians Zeus and Hera, condemned him to...be both murdered by the son he eventually conceived and replaced by him in his wife's bed. Thus, the famous oracle, sealing the destinies of father and son, did not spring into being as a matter of happenstance. Rather, it bespoke revenge—a retaliation for violations perpetrated by a man so caught up in his sadomasochistic desires that he is oblivious to a boy's needs. Oedipus is fated to *avenge* Chrysippus, his alter ego.
>
> When Oedipus was born at last, Laius ordered the infant's ankles to be pierced with a spike. Pinioned so that he could not crawl, the baby boy was to be left to the desolation and elemental violence of the mountain where he was to have died. [Instead, he was rescued by his mother.]
>
> Whatever the masochistic and homosexual submission which may be read into a father's

persecution and sacrifice of a son (Abraham and Isaac
come to mind), Laius's first cruelty toward his baby
remains basically an act of manifest *evil*. In a certain
sense, it needs no further interpretation, no
psychologizing. In its own right the deed serves to
climax an intricate allegory, encapsulating a whole
complex of delusion and moral failure.

Thanks to John Munder Ross' Laius complex, we can
see the remarkable extent of Freud's sin of omission. Why
did Freud identify so closely with Oedipus that he failed
to take into account Laius' background? "All men, even
Freud and Oedipus, need their gods and fathers," says
Ross. "And Freud, indeed, loved his dearly. At times sons
and daughters will do almost anything—assume a remorse
that is not theirs, emasculate, blind and kill themselves,
sacrifice or exploit their children—rather than dislodge
the defensive and self-sustaining idealizations in which these
imaginary and real patriarchs are ensconced. Need and
guilt conspire in the exoneration of the father—the need
for his protection, guilt as his internal proxy and as an
everpresent protector."

If Freud's reluctance to hold Laius (and his own father)
accountable grows out of need and guilt, then there are
many fathers today who share in this denial. Some have
broken through that wall. A friend who grew up thinking
of his father as "distant, cold, and narcissistic" found out
why only after the old man's death. Going through his
father's things the day of the funeral, my friend unearthed
a dozen letters from his grandfather to his father that had
been crammed in the bottom of an old trunk. Father had
never talked much about *his* father, and after reading the
letters the surviving son understood why. Each was a lengthy
discourse on the value of money and why Grandfather
refused to provide even a penny for his son's college education. "They were written like memos from God," says
the son. "An unfeeling, unloving, self-centered god." In

the same trunk were photographs of the grandmother hugging her son while Grandfather looked grimly on. "I think my father must have known that Grandfather resented his closeness to his mother. And I had the same warm relationship with my mother, so I guess he was just living out the father-son scenario of his past."

"Oedipal feelings are a reality," Michael Maccoby assures us. "It happens to all boys after the age of two. We all felt a sense of competition with our fathers, whether we admit that to ourselves or not. This resentment could have been strong or weak or anywhere in between, but it was definitely there. We all worried to some degree that we would lose our testicles to Daddy if we got too close to Mom. The resolution? Freud," says Maccoby, "saw it as a symbolic act of cannibalism—the 'swallowing' of the father by the son—that meant we had accepted what it means to be a male and could go on from there."

Accepting what it means "to be a male" also entails accepting a simple truth: For whatever reasons, there is ample clinical evidence that boys and men tend to be inherently more aggressive than women. This, it seems, grows out of those first oedipal clashes. "In fact," adds Dr. Ross, "little boys act to elicit what appears to be an almost instinctive aggressive behavior from fathers and other adult men. Challenging and provoking them, inviting them to roughhouse, they seek to enact the competitiveness so necessary to masculine development. Indeed, without this kind of actual aggressive interplay," Ross continues, "boys may not know the limits of both their own and their father's durability. Untested, their aggression will intensify and fester into what is experienced as a frightening well of seemingly pure destructiveness. Hence, the unconscious violence of so many men deprived of adequate, strong fathers."

Psychiatric hyperbole? Not if we look to two young Americans without "adequate, strong fathers" whose senselessly violent acts shocked the nation: Mark David Chapman and John Hinckley, Jr. Chapman aimed a revolver at John Lennon and within a matter of seconds one December night in 1980 brought a bloody and untimely end to the life of one of the titans of popular music. On March 30, 1981, less than four months later, Hinckley lay in wait for the President of the United States outside the Washington Hilton, firing shots that very nearly killed Ronald Reagan and Presidential Press Secretary James Brady and injured two others. Ostensibly, both Chapman and Hinckley consciously sought celebrity by these acts, though Hinckley's obsession with impressing actress Jody Foster was deemed sufficiently psychotic by a jury to judge him innocent by reason of insanity.

Whatever the desire for recognition that is universally ascribed to aspiring assassins of this ilk, there is a far deeper and more intensely personal reason for their actions. Both Chapman and Hinckley were out to kill their fathers when they picked up the gun. In an alarming interview with Dr. Lee Salk, Chapman virtually admitted this: "I was going to break into his home, and get him in his room alone, and put a gun to him and tell him what I thought about him and what he had *done to my mother*, and that he was going to pay for it; and then I was going to blow his head off. First I'd just frighten him to death because he's not a very strong man, emotionally. I'd be holding on to him and say, 'This is what you get, this is what is coming to you for what you've *done to my mother* and our family, and I hear you're scared to death that you're going to Hell, and this is it, Dad, you know. I'm not even going to give you another minute to live, I'm just going to blow you away and make you suffer; you're going to suffer in Hell for this,' and then I was going to shoot him."

Chapman's unabated hatred of his father stems from the fact that the elder Chapman beat Mark's mother and that he was aloof. Chapman has repeatedly painted his father as emotionally detached, uncaring (a frequent complaint is that father and son never hugged or shared any similar physical expressions of affection), even penurious. "He was always so cheap, he was always so worried about money, so bothered about it," Chapman told Salk. "We never went on vacation once, our whole time. We went down to Florida and took in the sights—that was only for about four days…"

Chapman has never admitted in so many words that as he stood in the shadows outside the Dakota while Lennon and his wife, Yoko Ono, climbed out of their limousine, he was taking aim at his father. But he seems to have no illusions about the impact of that relationship on the development of any child's personality. "I think the relationship between a father and son is even more important than the relationship between a son and a mother—between the kids and the mother—because the father is the head of the household," says Chapman. "He is the authority, he has the final decision." But John Lennon's murderer is clearly deluding himself when he insists that his craving for paternal love and approval is no longer an all-consuming need. "My father's reaction," he says of his first meeting with Chapman senior after Lennon's murder, "was very blasé. I think he told me that he was disappointed: that's par for the course.… I have tried to block my father out as much as possible. I don't care about him; I've killed him in my mind already."

John Hinckley's emotional abandonment by his father —again we see oedipal undercurrents—proved to be a key element in Hinckley's defense on grounds of insanity. At a time when he needed his parents' support, in the months before the assassination attempt, they took the advice of John junior's psychotherapist. They gave him a hundred dollars, drove him to the airport, and sent him on his way. On the witness stand in his son's defense, John senior, a wealthy born-again Christian whose life had revolved around his multimillion-dollar oil and natural gas exploration company, broke down in tears. "I am the cause of John's tragedy," he told the jury as his son sat expressionless. "We forced him out at a time when he just couldn't cope. I wish to God that I could trade places with him right now."

The John Hinckleys, senior and junior, are not alone in this world. It has always been commonplace for the father, in his overriding role as provider, to be absent from the day-to-day conduct of household affairs. A disturbing twist was added following World War II and the flight to the suburbs that has taken place ever since. The other important function of the father—that of moral leader—was abandoned in favor of a kind of emotional and ethical matriarchy. So long as Dad brought home a paycheck, he was fulfilling his obligations. But even with sociological shifts aggravating the father-child situation, it isn't hard to see that there are far deeper psychological forces at work here—the rivalry over Mother's love that can become ugly if not confronted and resolved.

Shifts in the physical balance of power between fathers and sons are also a decisive factor in the molding and shaping of their relationship. Most men can remember the precise day and the circumstances involved when it became apparent to them that the tide had turned and they had overtaken their fathers in strength. If a man is reaching his late 40s or early 50s as his son reaches his mid-to-late teens, this is the time when this turnabout, with its myriad implications, occurs.

This moment was nothing less than a milestone in the lives of the legendary Twentieth Century-Fox mogul Darryl F. Zanuck and his highly successful producer son, Richard. Although the elder Zanuck engineered his son's overthrow as Fox's president in 1971, Richard does not hesitate to say that "my father was clearly the inspirational force in my life.... No one person I've met in my life was more supportive than he was." Still, as a child, Richard feared his distant dad, a mythical figure in Hollywood, equally renowned for his talent and his temper. This fear was reinforced when he sat with his father near the projection controls in the family screening room. Often bored by the movie they were watching, Dad would start wrestling with Richard on the couch. In true Great Santini fashion, Darryl (a World War II army colonel, by the way) always ended their not-so-friendly roughhousing by getting the boy in a death grip and making the lad holler "Give!"

They went through this same ritual for years. "Then came the fateful night I'll never forget," recalls Richard. "I was 14, and I could just feel for the first time that I was stronger than he was. I got him in a perfect headlock, and I showed him no mercy. His face became all red, and his eyes were almost bulging. I just kept squeezing and asking him the question he had asked me all those years. He finally blurted out 'Give!' It's so clear in my mind. It was a turning point in my relationship with my father and the way he looked at me and the way I looked at him." From that point on, Darryl Zanuck never again wrestled with his son.

"My father and I *always* got along; we've always been great buddies. I never felt any anger toward him, and I never felt I was competing with him." The refrain is familiar. Denial is a perfectly logical response to the charge that each of us who grew up with a mother and father present directed murderous thoughts at the parent of the opposite sex. Incest remains such a strong taboo that neither Mother nor Father is willing to admit to the obvious war between father and son over Mother's affections. That conflict can even be humorous when the kid is, say, under 10, but on those unfortunate occasions when it continues unabated into adolescence, this internecine rivalry can become unhealthy, destructive. More often than not, however, the war is muted after puberty, and we grow into adulthood without ever admitting that these primal passions of the mind took place at all.

"Dad called me Tonto," says a 35-year-old Beverly Hills realtor. "But he wasn't the Lone Ranger in our house, Mom was. I was mother's little helper, and he seemed to like that a lot. Until one day when he came home from work. We had this little routine where he'd ring the door-bell and I'd come and ask for the password. Whatever he said—'Open Sesame!' 'Abracadabra!'—I'd unlock the door and let him in. Only this day he came up to the front door and gave a password, and I didn't open up. So he tried another, and another. I just stood inside in the hallway, wishing he'd go away. Dad started yelling, so I ran upstairs and hid in the closet. He finally walked around to the back door, where my mother was in the kitchen making dinner. She let him in and he walked straight to my room. He didn't get mad or anything, he just wanted to know why I wouldn't let him in. It's only recently, now that I have a little boy of my own and see for myself what is going on between us, that I realized why I didn't want to let my dad in the house."

Why haven't we tried to fathom—if not sympathize—with Father's unhappiness as forever being cast as the heavy? In some respects Dad has been his own worst enemy. He is the first to reject out of hand any possibility of competition with his son because of the sheer physical ridiculousness of it. A 165-pound Papa Bear jealous of his defenseless cub? Ludicrous, insulting. Mother is likely to share in this misguided thinking. He's "ours," isn't he? Daddy must share Mommy's protective instincts, she insists, so any serious trouble between father and son is out of the question. Fathers aren't petty, after all.

What everyone has failed (refused?) to acknowledge from the start is that Father was probably less sure than Mother about why he had taken this life-altering step called reproduction. His capacity for selflessness and coping with rejection was put to the test as soon as mother and child came home from the hospital. She was so understandably engrossed in the business of feeding, burping, and diapering that he was excluded at the outset. Abstract concepts of child rearing are one thing; rarely are we prepared for what happens when the baby is really there.

Even before the blackened umbilicus drops off, the

rivalry between father and child took on a certain sexual quality. To be sure, one of the first casualties upon baby's arrival (regardless of the infant's gender) was sex. Our fathers may have occasionally helped out with a diapering or a two a.m. feeding, but the nitty-gritty of child care then, as now, was primarily the province of Mom. More often than not during those first few months, baby's crib was set up in his parents' room over by the dresser, so they could monitor his every gurgle. There was now somebody else in the room when Mom and Dad were grappling for each other in the night. Dad may have thought this added a dash of excitement to the whole affair; sex had not been so furtive and deliberate since the days when Mom and Dad romped in the back seat of *his* father's Packard. She, however, was more likely to be a tad squeamish about making love while their angelic issue—looking as if he were resting up between takes for a Gerber ad—slumbered only a few feet away. Even when both parties tried their best to ignore the kid's presence, no mother could put orgasm above answering her baby's cry. If the infant stirred, Mom shot out of bed, leaving Pop behind, his pride and erection wilting. Even when Mom returned to pick up where they had left off, the lesson was unmistakably clear: Dad's ardor took a back seat to the kid's squeals.

This was the first of many such lessons to be learned by Dad. "The Oedipal struggle with our children," says writer William Reynolds, "gives Father his most anguished moments for most of his life, and his resolution of the situation varies, sometimes from day to day. Father as a man loves his child, but the stress of losing Mother's attention is truly angering to him."

What angered our fathers most was the evident one-sidedness of the situation. He cared for his wife more than his child, generally speaking, but she seemed to be giving the kid first priority. He had not lost any desire for her just because he had become a parent, but his sex life with Mother was dampened, and probably for good. Before long, kid and crib were moved out of Mommy and Daddy's room, but for the next several years Mother structured her daily routine around us children, sleeping when we slept and trying to keep herself whole.

Dad knew better than anyone that Mom deserved his gratitude and his admiration for her Herculean tasks, but that didn't make him any happier about this intrusion on their lives. In fact, it merely made matters worse by painting a veneer of guilt over two layers of frustration and a base coat of rage.

"I used to call Dorothy from the office around noon," recalls Hal, whose son is now 30, "and she'd be napping. By the time I got home at six thirty, little Todd was asleep and she was completely exhausted. She stayed awake just long enough to have dinner and tell me what the pediatrician had to say. By nine p.m. she was fast asleep in bed. I was too wound up to turn in that early; besides, during the first six years of our married life before Todd's birth we never went to bed before eleven. So, of course, when I *did* go to bed she'd be out cold. Sex became something very difficult to work out between us, and I was getting more and more angry that my own needs weren't being met. Dorothy called me selfish and ungrateful, and she was right. All this was harder on her than it was on me, I guess. But that didn't take away from my feeling frozen out. Our sex life had ground to a slow crawl. We never got back to the way things were, and I think I held that against Todd until he left home for college. Hell, maybe I'm still jealous. He's always known that there was a little bit of healthy tension between us, but I'm sure he doesn't have the slightest clue that underlying it all it's because he put a crimp on our sex life."

The appearance of this unwelcome rival often coincided with a period in Father's life when he could least afford it. Bill was 25 and had just been promoted from the ranks of his company's salesmen to the position of assistant regional sales manager when he began to notice the change in his 4-year-old's attitude toward him. "Curt gave me one of those 'if looks could kill' stares of his every time I got near his mother," says Bill. "If I offered to play a game with him or take him to the playground, it was always 'No, I want to play with Mommy.' Curt's mother kept asking what I had done to make the kid mad at me, as if I was twisting his arm behind his back when she wasn't looking or something. Meantime, there were career pressures on me like I'd never experienced before, and for the first time since our marriage I wasn't getting the support I needed at home. I wanted a loving pat on the head and lots of ego boosting, but he was the one getting all the attention. It was hard not to blame Curt, but we realized it was just a phase and we rode it out."

Not all fathers have been able to "ride it out." Psychologists have now pinpointed this oedipal stress as one of the principal causes of child abuse. Statistics show that in the United States each year over 700 children are killed, more than 100,000 battered, and 50,000 to 75,000 sexually abused, mainly by their fathers. Many studies of the causes of such incredible mayhem draw a parallel between the battering father and the pathologically violent son. As with alcoholics and drug abusers, the sins of the fathers are likely to be visited upon the sons.

"My father beat the hell out of me when I was a kid, but it got really bad after I turned 13," says a 33-year-old warehouseman whose bricklayer dad nonetheless never laid a glove on his two daughters. "The real terror was that I never knew when it was coming," claims the son. "Sometimes I'd bring home a report card with three F's on it and he'd just go back to watching the game on TV. Another time I'd come home from a date right on time and he'd let me have it across the back of the legs with a hanger because I didn't clean up my room two days before. It was crazy. He wasn't exactly wonderful to my sisters, but he didn't beat the shit out of them, either."

At 15, the bricklayer's battered son left home for good,

never suspecting that it was his closeness to Mother that Dad envied. It has taken him thirty years to admit it, but the warehouseman's father now concedes that it was jealousy—not so pure and not so simple—of the mother's devotion to their son that prompted him to pummel the lad without cause. "I didn't like myself very much at the time, since I knew why I was doing it," concedes Dad. "And I guess that just made me madder and more violent."

Not an insignificant part of Father's growing anger and resentment toward Sonny was due to the boy's growing strength and the threat it posed. At 13, the son was already his father's height (5 feet 9 inches) and weighed 140 pounds. More importantly, though, the strapping adolescent was beginning to remind Dad of himself at that age of budding sexual awareness. It began to bother him even to see mother and son laughing and talking together, and though Mom may have been vaguely aware of her husband's unspoken envy, she could not turn her son away when he came to her after a thrashing from Dad. The family had been drawn into a vicious circle. The more jealous Father became, the closer grew mother and son. All three eventually reconciled, but the scars remain. The bricklayer's son is in his sixth year of psychotherapy and vows never to marry or have children for fear of unleashing the dark forces that made his own childhood a nightmare.

These same dark forces know no economic or class boundaries. A San Francisco divorce lawyer admitted to me that, though his son wanted to attend one of the many good public high schools or private schools in the Bay Area, the boy was sent to a private school "back East" for the simple reason that he feared the boy was proving too strong a rival for his wife's attention. "Here I was representing men and women in court who probably would have hired a hit man to rub out their ex-spouse if it meant they would get custody of the kids," says the lawyer, "and I was sending my 10-year-old son away because *I* wanted to be the center of my wife's world."

Those of us who grew up taking a bus or being driven by Mom to a local public or private school may have always wondered how some parents could be so emotionally detached that they would put their own offspring on a plane a la Christina Crawford to be raised by strangers hundreds or thousands of miles away. But did we ever for a moment suspect that some of these hapless Fauntleroys might actually be the victim of upper-class oedipal feuds?

These feelings are sinister, explosive, strange—yet Father recognizes them. He will tell us they were the same feelings he had toward *his* father, the same tortured emotions that were either rationalized away or smoldered and ignited during adolescence—leading in many cases to that final, irrevocable break. The adult male who is close to his mother but has never been able to get past a strained, formal status in his dealings with Dad is commonplace in this country. Our affection for Mom only serves to complicate matters, for we must at once concede that we—subconsciously at least—wanted her all to ourselves, and that she was the oft-unwitting cause of our rift with Father and the anxieties that followed. Our generation at last has the opportunity to end this vicious circle by sweeping away the fallout of decades-old father-son rivalry. First we must admit to ourselves that in this sense at least, we may never have grown up at all. We must stop denying the obvious, stop fixing the blame where there is none. As sons, we will be able to recognize that we may be needlessly waging a war that neither side was meant to win. As fathers ourselves, we will finally be able to understand what is going on between us and our sons *while* it is going on, and to tamp down those oedipal fires before they erupt into a full-scale conflagration.

The tightrope that Dad walks in regard to his daughter is strung even tauter and higher and, as is also the case with a son, he walks it without a net. The Electra complex— a young girl's suppressed but equally natural feelings of competition with her mother for Father's affections—must be confronted by every woman who seeks to fathom Father/ Love and the impact it is having on her life as an adult.

When an infant girl touches her genitals, it is Mother's job to yank that hand away. According to Nancy Friday, this one event starts mother's "lifelong nay-saying in her daughter's eyes." Men, then, particularly Dad, take up the slack. They are the yea-sayers to sex, adventure, risk taking. "Men are not prim and proper prudes like mother," says Friday. "They are lusty rogues, sexy devils, and we yearn for our time with them to come." A time, we presume, when some male magically transforms them into sexual beings.

Of course, despite Mother's nay-saying, we were sexual beings from day one, and Daddy is the first male on whom a little girl practices her feminine wiles. At 3 or 4 or 5, when a boy first starts to proclaim his interest in marrying Mommy, a little girl flutters her eyelashes at Pop, or, before Mother gives her a bath, perhaps she dashes into the living room and performs a flirtatious fandango au naturel while Dad tries to catch the rest of the seven o'clock news.

Erica Jong, author of such best-selling novels as *Fear of Flying* and *Fanny,* grew up in an extended family with maternal grandparents in a huge triplex on Manhattan's Upper West Side. Her father, a frustrated drummer who gave up his musical career to become a prosperous importer, was "absent a lot," says Erica, "about six months at a time on trips to places like Japan and Hong Kong. He'd be gone six weeks at a time, so I really had a split father image: half my father and half my portrait-painter grandfather." Jong concedes, however, that whatever early sexual feelings may have stirred, they were certainly sparked by her father. "He was very young—only 23 when I was born—fun-loving and very beautiful. My father seemed more like a youth to me than a patriarch. He marked me erotically. He was adoring. The whole routine was very seductive, and of course there were oedipal currents beneath it all. It's impossible to stop it."

Oedipal conflicts can badger us for a lifetime. Consider the alarming statistics regarding the number of women in the United States willing to give up custody of their children: more than one million in 1982 alone. The reasons offered by some of these women are sometimes touching, nearly always desperate: "It was either run away or kill myself! I loved my baby, but I was afraid I would hurt him or end up hating him." "I felt I had no other alternatives, and I didn't want to see my children suffer anymore; I was emotionally immature...." "Had I stayed, I either would have continued to die a slow spiritual death or I would have literally died. Or gone crazy."

A 1975 study indicates that women who cannot cope with motherhood have stronger-than-average oedipal ties to their own fathers. This is confirmed by Patricia Paskowicz, herself an absentee mother and the author of *Absentee Mothers*. Paskowicz interviewed more than a hundred of these women and discovered that the incidence of the father's death when they were young children was *ten times higher* than usual. Daddy, then, was the object of unresolved fantasies that kept the daughter in constant competition with her mother. This, in turn, made it calamitously difficult for her to see herself as a mother. Observes Paskowicz: "Perhaps the most significant point is that not one member of the group (whose fathers had died when they were little girls) expressed ambivalence about her relationship with her father. No one described her relationship with her father as mixed or even neutral. Such clear-cut perceptions are often reason to suspect some departure from reality...and the kind of paternal idealization that occurs in the Electra version of the Oedipal triad." Only two of these women could say they have positive relationships with their mothers.

Father does not have to die to leave as his legacy these

lingering oedipal urges. He need only be gone. "My own father died when I was, chronologically, an adult," says Paskowicz. "Emotionally, I was a pathetic five-year-old. I had lost my father the first time, when I was *really* five, when my mother 'threw him out,' as she loved to boast. That was the time in which my subconscious had chosen to stay. I was passionately in love with my father, refusing to see his faults, glorifying his every characteristic, clinging to a treacherous cliff of possible conviction and desperate hope that he *did* love me. I held with ferocity the long-ago visions that proved how he really felt about me: the horsey-back rides to bed, our late winter suppers alone when I had waited for him to get home while my mother and sister had eaten earlier, the way he cried once while he held me on his lap. I was still in the full flush of attempting to gratify my Oedipal love when my father died at 58; I was 31." Paskowicz visited her father as he lay dying in the hospital, and the moment she walked in the room, he burst into tears. "I hugged him while he cried, and I felt that he was crying because he had to leave me in just a few days. I remembered that it was the very same reason he had cried the first time when he and my mother were separating. He *did* love me."

Paskowicz's father died two years after she had relinquished custody of her own three children "in a blind lurch," she says, "toward dealing with the child in me." She concedes that in spite of their tearful farewell, her father's final tears did not "mitigate my Oedipal complex. It seemed that now, when he had finally given me a sign, when he seemed on the edge of fulfilling my need for him, he had also withdrawn—now more profoundly than ever."

When does it all begin? "The influence of the father does not crystallize in some oedipal drama at age four," Dr. William S. Appleton, assistant professor of psychiatry at Harvard Medical School, is quick to point out. "It is a process that goes on for 30 years." But how important those first four or five years are. From the day she first starts parading about in the buff or batting her baby blues, the daughter begins to receive the signals from Daddy that will color the way she deals with men forever. If Father laughs at her naked dance, she is encouraged to be adventurous, to further polish her feminine wiles. Her positive self-image is also reinforced. If Daddy finds her attractive and amusing, that is the ultimate accolade for a 4-year-old.

Many adult women recall that their father was anything but approving when they first began to flirt. Daddy may have sat impassively, scowled, turned away, or even exploded with rage at his little girl's lack of propriety. For most women Daddy's reactions fell somewhere in between. One time he might respond with total delight, another with disapproval, more often than not with a look of mock outrage and a wink.

Maccoby, himself the father of two daughters, stresses that the inevitable erotic link that develops between Daddy and his little girl, as is often the case, be interpreted not as having incestuous overtones. "These feelings are healthy, even necessary in the growth of the child," he states. "The operative word here is *erotic*. And eros has nothing to do with fucking. A father may be interested in his daughter as a sexual being, but that doesn't mean he has even a subconscious desire to sleep with her." Adds Dr. Appleton: "To know your father sexually does not mean to known him incestuously. It means that you experience him as a man and that he responds to your femininity first when you are a girl and then when you are a woman. How your eyes meet, whether or not you touch, the way you play together, become the prototype from which you will later develop a style with your lovers."

"Unfortunately," claims Dr. Robertiello, "most men in our culture may be flattered by their little girl's attention, but they have such an incest taboo built into them that they ignore the little girl's sexuality."

When this happens, when Dad stiffens the way Lee Strasberg did when little Susan tried to sit on his lap, the results can be catastrophic. The little girl grows up to be an apprehensive, cold, fearful woman, so lacking in self-esteem and afraid to take risks that she either marries the first man who shows interest or opts for an asexual lifestyle.

At 38, Patricia has achieved some measure of success as a writer of television documentaries. Her personal life is something else again. Her father, an internationally respected professor of classical literature, is a typical product of Ivy League education in the late 1930s. Although, like Leonard Bernstein and Theodore H. White, he was one of the relatively small numbers of Jews attending Harvard during that time, Patricia's father did not share in White's humiliation at being called a "meatball" by his insufferably WASP classmates. Even then, the tall, strikingly handsome classics student was acknowledged to be brilliant and destined for greatness in his field.

One of the reasons he could command respect even at such a young age was that Patricia's father had affected an air of superiority that rendered him impervious to criticism. That same glacial quality transferred to his life at home, where his artist wife, herself a cum laude graduate of Smith, presided over their only daughter's strict, almost Victorian upbringing.

"I loved and respected my father; he was very attentive, very caring in his own way," Patricia now says. "It was my mother I could never really count on for support. She was the parent I really needed to help me grow up. She must have been a little girl too, I used to think. But all I ever got from Mummy was criticism. 'Straighten up! Comb your hair! Why don't you wear some lipstick?' Even when I see her now—and frankly I try to make that as seldom as possible—she nags me about my weight or my clothes."

Patricia insists that it was her mother's hostility that set the stage for her present predicament. When she is not scouting locales for documentaries on toxic waste disposal or substandard nursing homes, she fills her remaining time with chores (unnecessary trips to her gynecologist, orthopedist, dentist), language lessons, exercise classes, season tickets to the symphony and the opera, and also jaunts through Europe and Africa. She has only a few close friends of either sex, nearly all of whom are married. The only men she may go out with on a platonic date are contemporaries of her father. "There is no man in my life," she now says, "and I don't think there ever will be. *Of course it depresses me that I'll never be married or have children, but I'm resigned to it.*"

Her bitter attitude toward her mother is understandable, even justifiable to a degree. But can she really be unaware that it was her father who taught her by example that men were cold, unfeeling, aloof, and that she must be fearful of them? Patricia will complain that "there is no man in my life," but when pressed as to why she does not go out like other women of her age and actively seek them, she replies, "Because I haven't got the time." Time enough for trips and language lessons and opera and Africa, but not for a mature loving relationship with a man. In exclusively dating men who not only are her father's age but share many of his intellectual, physical, and personality traits as well, she all but announces to the world that in her late 30s she still craves the love Daddy never gave her.

Patricia is not wrong when she points to Mom as a key participant in the development of a daughter's sexual self. Mom's response to the unique bond forming between Father and his little girl is of paramount importance. A 5-year-old wants to feel that she has Mother's total approval of her newfound sexuality and the way she is showing off in front of Father. Trouble is, it is Mommy's turn to feel jealous. And if Mommy reacts with a sharp "Don't bother your father" when the little moppet is doing her playful striptease, Daughter hears the warning: If you want to keep Mommy's love—the best, warmest, most unconditional love—don't compete with her for Daddy.

Even when she allows her daughter the freedom to flirt with Pop, Mom, in her all but unavoidable role as the ultimate sexual nay-sayer, will still call an abrupt halt to that first overt expression of budding sexual self-awareness: masturbation. The fact that at such an early age both boys and girls begin exploring themselves, whether their parents know it or not, is little comfort to either parent. "Nice little girls don't do that" is what Mother will say when little Suzie starts playing with her genitals, and Daddy will try his best to look as if he's missed the whole embarrassing episode.

Dads who have been open and encouraging to their young daughters begin doubting their openness when they suddenly realize they are unwitting accomplices in their little girl's covert attempts at masturbation. A friend of mine told me he was rocking his two daughters, ages 4 and 5, back and forth on his leg—"playing horsey"—when one of them told him why they were giggling so hard. "Faster, Daddy, faster. It makes our panties tickle!"

"I put them both down right away. I guess I've been naive about this," he says, "but when I think of masturbation I still think little boys do it, and not little girls. Maybe I shouldn't let it bother me, but now I think twice before I play any physical games with the girls."

The repugnance shared by fathers and mothers concerning masturbation stems from their own shame and guilt over having been caught in the act by *their* parents. Beyond that unreasonable anger, there is no logical justification for either parent's tendency to panic when little Michael or Lisa starts playing with themselves. Pleasure for pleasure's sake is bad, we are taught—worse for our pretty, obedient, good little girls than for our raffish little lads. In some cases Dad himself is pressed into service in Mother's war against masturbation. It is a Holy War—an integral part of the Judeo-Christian antisex ethic that regards daughters as being somehow above carnal lusts. Against all these allied forces of guilt, even the most open-minded, least neurotic Dad can do little. He must, when it comes to masturbation at least, join in the chorus of "nays."

If Dad drew up his daughter's sexual blueprints during her early childhood, then it was during adolescence that building began. And now more than ever, he finds the possibility of clashes wih Mother greater than ever. Mom may cope with competition from her daughter for Dad's affections by glossing over his attractiveness, or, worse yet, denigrating him. "Mom and I used to band together against Dad," recalls the 33-year-old mother of twin boys. "He drank too much, she kept telling me, and was cheap. So I learned early if I wanted anything, Mom would help me get it from Daddy. An us-against-him mentality continued right through to my mother's death. I had moved across the country and had children of my own by then, and I brought them back home with me for the funeral. As we walked away from the gravesite, I walked up to Dad and, for the first time, put my arms around him without any ulterior motives. He broke down sobbing and I said, 'Dad, you've still got me and the kids.' He turned to me and said, 'Don't you still hate me?' My mother had to die before I realized how rotten we'd been to him. If he'd been the first to go, I probably never would have known what a lousy deal he'd gotten."

Similarly, a 30-year-old nurse discovered only after she had graduated from college and moved away to another state that many of the confrontations she'd had with her father over the years had actually been engineered by her mother. "My father was a welder, a tough union man, not terribly articulate and maybe not that thrilled at being saddled with a wife and four kids at such a young age," says the R.N. "He was always off at work or with the guys bowling or something, so practically everything between Dad and us kids was funneled through Mom. If I came home late from a date, she would always say 'Dad is hopping mad at you,' or if I wanted to buy a dress it was always 'Your father says absolutely not!'"

Just before she left home, Daughter stopped speaking to Father when Mom informed her that he was against her leaving. Months later Daughter called home to chat with Mom, and Dad picked up the telephone. "My mother was out shopping, and for the first few moments it was awkward. Then we sort of broke through that barrier that had always been between us and Dad told me that he had never been against my leaving. From then on I started calling him at his work or when I knew Mom was out and began comparing what they said. He didn't want to call Mom a liar; he just kept saying she got things all mixed up and was confused. But it dawned on me that she was pitting us against each other just so she could control things. I started wondering how many times I thought it was Dad who didn't want me to do something when *all the time it was Mom.* It scared me, but I eventually got up the nerve to ask her what was going on. She played dumb, but I knew I had struck a nerve." Realizing that she could not undo three decades of misunderstanding by ostracizing Mother, she took it upon herself to start building bridges to her father. "I talk to Dad on the phone two or three times a week," she says. "I just make sure Mom's not around when I do."

Still, a father is always a co-conspirator in his own demise. He can only be estranged from his children if he allows himself to. During his daughter's early adolescence, says Eda LeShan, Father ideally serves as a trial suitor. "Father is the first date, and in that way he can play a tremendously important role. My daughter Wendy was 12 when she finally got her father to take her out to dinner. When they came back in the front door, she ran up to me and said, 'Mommy, Mommy, do you know why a man is on the outside when he walks down the street with a lady? Because in the olden days the horses used to splash mud up, so the men got dirty instead of the women.' She was excited about telling me this tidbit, but it was more than just trivia—it was her induction into the world of grown-ups. No one is better equipped to serve as a young woman's guide into that world than her father."

He also soon came to be regarded as the authority figure against which to rebel. "The closer the relationship with Dad, the more the need to rebel," says LeShan. "When Wendy turned 13, she wanted a pair of sexy pumps. We went out and bought them and she came back and wore them around the house but her father didn't even notice. Wendy was furious. She wanted him to scream and yell and make her return them."

Sandy claims that, at 36, she and her father "get along okay." It takes less than ten seconds for her to explain why her endorsement of Dad is anything but ringing. "My mother was a real bitch; she ran the whole show," says Sandy. "My father just toed the line, and when I went to him for help, his attitude was always the same: 'Look, I understand what you're going through, but I've got to live with this woman. Don't expect any help from me.'" Sandy's father confirmed his daughter's opinion and resentfulness toward both parents. Sandy began seeing a psychiatrist at the age of 11, and it was not until shortly after her thirtieth birthday that she felt strong enough to stop.

Above all else, the most important man in a girl's life, her father, must pay attention to her. Detachment as a child and adolescent will result in either a hunger for male affection and/or a rage over this rejection that will burst forth in later life. If she never got what she needed from Father, the slightest flaw in a lover—a social faux pas, perhaps, or a momentary wandering eye—may ignite a fury that is wholly incommensurate with the transgression. If poor Bill spends too much time in idle chatter with the stewardess who occupies the apartment across the hall, holy hell can break loose. Daughter drives men away or tortures the few who remain.

Adolescence is one of the most painful periods in our lives, no question. We are all admonished to understand and forgive when little John and Suzie misbehave. But what of Dad? When his daughter is experiencing her teenage traumas, Dad (who is on average three to five years older than Mom) is reaching an emotional flashpoint of his own: middle age. If Suzie is turning 15, Dad is likely to be in his 40s, and like his daughter he faces crucial life decisions. Is he happy with his job, his career, his marriage?

Unlike his daughter, he does not have the luxury of time. She can change her mind: she is on the threshold of her life as an adult. His life is two-thirds over. "Now in his 40's," Dr. Appleton observes, "he is more like an adolescent himself, more sexual, harder-drinking, moodier, and likelier to get into trouble with work or women. But this is not necessarily bad for his teenage daughter. Fathers who do not develop and change over the decades can give daughters unrealistic ideas of what men are." This means that fathers who manage to maintain the equilibrium of their 20s and 30s, when they are striving like boy scouts to get that promotion and that club membership, linger on as heroes to their daughters. And if they are to ever stop performing as children in their relations to men, then daughters must understand that men are full of common human faults.

Robert Young was an unrepentant alcoholic during the years he filmed television's *Father Knows Best,* as was Dick Van Dyke when he played the ever-wonderful Richard Petrie opposite Mary Tyler Moore in the hit series of the early 1960s, *The Dick Van Dyke Show.* No matter how many times Young and Van Dyke confess to us that they were problem drinkers during the years they portrayed America's perfect fathers, it will not undo the damage such unrealistic portrayals in popular fiction, movies, and television have done over the years. Fathers are anything but perfect, and they seldom know best. Those women growing to adulthood with these delusions in mind—and there have been millions of them—will forever be searching for men willing to put up with their every foible and failing, to be daddies to little girls.

Ultimately, what the older and wiser teenage daughter now sees are the human frailties that afflict us all. What she did not recognize as Dad's penchants for gambling, womanizing, or overimbibing now become clear. He, meantime, may seem callous in his attitude toward his princess. As Appleton points out, *both must conspire subconsciously in his fall from grace if she is ever to become a fully mature woman.*

Most adult women now will tell you that when they lost their virginity, their thoughts were as much on Dad as they were on the lover they were momentarily entrusting their bodies to. For some, there was a genuine concern for what Dad might do to them for committing this heinous crime; for others, a concern for the pain it might cause Dad. At the bottom of it all was the simple recognition that there was no going back; things between Daddy and Daughter would never be the same. Would it mean the loss of his love, his adoration? Was this to be her ultimate fall from grace?

To be sure, the loss of her physical virginity can indeed threaten the loss of her father's unrequited affection. Contrary to the titillating fiction that this event occurs to most girls by the time they are 14, studies show that even today most females remain virgins until their late teens. For women who reached puberty in the 1950s and '60s, nineteen or twenty was the common age for the "first time" to occur. Both Daughter and Daddy need time to adjust to her new status, and given his preoccupation with his own midlife crisis and common standards of privacy, she can keep it from him for a while. And frankly, just as she does not want to know that he has a sex life, he would rather think of her as unsullied. Eventually, it is a fact that cannot be denied. They will never again share the unique psychological intimacy they have had. "The awful truth is out," notes Appleton. "He must share her with another man."

The way a father adjusts to this horrible new state of affairs will probably reflect the adroitness with which he has handled her flowering sexuality until now. If he has, as all fathers must do if they are to keep their sanity, treated her coming of age with a Zen-like cool and philosophical resignation, the transition will in all probability be smooth. She will interpret his silence as disappointment, and that may indeed be the case. But he will get over it. They will survive as a team even if she overreacts, as she inevitably will, to his signs of implied condemnation, real or imagined.

What a daughter and dad may not survive is the guilt inflicted on both parties by a father who treats the whole episode as if he were a scorned lover. Jean and Pam, both now in their late 20s, are condemned to lives of confusion by their father's obsessive protective behavior toward them. Like many, too many, women of their generation, they were subjected during their teenage years to surveillance that would rival the combined forces of the FBI, CIA, and KGB. The signs of their father's suspicious nature were there even before puberty. At age 8, Jean was spanked for talking with her male cousin on the front porch without a chaperone. The cousin was 6. Pam, less adventurous than her older sister, managed to escape her father's wrath until she was 12 and Dad discovered her walking home from junior high school with a Latino classmate. Pam still bears a scar on her upper arm from the whipping she received with a leather razor strop.

During their high school years and even into their early 20s, both Jean and Pam were pursued by their father into bars, parked cars, darkened living rooms, and boys' apartments. At 22, Jean left the Illinois town where she had grown up, moved to Portland, Oregon, and over the next year ran up a half-dozen arrests for prostitution. She later married one of her customers, divorced him after two years, and returned to the streets.

Pam fared better, but only slightly. After high school she went to work at the local supermarket and worked her way up to manager of the store's produce department. She moved in with a truck driver cum bronco-busting rodeo contestant with a jealous nature that rivaled her father's. Pam's boyfriend left her a mass of welts and bruises, and on one occasion she was admitted to the hospital for a concussion that resulted from his slamming her head against the pavement in front of their house. Her crime: supposedly flirting with a Safeway boxboy.

Still, Pam never tries to leave or press charges against him; her life might have been forfeit if it weren't for the fact that the day after he gave her a particularly nasty bashing, he was thrown from a bronc and killed. Amazingly, while Jean did everything she could to escape her father's surveillance (they have not seen each other since she moved to Portland), Pam sees him for dinner from time to time and seems unaware that she is still explaining herself to Dad.

The reasons behind Father's suspicious nature can be traced to his own adolescence. He remembers that as a 16-year-old, his sexual urges were so great that no girl who came near him was safe. The lustier he was as a youth, the harder he tried to shield his virginal daughters from all the young cannibals—in other words, any and all males with whom they came into contact.

In talking to Jean, Pam, and their father, I wondered how many women are fated by their father's irrational protectiveness to repeat the mistakes of the past. A father's unrelenting pressure on his daughter to remain his "good little girl" and refrain from intercourse is a leading cause of sexual guilt, inhibition, and frigidity. Does such a father know that in policing a daughter's life to such an extreme degree at 17, he has condemned her and her husband to a life of frustration and unhappiness twenty years later when she is a married woman of 37? Or worse yet, that he may be passing a lifetime sentence of guilt onto her, and that she will spend the rest of her days seeking out men to punish her the way Daddy did?

The answer is no. No more than the cold, aloof father deliberately sought to render his daughter sexually crippled or confused, or Darryl Zanuck deliberately sought to keep his son Richard in a perpetual psychological hammerlock.

"Fathers change," Dr. Appleton tells us. "They do so as daughters grow older. Your father's current views may be unknown to you. You will be surprised to learn he now regards you as a sexual woman, not a little girl. Both of you—father and daughter—have grown and developed. It is possible your father has remained closed to your having become sexually mature, but you owe it to both of you to give it a chance. You may be in for a pleasant surprise." As for the sons, Richard Zanuck and the bricklayer's boy will never forget their earlier rivalries with father.

In his late 70s Laurence Olivier confessed to me that his lifelong oedipal search to replace the mother who died when he was 12 ended only when he met his third wife, Joan Plowright. "I've always suffered from an Oedipus complex," he said, "and Joan comes closer to being like my mother than any person I've known." We cannot deny that those long-buried feelings of competition with Father for the affections of Mother will forever influence us. But neither can we forget the days we kept Dad locked out of the home when he most needed to come in from the cold, no matter how many times he gave the password. The password is: "Give!"

When I was a boy of 14, my
father was so ignorant, I
could hardly stand to have
the Old Man around. But when
I got to be 21, I was astonished
at how much he had learned
in seven years.

—Mark Twain

CHAPTER VI _____

The Real World

"It's a jungle out there." "It's a cold, cruel world." "It's dog-eat-dog." "Every man for himself." From the beginning it was Father who provided us with a view of the harsh realities of the "real world," of the fierce struggle awaiting us in school, on the job, even in marriage. And once again it is through first-person accounts that we see how Father's successes, failures, dreams, and apprehensions molded our own psyches and determined the way in which we function in the real world.

Perhaps more than anything, Father has left us with a palpable legacy of fear. He has told us there are rules we must live by as children, and stresses that the rules that will govern us as adults are even more rigid. In most cases he did not dare to break those rules. He wonders in the back of his mind what he might have achieved had he taken risks and defied his own father's warnings, but rare is the father who has the courage to admit to himself that he may have made a mistake, much less a father who will admit to his son that he might have been wrong.

Things were different early in the game, as a son's dreams and aspirations were indulged to the fullest. For even at 5 and 6 and 7, while fathers encouraged little boys to pursue their dreams of becoming a fireman, policeman, Indian chief, or even president, their daughters were given an altogether different agenda to live by. "All right, you can have a career, too, but first you will be a wife and mother." What is not taken into account is the undeniable fact that in this society, a full-time career and full-time motherhood can be managed, but only by a minority of superwomen. It has always been easier for Father to spare his daughter, his wife, and himself the pain and frustration of setting unrealistic goals for his little girl. Girls are supposedly the loving sex, the *passive* sex. They do better to learn how to follow, not lead in the waltz of life. They nurture, support—and suppress their own fantasies of excelling outside the domestic arena.

To fully understand why most fathers conspired to keep their beloved daughters second-class human beings, we must first consider what role fathers played in shaping the destinies of sons. Fathers, our first emissaries from the outside world, deserve much of the credit (or the blame) for the way in which we perceive the challenges that await us after we leave home, and our capacity to meet those challenges. Scour the library shelves for the biography of the accomplished person who does not owe some measure of his success to a father or father figure and you will be hard pressed to find it—even when the mother was clearly the overriding influence, as was the case with Winston Churchill's American mother, Jennie. She was the quintessential political stage mother, but her husband actually played out the first act, serving as an example for her son. From Lord Randolph, who became a major force in Parliament only to succumb to syphilitic insanity, Winston learned not only how to govern, but also how to understand the cruelest twists of fate.

Dr. Bernard Saracheck of the University of Missouri at Kansas City studied the lives of 187 entrepreneurs, many of them legendary business figures like John. D. Rockefeller, James Cash Penney, and Henry Ford, and discovered that although most of their fathers were self-employed, none were successful. The fathers' self-reliance strengthened their sons' resolve to pursue independent commercial activity, but equally important was the father's bitter lesson of failure. Knowing how horribly dehumanizing poverty could be, these men vowed that this would never happen to them. The only instances where the son completely rejected Dad as unworthy of emulation occurred not in response to any business failure on Father's part, but only after the father spurned his son because of dislike, disinterest, or distrust.

John is a 34-year-old newspaper columnist, and while his lawyer wife earns twice his salary representing insurance companies in arson cases, he is almost insufferably pretentious. He buys his clothes only at Brooks Brothers, drives a preppy-perfect cranberry-red BMW, and after he has ordered the most expensive bottle of wine at a restaurant, he goes through the whole ritual of sniffing the cork, holding the glass up to the light, and then swishing it around noisily in his mouth before invariably rejecting it as unsuitable.

John is an aspiring snob, and only after broaching the subject of his lower-middle-class Pennsylvania upbringing did it become clear why. "My father was a haberdasher—a failed haberdasher," says John, "and Mother never let him forget it. She ran things, pushed him around, told him off in front of other people. Her favorite phrase—and this really got to my father, you could tell—was 'not for the likes of us.' If we stopped in front of a store window or a nice restaurant, or if my uncle Harry just told us he was taking his family on a vacation to Hawaii, Mother would shake her head and say 'Not for the likes of us. We can't afford it. Don't ever be a failure like your father, John,' she'd say. 'Make enough money so you can *enjoy* life.' I hated the way she made him feel, but I guess I've tried to do what she said. Living well *is* the best revenge, after all."

In the most superficial sense John is trying to live well with a vengeance. Yet, like his father, he has abrogated real power to his wife. She is the manager of the family finances, the bigger breadwinner, and he defers to her in all but trivial matters, like selecting the wine in a restaurant. But John has not been able to get beyond his own sense of inadequacy.

Lewis Yablonsky's story is remarkably similar. "I vividly recall," he wrote in his excellent *Fathers and Sons*, "sitting at the dinner table with my two brothers and father and cringing at my mother's attacks on my father. 'Look at him,' she would say in Yiddish, 'his head and shoulders are bent down. He's a failure. He doesn't have the courage to get a better job or make more money. He's a beaten man.' He would keep his eyes pointed toward his plate and never answer her. She never extolled his virture of persistence or the fact that he worked so hard; instead she constantly focused on the negative and created an image to his three sons of a man without fight, crushed by a world over which he had no control."

Yablonsky concedes that his father's refusal to counter his wife's charges tended to confirm this unfortunate image in their children's eyes, not to mention leaving all three boys with a rather grim view of marriage and of women as life partners. In the Yablonsky household, Mother was the smudged lens through which the children saw their father. What Lewis, the middle brother, did not realize until his older brother told him many years later was that their dad had not always been such a weakling: During the early years of his marriage, in the 1920s, the elder Yablonsky was unquestionably the boss in the family, the head of the household. It took the Depression, and the arrival of his mother-in-law and his own mother to join with his wife in the chorus of kvetching, to leave Lewis Yablonsky's father a broken man.

Milton Berle offers yet another glimpse of the defeated dad when he speaks emotionally of his father, Moses:

"Everybody asks me about my mother, and I was very close to her and loved her dearly. But nobody ever asks me about Pa. I can describe him in one word: lost. My mother was a department store detective, and she was too strong for him. He was a creative man who built castles that evaporated, a dreamer whose dreams never came true. Not that he didn't try. One time when I was a little boy, I remember he was in the basement and Ma said, 'What are you doing down there?' He'd say, 'I'm dipping cherries in chocolate.' 'Stop that nonsense,' she'd yell. 'Dipping cherries in chocolate. Where is that going to get you?' Of course, years later somebody else invented chocolate-covered cherries and made a fortune. Another time, he was stuffing perfumed powder in little packets, and she berated him again. Sachets are very popular now. Can you imagine what he might have come up with if he had the courage?"

Berle's mother took charge of her little boy's career as a child actor and traveled with him on his vaudeville dates around the country. "Pa stayed home while my mother and I went from city to city, and one time, we were in San Francisco I think, we got a letter from him that I'll never forget. He talked about how he'd just mended something, and how he just cooked a pot roast, that sort of thing. It was just very sad, as if he was the mother and she the father."

All these men look back on fathers whose bitter disappointments probably served to fuel their ambition. A domineering mother added to their determination, though perhaps at the cost of making them resentful and suspicious of women. In families where roles seem to be switched and the mother is an inordinately strong character, the father need not acquiesce to the point of allowing himself to be depicted as a weakling.

Gay Talese's father is a furrier, tailor, and owner of his own dress boutique in Ocean City, New Jersey. "Back when he was supposed to go to college," says Gay, "my father told his father to take him into the family clothing business and not to waste the money. My mother was well ahead of her time, a woman more interested in business than her family. She was a department store buyer in the 1920s, and if she had never married and never had children, she would have been happy with just a career. It was my father who wanted a family. He was much more responsive; he took charge of the home as well as the business. Unlike the commuter father, who may have practically nothing to do with the home, he was the commanding force in both places. My earliest memory—I must have been three years old—is of waking up in the middle of the night and wanting some hot milk. It was my father who brought the hot milk, not my mother."

Talese remembers that his father was also a disciplinarian, a man "not reticent to voice his opinion. He was very religious, politically conservative, unequivocating in his principles. He often made your mind up for you, and there are times when you want that, when you don't want to deal with options. Because both parents were strong, there was no female in the family, in a sense."

For all his decisiveness, Talese's father also displayed a cautiousness characteristic of most Depression dads. "My father always said don't count on anything to happen. Do nothing speculative, because nothing could be assumed. He carried with him a sense of impending doom, a wariness, a caution. As a son, that's not a great thing to carry around with you."

The senior Talese's own anxieties did not prevent him from encouraging his son to try his wings as a journalist. "He was always influential in my life," admits Gay, "because he alone out of all the authoritarian figures in my life always believed in me. I was not academically outstanding, but he was my steadfast supporter—a party of one." Gay worked as a writer at *The New York Times* for a decade before quitting in 1963 to write his best-selling history of that newspaper, *The Kingdom and the Power*. These days Talese still makes a point of spending his summers with his parents in Ocean City ("I'll always go there; it's the tie that binds") and is wistful about the family business, which will probably die with his parents. "My father never coerced me to follow in his footsteps," says Talese, an only son. "Now there's nobody to carry on. It's sad."

Gay Talese took the best of what his father had to offer, true. But we would be neglecting half the story if we did not point out that like his father, Gay also married a woman who was in the same profession and every bit his match: publishing executive Nan Talese. Now Gay relates with a trace of bitterness that he, like his father, is taking the active role in the raising of his children, two teenage daughters. "Nan is at the office all day, but I'm here at home writing. When the man comes to read the meter, *I'm* the one who lets him in. When my daughters come home from school, it's *me* that's here; I'm the housewife!" What lessons has he learned from his father that apply to his brood? "Be firm. The tragic alternative is the vacillating, equivocating parent. Kids don't want Dad to be a marshmallow, even if they are only looking for something to rebel against. Take a position!"

There is a sentiment afoot these days in feminist circles that men's hidden strength is in their ability to communicate, to plunge into healthy competition on the playing field or even at the office and come out the best of friends chatting about it locker-room style. Hogwash. Women are the kaffee-klatchers, the kibitzers, the sharers of intimate secrets that would make subway graffiti artists blanch. Under the proper circumstances, women have always been permitted to tell "the girls" about everything from their lover's most recent sexual predilection to the excruciating intensity of their menses. Our mothers, however demure they may have seemed to us as we curled in front of the set to watch Jackie Gleason or Ozzie Nelson, had ready access to this emotional outlet. Every Lucy on the block had an Ethel, or more likely several Ethels, to tell her troubles to. Not so their husbands, our fathers. Men in

America are not particularly given to confidences, to opening up to one another. Psychoanalysts will tell you that, of all their patients, the most difficult to get to unburden themselves are men 50 and older, men our fathers' age. Most of what we learn from Father, we learn by observation.

"I never talked about my doubts and fears," says one 58-year-old father of six, "because I really didn't want to let on to the kids that I was anything less than perfect. It's tough enough to get children to obey you unquestioningly these days, and I knew that the minute one of them heard me say, 'Well, maybe I blew up at you this afternoon because I'm scared shitless that I'm going to lose my job,' then it would be all over. They'd never listen to me without trying to second-guess my motives, my problems." This father came to learn, however, that "kids aren't stupid; they figured out what was bugging me. So now I have a 32-year-old son who works for a construction company and is *twice* as nervous as I ever was about being laid off. Now that I can see how his attitude is screwing up *his* kids—my granddaughters—I just wish to God I'd been a little less anxious when my son and his brothers and sisters were growing up. If I'd just talked about my troubles with other people, and not brought my suppressed worries home with me, life just would have been more enjoyable."

This father is not the only Depression Era kid who regrets having cast a pall over his children's expectations. "My daughter is careful about her budget—too careful," admits one. "She watches every penny, and she doesn't have to. But I know who's responsible for that: me." Just as often, fathers who grew up fearing poverty regret their negativism because it had the opposite effect on their children: it made them irresponsible, reckless. "When he was 17, my son told me he wasn't going to college because he wanted to be 'free'—free of the fears that he knew still plagued me and I guess always will." Now in his late 20s, the son skips from menial job to menial job, from town to town and girlfriend to girlfriend. The young man revels in his rootlessness, but that is little comfort to his father; now the "old man," as his son calls him, frets for both of them.

Not all fathers who grew up during hard times are defensive about their cautious outlook, certainly. In fact, while most of those men falling into that category admitted that this was something of a burden—a phantom that would prevent many of them from spending money freely and enjoying it—at bottom they felt that their words of warning were wise. "I wish to God," said one, "that my grandfather had warned my father to be at least a little scared, a little reticent. That way when the Depression came he would have been prepared for it." As it was, the man's father lost everything and ended up drinking himself to death.

New York investment banker Todd Rutledge was proud that both his children followed his footsteps into the business world. He was therefore stunned to find that, while they respected him, they also resented him for making them all essentially driven careerists. Says Rutledge: "It's bewildering to discover that your kids are willing to take your financial and personal support, to reap the financial and personal rewards once they've made it—and then turn around and say *you* have somehow made them unhappy people. But they must have thought *I* was a happy man, or they wouldn't have pursued the same goals, right?" Well, yes—and no.

A father's influence on our lives outside the home is determined by many things. If the son has a deeply felt affection for his father, if Father is himself a professional and personal success, if Mother supports Father as a model to emulate, chances are we will be influenced to follow in his footsteps. Conversely, if few or none of these conditions exist, in all likelihood the son will reject his father in whole or in part as a role model. Hence the boy who worships his cellist father doggedly pursues a musical career and eventually wields a baton as one of the most celebrated conductors of his day. His name: Arthur Fiedler. Another young man, the son of a mathematician, discovers rather early in his academic career that he, too, has a sizable aptitude for abstract thinking. Yet the boy enrolls in college and majors in journalism, a field in which he has never exhibited any particular interest and for which he is clearly not suited by either intellect or temperament. Why? Because (1) he has seen that, despite his father's eminence as a mathematician, Dad remains an unhappy, withdrawn man, and (2) the son does not wish to spend his entire life forever being compared to his noted father.

Another family arrives at a strange compromise. The retiring board chairman of a Fortune 500 firm has always wanted his only son to take his "rightful place" in the company, but only after the lad has taken the prescribed route. He must attend the proper schools, join the right clubs, and enter the firm as a trainee so as to at least give the appearance of a proper apprenticeship (not to mention avoid embarrassing Dad). The son goes to the schools selected by his father, all right, but when it comes to going to work he has his own ideas. He circumvents his father's carefully thought out plans by engineering his own entry into the company at a high level; he convinces a family friend who is also a senior vice-president in the company to take him on in a job for which he is profoundly unqualified. The father is enraged, embarrassed in the eyes of his peers. Meantime, the son has granted his father's wish that he join the company—but only under Junior's terms, not Dad's.

Beyond wanting their sons to achieve a level of professional and personal happiness, most fathers do not map out their sons' lives for them. All fathers do indulge themselves to some degree by imagining their little boy as, say, a future occupant of the White House. Movies like *The Jazz Singer* (in which the son thwarts his father's expectations by not carrying on in the family tradition as a cantor) or Rodgers and

Hammerstein's *Carousel,* where Gordon MacRae belts out "My Boy Bill," also remind us how powerful those dreams can be.

And how destructive. Cain struck down Abel, the Old Testament tells us, because Adam loved Abel more no matter how hard both sons tried to please him. The tale is twice retold in John Steinbeck's *East of Eden,* the saga of two generations of sons caught in similar battles for a father's affection.

Practically everyone I interviewed, however, thought they knew what course their fathers wanted their sons' lives to take, but admitted Dad never said, "Be a doctor" or "I'll want you to take over the family hardware store when I'm gone."

Was there ever need for words? Ted Turner is a case in point. His father, Ed Turner, came off a hardscrabble farm in Sumner, Mississippi, and went into the billboard business. After a stint in Cincinnati, Ed moved to Savannah, Georgia, and immediately shipped off 9-year-old Ted to Georgia Military Academy outside Atlanta. Father and son somehow managed to remain close, but Ed Turner saw to it that life at home was no softer than at military school. He used a wire coat hanger from time to time, Ted recalls, "to get my attention." Then there were endless chores to earn his pocket money, and by the time he was 17, Ted was being charged rent by his father for the time he spent at home during summer vacation.

Ted wanted to attend the U.S. Naval Academy at Annapolis, but his father insisted on an Ivy League school. At Brown, Ted immersed himself in the Greek classics; he had been enthralled by the mythic heroes of ancient times— and his father disapproved. "I am appalled, even horrified that you have adopted classics as a major," Ed Turner wrote his son. "As a matter of fact, I almost puked on the way home today. I am a practical man, and for the life of me I cannot possibly understand why you should wish to speak Greek. I have read, in recent years, the deliberations of Plato and Aristotle, and was interested to learn that the old bastards had minds which worked very similarly to the way our minds work today. I was amazed that they had so much time for deliberating and thinking, and was interested in the kind of civilization that would permit such useless deliberation. I think you are rapidly becoming a jackass, and the sooner you get out of that filthy atmosphere, the better it will suit me."

There was only one way for Ted to get even with his father: He published the contemptuous letter in the Brown University newspaper.

Eventually, Ted switched his major to economics, then left Brown and joined his father in the billboard business. The apprenticeship was intense. "Driving to work," recalls Ted, "my father told me about the tax laws, amortization, depreciation, sales, management, construction. He told me how he got started, what happened in competitive situations, how he lost business and how he got it." Ed instilled in his son ambition, yes, but more important the fear of failure that drives such men on. "All my life I have had this gnawing pain that I might not succeed," said Turner. "It is only in the last four or five years that I have put that ghost to rest."

Ed Turner had become a millionaire by the time his son joined his firm. He expanded, bought companies, then fretted that he should not have tried to grow so fast. He signed an agreement to sell his Atlanta division, drove off to his plantation in South Carolina, and in 1963, at the age of 53, he shot himself.

"My father died when I was 24," Turner says. "That left me alone, because I had counted on him to make the judgment of whether or not I was a success." Ted managed to hold on to the billboard business and eventually built it into a sports and communications empire. But for all his success, Turner is obsessed by the violence of his father's death. "He talks about death incessantly," says a friend of Ted's. "Over the years, killing himself was a high-priority topic of conversation. Most of the time he was flippant about it. He would talk in this joking way about how, if things did not work out, he could always sell the business, how all he needed was a roof over his head and some food. Then he would say, 'If things get really bad, I can always kill myself.' He could not go several days without talking about suicide." Ted Turner is clearly his father's son.

Often a father sees the light in time to turn his own life around, but, sadly, not his children's. Spencer is 45 years old, and his two sons are 24 and 22. At the age of 42, he collapsed at his desk in the trading room of a major New York brokerage firm and was operated on for an aortic aneurism. Until that moment work and winning were everything to Spencer—a philosophy of life that he unhesitatingly passed on to the boys. "I taught them," he recalls, "that Vince Lombardi was right, that winning was the only thing. It didn't matter if we were talking about football or chess, grades or getting the prettiest girl in school to go out with you. When I got out of college and the service, all my energies went into making a million dollars. And once I did, I wanted ten million dollars. It sounds completely trite, I know, but I never stopped to smell the roses until I almost died at 42. Jesus, *42.* Both the boys are in business school now, and they're just like I used to be, scrambling for straight-A's. When I tell them to take it easy, they get this funny look that says, 'We know you're running scared, Dad. What happened to you will never happen to us.' What they don't realize is that I was running scared back *then,* that at last I'm not afraid. I just know I'm not invincible. But they don't hear me. I created my own monsters; I've got to take the blame."

My father walks too fast. In a supermarket or department store he strides swiftly ahead of my mother, jingling the change in his pockets, even though she is the one doing the shopping. When he visits us in New York, he is always fifty feet ahead of the rest of us. No matter that he is unfamiliar with the city and that I must run ahead to tell him that he has overshot his destination by a block. True, this is all part and parcel of his restless builder's personality. And in groups it obviates the need for idle chatter. The purpose of walking is to get somewhere, right?

I watch the way other men his age behave on the street, and see that in nearly all cases they zoom on ahead while wives and children stroll behind. They must share with my father some dread of what will happen if they remain stationary. Movement, perpetual motion, burns up nervous energy and helps us to forget in those anxious, inert moments that mortality is nipping at our heels. As Satchel Paige so sagely advised, "Don't look back. Something may be gaining on you."

The fears that propel my father and his generation through supermarkets and along sidewalks also appear to take hold behind the steering wheel. Though as many women as men drive, men account for 70 percent of all speeding violations nationwide. Anyone who ever took a long-distance ride with Dad at the wheel will recall that he pressed on while the rest of us tried to keep our minds off the fact that we were weak from hunger and our bladders were about to burst. Mr. Mileage—that's what we called Dad.

As if governed by some set of regulations that applied only to the men of his generation, my father often seemed bound to obey some invisible authority. In a restaurant, he never asked to be seated anywhere special; if he was plopped in front of a swinging kitchen door, that was just the way things were. He thought it the height of rudeness to ask for anything that was not on the menu, and food that arrived at the table in an inedible state was nonetheless never sent back ("They'll just spit on it and throw it on the floor, and then serve it to us again.")

In a store, if you could not find it yourself, you left without the merchandise you needed. Asking for directions was not any more acceptable under those circumstances than it was the time we were driving across country and somehow found ourselves in a holding pattern around Boston. (In a scene straight out of *Twilight Zone,* we circled the city for an hour before finally breaking free.)

Men don't do these things. They never complain, and they never explain. Perhaps it was World War II, or the mere fact that my father was a career officer, a believer in duty, a follower of orders. Maybe it was the bitter lesson of growing up poor in the Depression How many times have we heard our parents tell us of stuffing cardboard in the soles of shoes that had long since worn out, of trying to save up a nickel for a movie, of shameful days watching relatives and neighbors queue up in breadlines—if you didn't have to yourself. That that generation of men and women not only endured the dual calamity of the Depression and the war, but transcended it, is nothing less than a triumph of courage and human spirit. Those of us whose mothers and fathers took the world by the hand and led it through those most turbulent of times will always be in awe of them. Just as we will always bear their scars.

It is that legacy of fear that, as Ted Turner must attest, keeps driven men going. Actor Robert Blake, whose topsy-turvy career began when he was a child star in the 1930s and peaked with his hit television series *Baretta,* couches the lesson he learned from his father in, well, vivid terms. "Every time you think you got it made," smiles Blake, "old Mother Nature kicks you in the scrotum."

As a boy, I imitated my father; I even wore a seersucker suit exactly like his. On the coffee table in our living room sat two wooden likenesses of us hand-carved by a Yokohama craftsman. The figures are identical in all but a few minor respects: his crew cut has been painted in black and his eyes are brown; my hair (also a crew cut) is light brown, the eyes blue. My figure is half the size of his. The career I chose is one that he would never have considered, and I think he respects me for that. Certainly I would not have had the gall to go to work as a reporter and editor for our local daily newspaper when I was still a junior in high school, or to start writing feature pieces for *The New York Times* at 19, or to become a correspondent for *Time* magazine at 20 or to write my first book at 25, if it had not been for the influence of both my parents. But I sit where they put me in restaurants, berate my wife (as my father berated my mother) for asking for items not listed on the menu, and stop myself when I suddenly realize much to my horror that I am absentmindedly jiggling the keys in my pocket. I also worry about taxes, the Middle East, and how we can possibly afford to send our daughter, Kate, to school in New York when kindergarten already costs more than what I paid for an entire year's tuition at Berkeley. They also tell me I walk too fast.

In terms of the way they wind up viewing the harsh realities of the outside world, women are, just as much as men, what their fathers made them. But there is a crucial difference. Exploitation, not failure, is what women fear most. They do not want to be used either domestically or in the marketplace. That is something they may have seen firsthand as children, and they know how bitter it has made their mothers.

Father plays an enormous part in molding his daughter's perception of men as co-workers as well as sexual beings. Weak fathers may make daughters unduly fearful. For these women, mothers are in command, men are to be manipulated. Detached daddies make their daughters lonely, unable to sustain any solid relationship with a man in the bedroom or the boardroom. Tyrannical fathers may instill an irrational fear of the opposite sex and leave a daughter suspecting a man's motives. Under those circumstances, she is either left to seek lovers and colleagues she can push around, or resigns herself to a life of martyrdom at the hands of autocratic males.

Mommy, of course, and society conspire in the handicapping of female children. Baby girls are perceived to be more delicate, more vulnerable, despite the medical fact that they are sturdier, stronger, and statistically far less likely to fall seriously ill during infancy. There have been studies in recent years indicating that children's cries are interpreted along sex lines. If the child crying was a girl, mothers and fathers thought the cause was fear; if it was a boy child, they assumed he was angry. Consequently, mothers responded more readily to their infant daughters' cries, picking them up and cuddling them, than they did to their sons' wailing.

It is fascinating how the authors of popular women's books have chosen to interpret these findings. In her intelligent best seller, *The Cinderella Complex*, Colette Dowling saw that such a difference in the handling of male and female children was crippling to girls because it made them more dependent. If they cried long enough and hard enough, someone—Mother, in most cases—could be counted on to come and comfort them. But Dowling also suggests that this is a plus for the sons. "Because male infants are thought to be tougher," writes Dowling, "Mom doesn't trip over the vacuum cleaner running to comfort her baby boy. As a consequence, he is not systematically reinforced in the idea 'Help will come speeding my way if I cry for it.' There are times he has to solace himself. Occasionally, he discovers, this works *for* him. He is able to comfort himself. Bit by bit he learns to do this on a more regular basis. Bit by bit he learns to become his own emotional caretaker." *As if being left to fend for oneself in infancy were a blessing!*

Dowling is correct, however, when she pinpoints this as the start of a woman's lifelong dependency. Tommy is the "little man"; he is encouraged to explore, extend. He will get over the inevitable bumps and scrapes. Not so Suzy. She must be protected at all costs, and Dad in particular can be forgiven his tendency to overreact when Daddy's

Girl stumbles to greet him at the door. Cautiousness and timidity are thought to be inherently feminine qualities, and therefore we encourage these in little girls. Mother is happiest when her daughter does what she does: obeys the rules.

Don't make waves; be a lady. Daddy, once again, is the prime reinforcer of these qualities. "My mother has never wanted to make waves," says a Hartford-based insurance executive who admits to downing more Valium than she should to get through senior staff meetings. "Her life was lived in my father's shadow; when we got older my sister and I called him the General behind his back. My mother didn't think it was funny then, any more than she does now. Her accomplishments, whether it was preparing a perfect veal cordon bleu or getting elected to the school board, meant nothing to her if the General didn't approve. He defined her life for her. Even on the school board, she really cast her votes the way he wanted her to. As long as she behaved, things were fine. He took her out, brought home little surprises for her, never forgot a birthday or anniversary. They've been married almost forty years, and to everyone who knows them they are the perfect couple. But I can't help thinking Mother knows that a part of life passed her by."

Yet how many women make that choice, and gladly pay the price for surviving within the fortress of marriage? Rather than deal with the turbulent world outside, they seek the marriage partner offering security in exchange for dependence. Most adult women today had mothers who made such a pact, and in doing so seriously jeopardized their daughters' chances of ever breaking down those marital fortress walls and embarking on successful careers of their own. "For a woman to live in a manner for which she has not been raised, to act in ways never observed or practiced in childhood, is not easy," writes Dr. Appleton. "The examples set by her parents often do not serve to guide her career path." Indeed, Mother's domestic chores were there for all to see. Laundry, cooking, cleaning, shopping, chauffeuring the kids from school to dance class to dentist to home, showing up at PTA meetings—these often underrated tasks were performed by Mom daily, right under our noses.

What did Dad do? He went off to that mysterious place called "work." Frequently, Mom was not even that precise about what her husband did for a living, so how were his children supposed to know? In my interviews, I discovered that the majority of daughters never visited their fathers' place of business—whether it was a loading dock, a doctor's office, or an executive suite—and most of the *sons* had (though even then seldom more than once a year).

Much of my childhood was spent on a series of military bases, tantamount to living over the shop. But I remember only a handful of times when I ever got a glimpse of an airplane cockpit or an operations room. Yet all of us knew as children that whatever it was Dad did, he was responsible for keeping us afloat as a family. If he came home buoyant, we were excited and put everything aside to be with him. If he was fatigued, Mother shushed us into silence while he tried to recover with a nap before dinner. Dad was aggressive, daring, independent. Mom and the kids were submissive, hesitant, dependent. But then, we kids would grow out of it. Wouldn't we?

The baby-boom girls were, for the most part, given more of a chance to carve a niche for themselves outside the home than were their mothers. A father's ambivalent feelings toward his daughter's sex life were one thing, but that did not mean he wasn't proud when she got good grades, moved on to a well-paying job and worked her way up the career ladder. In grooming her intellectually, he often became a pal to his daughter during her adolescent years.

Samantha's blue-collar father never told either of his daughters they were attractive ("We had to rely on our mother and our uncles for compliments about the way we looked"), but he did lavish praise on Sam for what he spotted early on as a "head for numbers." He compared her to his own older sister, a regional director for the IRS. "Coming from him," Sam says, "that was the ultimate praise." When she was still a straight-A student in high school, Sam went to work part-time in the credit department of a local department store. Her father's pride grew; hadn't he predicted she would be a success in business? What he had not predicted was that she also had a talent for languages and a love of Spanish literature.

Instead of enrolling in the nearby state college, as Dad had wished and as her older sister had obediently done, Sam applied to Stanford University and was accepted. Her twin major: Spanish and German. Sam had been awarded a number of scholarship grants, but she still needed her father to co-sign a school loan to meet all her tuition costs. He refused, demanding that she either go to the cheaper (and considerably less prestigious) state college or go to work for the department store full-time. "I wouldn't take no for an answer," Sam recalls. "I stood there in the kitchen and told him there was no risk. It was such a small amount— twelve hundred dollars—and he knew I'd pay him back as soon as I graduated. But without that money I couldn't go to Stanford. I kept asking 'Why? Why?' and he just stood there clenching his fists, saying nothing. All of a sudden his hand came up and he socked me in the face. I had a black eye for days and I didn't try to hide it from him. He never apologized, but I guess he was ashamed. He co-signed the loan the next day."

Where was Sam's mother during the fight scene? Standing there silently, not attempting to intervene. "I guess she thought I was being impudent or something," says Samantha, obviously hurt then by her mother's lack of support. Mother had been an obedient daughter and wife, and she apparently expected nothing less of her female offspring. As it turned out, Sam's father was not incorrect in his assessment of her financial acumen. After she graduated from Stanford with honors, his daughter moved to New York and before she reached 30 was appointed assistant vice-president in the international credit department of one of the world's leading banks, handling hundreds of millions of dollars in loans to foreign concerns.

Even then, his own fear of seeing his daughter getting too far ahead for a woman prevented Sam's father from ever fully acknowledging her success. "Before being promoted to assistant vice-president there were a number of steps: assistant manager, assistant treasurer, assistant secretary—'secretary' as in corporate secretary, a high position in the company," explains Sam. "When I was made assistant secretary and sent him one of my business cards, all he said was, 'Eh, all those years in school and you're not even a secretary yet. Just an assistant.' He wasn't kidding. I could never make him understand that I wasn't some secretary's assistant. Whenever I'd visit home for Thanksgiving or Christmas, all my relatives kept asking me when I'd get promoted to teller."

Sam's sister, meantime, has done what her father told her and given up hopes of becoming an artist to major at that nearby state college in preschool education. Now she is the mother of four and occasionally does some substitute teaching. "Dad understood his daughter becoming a schoolteacher," sighs Sam. "What I did he couldn't understand, or he wouldn't accept."

The first guilt comes when father and daughter seem teamed up against Mom. Often the mother is left out as Dad tells his little girl how much she reminds him of himself at her age, how bright she is, how far she can go. Mom may sit quietly, seemingly oblivious to this, or go about setting the table or folding towels. The daughter often feels sorry for her exclusion from the proceedings. Little does she suspect that Mom isn't upset for one reason only: She knows better. She was the daughter once herself.

What mother understands is that, eventually, Dad will

in all probability slam on the brakes once he begins to feel that he is in danger of being upstaged by his Good Little Girl. "I was obeying his wishes to the letter and that seemed to anger him," wrote Simone de Beauvoir of her relationship with her father in *Memoirs of a Dutiful Daughter*. "He had destined me to a life of study, and yet I was being reproached with having my nose in a book all the time. To judge by his surly temper you would think that I had gone against his wishes in embarking on a course that he had actually chosen for me. I kept wondering what I had done wrong. I felt unhappy and ill at ease and nursed resentment in my heart."

What de Beauvoir and others have experienced is essentially the same form of parental competition that one most associates with fathers and sons. Once the daughter has exhibited many of the same qualities in the workplace and hence ceases to be so totally feminine (i. e., dependent) in her father's eyes, then jealousy rears its head. Go ahead and succeed, but do not threaten to surpass Father. His ultimate weapon is the one that will hurt her the most, and he knows it. A son may never marry or father children, and his father can live with that. All Sonny need do is one thing: succeed. For the daughter, there are other things she must do to satisfy Daddy. She may have the career, but Daddy's little girl will never be a "complete woman" without also having a husband and child, preferably both.

Marilyn was urged by her father to abandon her plans to become an archaeologist even after she had been admitted to Harvard's graduate program. Daddy told her to marry the first man who asked her, and she did. Now 40, she is divorced, her husband has custody of their teenage sons, and she is a librarian in a Connecticut village. She will probably never pursue her original dream of assisting well-known archaeologist Iris Love in a major dig. "Whatever confidence in myself," she sighs, "was drained out of me by my husband. And," she adds, "by Daddy."

The woman whose father encouraged her to excell in school and to pursue a career becomes understandably confused, even enraged, when Daddy's fragile ego won't allow him to see her through to full independence. Relations between the two are strained as he senses that she is slipping away from him, and in the most extreme cases a rapprochement is never achieved. Father may die before his daughter can ever bring herself to comprehend the fact that he has doubts and fears too. His intransigence is more forgivable than his daughter's once battle lines are drawn. By now Dad has been conditioned over a lifetime to think of himself as protector and provider for his wife and daughters. His daughter, for all her righteous indignation, comes at this from the perspective of one with her whole life *ahead* of her. If there are lingering feelings of betrayal, it is the grown-up daughter who is best equipped to make the first move toward emotional independence. She can, as a mature and accomplished adult, stand back and see Father as she might see any man in his situation at his time of life. She can stop asking, "Why doesn't he try to understand me?" and try to see for the first time that he is faced with apprehensions as great if not greater than her own. She owes him that.

Still trying to come to grips with his own feelings for his long-dead father, Laurence Olivier concedes that his own conservative attitudes toward money stem from his impoverished childhood and his father's penny-pinching. And though he confesses to somewhat resembling the miserly James Tyrone character in Eugene O'Neill's *Long Day's Journey into Night,* his white Bentley, his memorabilia-crammed London townhouse, and his large country home offer ample proof that he is perfectly capable of enjoying all the perks of his position. Aside from what he calls his "insufferable guilt complex," Olivier is clearly not a fearful man. He sees himself and his third wife, actress Joan Plowright, as "rather good" parents. "Most people think of people in my profession as being rapacious when we're really very domestic," he muses. Indeed, the Oliviers' son, Richard (Dickie), and daughter, Tamsin, seem to have been given an upbeat view of the world—and, specifically, their parents' profession—since both have chosen to enter the theater. Does Lord Olivier worry that there will be the inevitable comparisons? "I won't be around to be compared *to*," he shrugs. "I've timed it all perfectly." He becomes somewhat less sure, however, of how things stand between himself and his youngest daughter, Julie Kate. "I've tried to get close to her, but there is always this distance," he allows. As of late 1983 she had not made known whether she would also go into the theater or choose an altogether different profession. "We, shall we say, have a mutual understanding," explains Olivier. "But their mother and I have done what we could to show the most important thing in life: domestic bliss, the joys of warmth and love and having a family to share them with. A career? Yes, *anything* that makes them happy."

Consider how much more difficult it is for the daughter whose father has always sought to discourage her. Author Susan Brownmiller remembers her father as being "distant" from the start. "He didn't think I should go to college, just marry and have kids. Part of my competitiveness came from having to constantly fight him." Brownmiller's dad was, she says, "an unsuccessful garment salesman, a bitter man stuck in a profession for which he was not suited. My mother was the one who worked and supported us, so I grew up not being in awe of Daddy despite his insistence on making me feel inadequate. I didn't grow up thinking men were all-powerful, which made me perfectly comfortable with the women's movement. People are always talking about their parents, particularly how much they hate their fathers, but for me this subject is a closed door. My mother and father are both dead, and I am free."

Brownmiller's case is clearly the exception among women of achievement. Most will, without hesitation, credit their fathers with instilling in them the self-confidence, intellectual curiosity, and ambition to move forward. Author Florence Rush claims her father "was my model, definitely not my mother. He was a wonderful, nurturing man. I loved him, we all did." Eda LeShan also credits her father with giving her the "push" to excell in school and in her career as one of the country's leading psychologists.

No one speaks more movingly about her father than Dr. Joyce Brothers. "I was enormously close to my father," concedes Brothers, both of whose parents were attorneys. Brothers recalls that he treated her and her sister, who is now also a practicing lawyer, "like his sons. I imagine we were treated the way boys are treated. Dad insisted on discussing politics and world affairs at the dinner table. He wanted us to think, weigh facts, form opinions. He had more of an impact on preparing me for the outside world than my mother, even though she was an attorney, too." Brothers now admits that she may have relied more than she should have on her father for love and approval. "My relationship with my husband got better after my father died. There was this feeling on the part of my husband that I was comparing the two of them, that all men had to play second fiddle to my father. As it turned out, I was *too* close to my father." When her father died, Brothers had already been a household name for two decades. That this dispenser of advice on mental health to millions of Americans still required Daddy's approval bespeaks the central problem of women surviving (or even thriving) as professionals.

It is frustrating when Pop suddenly applies the brakes. Not nearly as disturbing, however, as when he presses so hard that he forgets his daughter still wants to be loved for being his child, not for her accomplishments. "He was not there for me when I needed him as a little girl," says

Erica Jong of her father. "He never talked to any of his three daughters about getting married, but he expected us all to graduate from college. As I grew up, we had battles. I felt that I was only loved for being an over-achiever. I had to earn all the medals, get all the grades in order to be loved."

Jong did not sort out her feelings and confront her father with them until she was 31 and *Fear of Flying* had already taken off. "When *Fear of Flying* went to number five on *The New York Times* Best Seller list, my father said, 'Well, why aren't you number one?' I exploded. 'I've gotten enough number ones and enough A's for you to last for-ever. If I never do another thing in my life, you'll *have* to love me.' It was a great moment of contact between us."

Her father, it turns out, may have seemed eternally dissatisfied with her performance because of his own thwarted dreams. "He was a drummer and a theatrical manager for a time," says Jong. "But he married at 21, and he was pressured by his wife to go into the export business. He was spectacularly successful, but he's always been frustrated because he gave up a career in show busi-ness." Now, Jong describes her relationship with her father as "very close. Rebellion is painful, but essential. You can get through to that adult level of love and emotional re-spect, but it's a point you reach only through maturity, exhaustion, attrition."

Not to mention courage, tolerance, and a forgiving heart. Father began shaping our view of the outside world long before we ever even remotely considered venturing out on our own. No matter how good his intentions, how rational and considered his advice, we all wound up with an image as warped as any found in a funhouse mirror. Those distortions turn out to be just as important, we dis-cover, as the portion of the image that is accurate. Fear and dread of failure inherited from Father may have made us restless and unhappy, but it also may have made us strive for something a more contented person might easily do without. How could Father encourage us to acquire the education, the ideals, the goals to function as adults, then burden us with his own bitterness and anxiety? But, in fairness, how could he not?

He was more my father than my father.

—Erica Jong

CHAPTER VII ⸻⸻⸻⸻

Surrogates and Mentors

"Oh, God, yes! Alternatives to Mother!" shouts Dr. Sirgay Sanger, director of the parent-child program at Luke's Hospital and an instructor at New York's Columbia College of Physicians and Surgeons. "Mother is so absolute. She knows how she wants her daughter to be. 'Be like this, be like that, be like me!' If the girl has an aunt, an older friend, a grandmother, a teacher, a great lady like Eleanor Roosevelt who's impressive as a woman—that's terrific. Even knowing men who like women to be independent can be helpful too. It doesn't have to be direct; it can be indirect and still be useful."

This is no less true of a daughter's search (unconscious or otherwise) for alternatives to Father. In other relatives, perhaps—grandfathers, uncles, older cousins, in-laws— or in older friends. Once more, from our current perspective as adults, we may recall this period with pain as well as fondness and even a vague sense of shame.

Erica Jong speaks of her grandfather, a portrait painter who lived with the Jong family in a sprawling triplex on Manhattan's Upper West Side, as being the household's preeminent male figure during her father's long absences on business. "My grandfather was a warm, loving, sensitive man," she remembers. "He was the other half of my split image of Father. For these first years of my childhood, he was more my father than my father."

There are only words of praise for this artistic soul who read little Erica bedtime stories and took her to the zoo. But he could only partially fill the void left by Erica's real father while the younger man chose instead to travel the globe drumming up business. All of Jong's phenomenal success as a novelist cannot erase this fact, and even though her relationship with her father is now cordial, it will always be colored by his first decision to stay away from his children for long stretches of time.

In his superb book *A Man in the Making*, Dr. Richard Robertiello describes a similar situation. Robertiello's own father was, says Robertiello, "busy glorifying himself as a doctor. My paternal grandfather became more of a father to me than my own father. Michelangelo Robertiello apparently decided the day I was born and was male that he would take me over, raise me, train me, and help me to become all the things he had always wanted to be. Everyone else in the house was too frightened of him and his temper to offer any opposition."

Robertiello's self-effacing mother was a conspirator in this arrangement because she was essentially submissive, having been dominated by her own strong-willed father. As it turned out, the elder Robertiello's Pavlovian approach to training his grandson—for example, sitting at the kitchen table for hours with the boy going over his homework again and again until every word was spelled perfectly—involved little emotional interaction. But this was not confined to Robertiello's relationship with his grandfather; the noted psychiatrist believes, and rightly so, that this is the sorry situation that existed in many patriarchal households: "I have never really communicated very well with my grandfather or my father or my male cousins or uncles or with my son or stepson. And they have never com-

municated very much with any male in their life—certainly
not with one of their relatives. As a result, almost all of us
men have been entirely dependent upon our women to
provide us our feelings, or at least the outlet for our feelings. And we have been so afraid of losing that connection
to our unconscious that we have at times fallen prey to the
temptation of seducing our women, and controlling them
so they cannot leave us."

Richard Robertiello has always recognized his grandfather's role as his surrogate father; what he did not realize
until he was 51 and had been through years of analysis
was that an uncle of his may have actually been the most
important man in his childhood. "He'd just never before
appeared on the scene in my conscious mind...he's been
completely repressed all these years."

Robertiello is not alone. Most men and women will
deny that there ever was one person aside from their parents who served as a surrogate or a model for them while
they were growing up. Some of this selective forgetfulness
when it comes to putting together the puzzle of our early
lives may be due to the fact that our parents are deliberately
withholding certain pieces. As young children, we may
have relied on a father substitute because the real item
made pursuing career goals his first priority. If, say, Uncle
Ned took us to the circus for the first time or taught us
how to ride a bicycle, Dad may still feel guilty. Consciously
or otherwise, he may want Uncle Ned to remain only a
dim memory to us. A 25-year-old remembers that his great-
uncle, a retired schoolteacher, used to take him to the roof
of their Brooklyn tenement to fly kites and talk often for
hours on end. The great-uncle died when his nephew was
seven, and though he possesses qualities of curiosity and
thoughtfulness that are not found among the other members of his raucous family, all he knows is that his passion
for kites came from his great-uncle.

We daughters and sons aren't entirely off the hook,

either. Early surrogates are consigned to oblivion because that is where we want them. Denial of this sort may not be taking place on a conscious level, but it is denial nevertheless. "I think this kind of forgetting," Dr. Robertiello has said, "may be a feeling it is disloyal to our parents to recognize how important these other people were. If only unconsciously, we realize that we owe the role models of our youth too much, and tune away. This is a kind of defense of our old notions of omnipotence. We may acknowledge that our parents were formative to us. After all, that's normal. But that we needed other people too? Oh, no!" We feel shame because we "betrayed" our real father; how could we have these feelings of trust, even love, for a surrogate?

The models and mentors of our adolescence are altogether different creatures than the ones we had earlier. Unlike uncles and grandfathers who took it upon themselves to guide us as small children, these individuals have not been assigned to us. We have chosen them to fill our specific psychological needs. For both boys and girls, a teacher usually filled the bill nicely. It may be that while we are more conscious of the role these models played in our lives, we are only slightly better at giving them credit for their contribution. Who has not been influenced so strongly by an English or math teacher, a football or swimming coach, who temporarily served as a father figure? And how many of us can summon up these surrogates in any detail, if at all?

"Women don't have mentors," a 30-ish financial consultant and mother of a 2-year-old boy tells me. "Men have mentors. Women have office affairs." A woman's first contact with male authority figures outside the home is in school, and by the time she teeters on the verge of puberty, she may already have chosen to look upon some of her male teachers as surrogate dads. Most women I interviewed, if they were able to recall any teachers who influenced their lives at all, singled out a woman. But there were those who admitted that they took away from their relationships with male biology or Spanish or history teachers something more than just the basics. One woman credits her freshman physics teacher with tapping her natural aptitude for science—an aptitude that had gone unrecognized by her own family and all other teachers she'd had before. "He opened up a whole new world," she now says, "not just intellectually but personally. My self-esteem grew enormously once he pointed me in the right direction. My father, well, he was a truck driver. He wanted me to learn, to grow. But he wasn't equipped to help me the way my physics teacher was. I think he understood that. He accepted it." The woman stops short of conceding that she had romantic fantasies about Mr. Physics Teacher. She doesn't deny it, either.

Hormones rage during adolescence; that's what this difficult transition period is for, after all. So we cannot be surprised to learn that Daddy takes a back seat, if only for a short time, to Daughter's first mentor and first "older man" crush. Oedipal feelings that once involved Dad and Dad alone are now transferred to Teacher. Women looking back on that first tug-of-war between father figure and father may laugh it off as girlhood silliness. They suppress the genuine anguish they may have felt at the time over what they perceived to be a betrayal of Dad. Again, guilt. Always guilt. Guilt that may well be compounded when a woman takes the same confused feelings she had toward her first teenage mentor and applies them to other mentors as she proceeds through life.

With the exception of the comparatively rare homosexual student-teacher liaison, adolescent boys are spared this added ingredient of sex in their dealings with surrogate dads. There are tremendously influential teachers, to be sure. Think back. How many times do we hear ourselves saying to our parents "Mr. So-and-so thinks this" and "Mr. What's-his-name says that." It is astounding to imagine that our parents, often educated, accomplished people in their own right, would listen so patiently to us as we confidently quoted such unimpeachable experts on history and mathematics as our eighth-grade teachers. The son of a Nobel prize-winning biochemist remembers how convincingly his father feigned surprise as the 13-year-old delivered an impromptu lecture on chromosomes and DNA—facts he had learned from no more authoritative source than Mr. Bronstein, who divided his teaching schedule between biology and auto shop.

"It was only normal for a teenage boy to want to impress upon his father that he was not dependent on me for all his information," says the Nobel prize winner. "I wasn't hurt at all by it because I recognized myself at that age; my father and I had precisely the same battles. And with my own son, I didn't want to risk souring him on science by questioning his teacher's qualifications."

Wise parents allow their children this freedom to pick their own authority figures outside the home. In the case of the Nobel laureate, his decision not to upstage the boy's newfound mentor at school was inspired. Unlike other children who have withered in the shadow of a famous father, the biochemist's son, now 30, claims that he never felt overwhelmed or was doomed to a life of constantly being compared to Dad.

A father commits a major blunder when he fails to recognize that his son must be allowed to choose other males aside from Father whom he can respect. One 40-year-old realtor, himself a father of three boys, remembers when he was 13 and proudly brought home a math test on which he had scored 95. His father, an accountant and tax specialist, sat the boy down at the dining room table to show him how to solve the few problems he had missed. "I told him, 'Oh, what the hell do you know about it? The teacher's the expert, and *he* said I did terrific!' Then I tore the test up and stormed out. It was silly, of course. My dad knew more about math than that teacher ever did. But it was just something I felt at the time. After that, he never offered to help me on my tests or my homework again."

Another father in a suburban household remembers how his son and two daughters, all now in their early 20s, cleaved to a particularly charismatic social studies teacher. "I had always been the last word in the house on all subjects," he remembers, "and I didn't like it *at all* when the kids started trooping home with pearls of wisdom from their teacher. We used to talk about current events at the dinner table, but it got to be *The World According to Mr. Robinson.* Everything their teacher said was gospel. What made the whole thing really unbearable was that each of the kids—they're a year apart—was assigned to Robinson, so I had to listen to three years of that stuff." In this instance Father learned too late that this was no coincidence. Because it so riled their know-it-all dad, each child had requested to be placed in Mr. Robinson's social studies class. Sighs Father: "If I'd only kept my mouth shut."

Dad had to give us the room to seek out surrogates, models, and mentors. But he was also well-advised to quietly monitor those teachers we chose to emulate. Like any given segment of the population, the teaching profession is not without its neurotics and even psychotics. Here, however, there is a difference. Just as he is in the position to make a tremendous contribution to the lives of his students, he is also in the position to do tremendous damage. We may not have ventured into a classroom in twenty years, but that does not mean that many adult men and women do not still bear the psychic scars inflicted by emotionally disturbed or overtly cruel surrogates.

Athletic coaches often serve as surrogate figures during a male's teenage years; Knute Rockne, Bear Bryant, and Vince Lombardi are just a few of the legendary coaches who entered the pantheon of sports greats because of the positive fatherly influence they exerted on their young players. There are thousands upon thousands of men across the country making much the same contribution as they coach everything from Little League to intercollegiate football. Because coaching also attracts a not inconsequential number of frustrated jocks, the opportunity for wreaking emotional havoc is definitely there.

I was a lousy Little League player. My throw was pathetic, my catching abysmal. I struck out routinely. My fate was sealed: to spend an eternity daydreaming in right field. I did have one asset to offer: I was sneaky, and that made me proficient at stealing bases (provided, of course, that I had somehow managed to hit the ball or walk).

My best friend at the time, Rick, was the star of our team; he possessed all the athletic acumen I did not. What he did not possess, however, was a stable coach. Whenever Rick slammed a home run, leaped up to snatch a fly, or slid into first, our coach cheered the loudest. But if 9-year-old Rick failed to perform up to the coach's expectations, the coach did not hesitate to grab him by the scruff of the neck, drag him behind the dugout, and berate the boy. What the rest of us found most astonishing was Rick's own father's attitude. He often saw what was happening, but declined to intervene. I eventually learned from Rick that his father had been a college ballplayer, and that he lived vicariously through his son's triumphs on the field.

The whole messy affair came to a head during a championship game that our team had miraculously blundered into. I walked, then proceeded to steal my way home. My father, who was mercifully too busy to attend most games, showed up at this one and cheered from the sidelines. Then he watched as Rick came up to bat. As usual, Rick clobbered the ball, and though it enabled two of our teammates to score, he tried for second base and didn't make it. Fighting back the tears, he walked back to the dugout. Only this time the coach did not wait to drag him off to the sidelines. He walked up to Rick and struck him on the head with an open hand, knocking his cap to the ground.

Rick's father jumped down from the bleachers and ran to his son's defense, shoving the coach aside. After firing a few blistering expletives at the coach, he walked away with his arm around Rick. The star was out of the game for good. Needless to say, we lost. But Rick, clearly if belatedly, walked away a winner.

A surrogate-mentor can be as valuable to the adolescent as an inspiring teacher or as detrimental as Rick's coach. He can be that other male authority figure in our lives who reinforces our positive feelings about ourselves and the world that awaits us, or someone who has betrayed our trust by burdening us with his own unresolved inner conflicts and neuroses. Whether or not we are consciously aware of it, most of us remain profoundly influenced by these phantoms of the distant past.

By the time we embark on a career, most of us have already begun to forget the models of our adolescence. "Getting ahead" is our first priority, and we greedily search for those who can help us in the most ignoble endeavor. We are, as F. Scott Fitzgerald said of the young Ernest Hemingway, "always ready to lend a helping hand to the fellow on the rung above us." Not that such relationships need be mercenary. What of mentors who catapult protégés into intellectual prominence—as Socrates did with Plato, Plato with Aristotle, Aristotle with Alexander the Great?

In fact, many of us get our first taste of what it is like to be an apprentice in college. Wellesley College President Barbara Newell spoke of "the impact of having a faculty member say to a student, 'You are good' and giving him a sense of worth." This is only a logical extension of the teacher-pupil bond, however, and even in those instances where a professor takes a warm and fatherly interest in a student's progress, it is generally understood that they will remain mentor and protégé only so long as they occupy the same classroom.

At its simplest, mentorship involves higher-level managers taking a limited interest in teaching and guiding a subordinate. At the other end of the spectrum, it can mean a close personal friendship and a willingness to use power on behalf of a protégé's career.

Dan Rather's father, Irwin ("Rags") Rather, was a Houston pipeliner—a ditchdigger for twenty years. Irwin Rather was also a voracious reader of newspapers. "My father was an impulse subscriber," recalls Dan, "and a man of sudden rages who would leap from his chair and cancel whatever paper had offended him. We went through every newspaper in town. My father would read something in the *Press* that riled him and he would shout, 'Mother, cancel the *Press*. We're through with that paper forever. I don't want to ever see it in here again.'"

When Dan announced his plans to become the first Rather in memory to attend college, his father was anything but thrilled. "My dad thought it was madness," he remembers. "The final jolt came when I informed my father I intended to major in journalism. That was not a word he could define and it was never clear to him how I thought I could make a living at it. He understood newspapers. But if one was going to college, it was to become a teacher or an engineer or a lawyer." Rather's father was also a listener of radio newscasts ("he cared nothing for music"), and Dan told me that as a lad, he tuned in to Edward R. Murrow, Eric Sevareid, and Charles Collingwood.

Who was the major influence on Rather? Not Dad, judging from Rather's autobiography, *The Camera Never Blinks*. "The dream begins," writes Rather, "with a teacher who believes in you, who tugs and pushes and leads you on to the next plateau, sometimes poking you with a sharp stick called truth. Mine was named Hugh Cunningham and he taught journalism in 1950 at Sam Houston State Teachers College." Rather goes on to ask how "Hugh Cunningham happened to end up there, with a master's degree from the Missouri School of Journalism, young with a mind that could light up a room. But it was a break for me. Otherwise I would not have lasted in college longer than three weeks and most likely would not have gone on to whatever career I have had. That may be putting too much on one man's conscience, but I owe a debt to Hugh Cunningham." Nowhere does Rather acknowledge a similar debt to his news-hound father.

We are at our most comfortable when we make clear to father that, even in our careers, he is the number one influence. Lee Iacocca does not hesitate to name one-time Ford Motor Company Vice-President Charles Beecham as a mentor. "I was really very lucky," Iacocca told me. "I had Charlie Beecham for thirty years. He took the time to talk to me, and I listened." The Chrysler chief is equally quick to say that his father, Nicola, had the greatest influence on his life. Nicola came to the United States from southern Italy when he was 12, soon bought his first Model T, and within eight years had parlayed it into a thriving rent-a-car business that grew to a fleet of thirty-three cars, mostly Fords. A millionaire before the Depression, he made and lost several fortunes in a variety of businesses before his death in 1976.

Because of his father's love for automobiles—specifically Fords—Lee never wavered from early youth in his desire to go to work for Ford. Iacocca was taking advice from his father—they talked on the phone every day—right up until the week Nicola died. "'Gamble all you want,' my father would tell me, 'but always have a nest egg. Put something under your mattress.'" The Depression Era mentality reverberates in Nicola's admonishments to his son: no free lunch. You get nothing for nothing. When Iacocca senior owned some restaurants, Lee watched him as he dealt with a waitress who was not getting along with customers. "Why don't you just get out of this racket?" Nicola told the woman. "You don't get along with people and that's all we serve. We don't serve monkeys, we serve people. If you can't be the best damned waitress in the world, go do something else." Iacocca heard his father's message loud and clear: If you can't be the best damned auto man in the whole world, go do something else. To accomplish that in Detroit, Nicola knew as well as anyone else, Lee needed a mentor—a man like Charlie Beecham.

Even when a mentor's influence seems devoid of any particular personal affection, we can be left with an uneasy sense of disloyalty. Henry Kissinger was always extremely close to his father, Louis, who died in 1982 at the age of 92. The elder Kissinger doted on his celebrated son, but Henry Kissinger's intellectual mentor was Fritz Kraemer, who retired in 1978 as political analyst for the chief of staff of the army and who had taught in the United States War College.

The intensely close relationship between Kraemer and Kissinger made the future secretary of state feel as if he had somehow forsaken his real father. "Kraemer," wrote political and economic analyst Peter F. Drucker in his *Adventures of a Bystander*, "largely made Henry Kissinger. He found him, he formed him, in fact he largely invented him.

"The story has been published in accounts of Kissinger's early life. Young Henry, shortly after his arrival as a German refugee, was drafted into the American Army. During basic training he heard a lecture on the European War given by a private first class, a fellow German whose name was Fritz Kraemer. The questions which young Kissinger asked so impressed Kraemer that he sent for the boy afterwards. And from then on, Kissinger was Kraemer's protégé."

After the war, Kissinger was advised by his father to go to New York's City College. But Kraemer took him aside. "I can hear him say it in his most languid guards-officer voice," relates Drucker. "'Henry, a gentleman does not go to City College. He goes to Harvard.'" So Kraemer proceeded to accomplish what Henry's father could not: He arranged for Kissinger's admission to Harvard and for his being taken on as a favorite student by the leading government professors there. "He remained Kissinger's friend, mentor and advisor," says Drucker, "until his protege had finished his studies and obtained his first Harvard teaching appointment, if not well beyond that time. What has not been published is that Kissinger's thoughts as well as his actions as Secretary of State under Nixon and Ford are pure Kraemer."

Louis Kissinger never tried to stand between Kraemer and Kissinger, and the fact that Kraemer shunned publicity of any kind served to reduce tensions between father and son over Henry's intellectual allegiance. Feelings of guilt can run high, however, when the chosen mentor eclipses the father. An administrative assistant for a prominent congressman admits that he occasionally suffers a twinge of regret when he realizes he is now far closer to his boss than he is to his father, a Midwest farmer who never got past the tenth grade.

Nowhere has the mentor system flourished more than in official Washington, where an aspiring politico or bureaucrat must first find a way to affix himself like a barnacle to the ship of state. Sam Rayburn had his Lyndon Johnson, Johnson his John Connolly, and so on. That means becoming a protégé. "Even today," says Brett Duval Fromson, who first went to work in President Ford's offices at the age of 21, "if you go into Sarsfield's, the Hawk 'n' Dove, or any of their usual hangouts, you might hear conversations between otherwise intelligent, self-confident young people that go something like this: 'Glad to meet you. I work for Congressman Deano. I'm a legislative correspondent [he writes letters to constituents]. Where do you work?'

"'Senator Kennedy's office. I'm one of his top aides. You say you work for Peano?'"

"'No, *Deano,* a freshman congressman. A Republican.'

"'Oh,' the person from the Kennedy office says politely. 'What state is he from?'

"This last question is a severe ego blow to the young

staffer from Deano's office that should send him sulking to the other end of the bar. It is intolerable to him that he should work for a nobody, because he too becomes a nobody, just as the fellow from Senator Kennedy's office is a somebody by virtue of his boss's surname and reputation.

"Ultimately," Fromson argues, "these protégés lose sight of their ideals and their willingness to take risks. Because their personal success depends on how well they further the goals of their superiors, they learn to fit in, not stand out: at the office, to write legislation and recommendations that will not upset the boss's constituency; at parties, to make 'contacts' who may later help them rise within their part of the Washington establishment, cautious manipulation becomes a way of life." Frequently, the up-and-coming bureaucrat's first act is to unabashedly allow his father to be supplanted, even giving a mentor prerogatives and powers a son might never have given Dad.

The business of apprenticeship at the foot of a master has as much to do with the mentor as the protégé. As Yale psychologist Daniel Levinson first pointed out in the mid-1970s, there is a "mentor phenomenon" that occurs in middle age when a man feels the need to promote the fortunes of a younger worker. Inasmuch as a corporation can serve as an employee's "other family," the desire to take a young worker under one's wing has its altruistic components. Why not nurture talent and ability? Why not pass along what you have learned, in the manner of even the most primitive tribal societies?

There is much satisfaction in that, but seldom are the motives of a mentor so simple. Often, having reached a plateau in his career, a mature worker has given up the game and now only wants to make his life simpler, his workload lighter. If he can groom a younger man to take on these responsibilities, he may have solved that problem—at least until the protégé smartens up. If the older worker is still very much in the race for the top, he may take on a protégé to step into his shoes once he is promoted. Many a middle-level executive has been frozen in one job because he has not been wise enough to train and then beat the drum on behalf of his back-up person.

Males with male protégés may also seek in their office underling the son they never had. Jed Silverman is a 35-year-old vice-president of a San Francisco–based shipping line. At the age of 24, he went to work for Ernest Blau as Blau's personal assistant. Blau was then, as now, a vice-president in the firm and 25 years Jed's senior. He also had an art student son one year older than Jed. Although Jed never questioned his boss about his family, Blau constantly despaired about his son's lack of ambition. Accordingly, Blau frequently invited Jed to golf with him on weekends, and the two lunched at the boss's club in town twice a week. Jed rose swiftly in the company and after just six years was promoted to assistant vice-president, with Blau as his immediate superior.

Jed remained in the same spot for four years while others were promoted around him. He did not believe what co-workers were telling him: Now that Blau had his hardworking number two in place, he was not about to allow Jed to be promoted out of his sphere of influence. If Jed was appointed vice-president, Blau, now awaiting retirement, had no one to replace him. It was not until Jed walked into the president's office and asked to know why he had been passed over that he learned the truth: For over a year the board had intended to make Jed a full vice-president, only to have Blau inform them that his protégé was not yet ready for the task.

The relationship, which is now somewhat more distant but still cordial, had its impact on Jed's standing with his own father, a retired physician. "Whenever we had dinner or talked on the phone," says Jed, "I was constantly catching myself before I mentioned Ernest for the hundredth time. It wasn't as if my dad ever showed even the slightest resentment toward Ernest, or that he ever seemed peeved at my mentioning him. But I could hear myself saying 'Ernest says this' and 'Ernest says that.' My boss was a major part of my career, and a pretty colorful character in his own right, so naturally he would crop up in much of my conversation. I think my folks understood that, but I had the damnedest time not feeling guilty about it." So did Blau, Jed came to realize. "Ernest and I would go to this club for lunch, say, and he really was pretty loose. But one time a waiter at the club asked what his son would have to drink and he blew. It wasn't vanity, I don't think. But the waiter obviously hit a nerve. I was his son, in a sense. And he was betraying me by thwarting my promotion."

Fathers themselves offer widely varied reactions to a son's becoming someone else's protégé. Much, of course, depends on just how all-pervasive that master-apprentice relationship is, and if it seems to have been forged in lieu of a stronger father-child bond. Should the mentor and the father be in the same field, then the possibilities for resentment on the father's part are considerably greater. If, say, a young man has a successful sales manager as a father, why would he go to anyone else for guidance? One retired police detective complains that his rookie patrolman son no longer comes to him for advice, but instead to an older man still serving on the force—a detective sergeant who at one time fifteen years earlier had been his father's partner. "It hurts like hell," says the rookie's father, "but at least my boy's turning to someone I used to work with and respect." It is not all that difficult to figure out why, after following in his father's professional footsteps, the rookie cop makes a point of *not* relying on Dad for day-to-day career counseling. By establishing a mentor-protégé link with his father's old buddy in the department, the son can declare at least some degree of personal independence and integrity without rejecting his perhaps overly sensitive dad. "Maybe," allows the father, "but I still think he'd get better pointers from me."

The father's own career background has much to do

with how he perceives his child's protégé status. Men who never found the need for a mentor during their professional lives are certainly more likely to feel confused if their son or daughter chooses that route. "I made it myself," said the prosperous owner of an employment agency. "You need contacts, friends, people who know the ropes, of course—but never let one person think he's responsible for what you've accomplished. My children have all decided to take the easy way and just glom onto somebody else in the hope that when they go to the top, they'll take you with them." Concurs a retired land developer whose 37-year-old son has risen to the vice-presidency of a major cosmetics company on the coattails of a mentor: "It's dangerous to hitch your wagon to somebody else's star for too long, because if he turns out to be a falling star, you go down with him."

Neither of these fathers admits to any jealousy on their part, though it seems clear to even the most casual observer that some tension exists between father and son over the son's allegiance to a mentor. "There have been times," says the employment agency owner, "when I've wanted to tell my son, 'Why didn't you ask *me* instead of him?' But that's really not the problem."

The "problem" is less likely to exist where the father has at one stage or another in his career been either protégé or mentor. "You can't make it today in business without finding someone to bring you up," contends one top airline executive. "I found someone to help me when I joined the company in 1956, and in the last dozen years or so I've brought some young people along myself. If my son or daughter didn't have that kind of support from a superior—somebody they can count on to look after them, see that they learn what they have to do to make it—then I'd tell them to hurry up and find that person." Even then, an occasional twinge of fatherly pride is difficult to avoid. "When my daughter tells me she's just had this wonderful heart-to-heart talk with her boss, then of course I think,

'That's the kind of conversation *we* should be having.' It's only natural. But I don't let myself get carried away. This is just reality. If you know your children love you, this is a small price to pay for their success."

Of course, American business is dominated by executives who were anointed by their superiors much earlier in the game. As the superiors rose in the company, their protégés were never far behind. Old-boy networks of this sort worked fine—for old boys. What of women? Was my friend right? Do women not have mentors? Seattle journalist Jane Adams, author of the book *Women on Top*, concedes that many of the women she studies had mentors, but hastens to add "that's a paternalistic relationship, not sexual. When a protégé takes another job, for example, the mentor feels as if a daughter married and left home. Older women chose the heads of their companies to be their mentors. Today's women are picking them from middle management."

Adams also encountered successful women serving as mentors for younger women: "Women over 50, in particular, find it's one way they can fulfill the strong need in their professional development to have an impact on someone else's life. It's a kind of motherly pride. But women under 50 are usually not secure enough in their position to be mentors—they're afraid of being supplanted." Adams' conclusion that women at the top are generally more willing to take on protégés is bolstered by a Korn/Ferry International poll of female senior executives at major concerns. The polls showed that 80 percent of women in key executive posts serve as mentors for other women. All of the remaining 20 percent conceded that they do not serve as mentors because they never had women advise them on their rise to the top.

Even for these senior women willing to counsel their youthful counterparts, the task was not always easy. With women as half her office's new employees, Touche Ross supervisor Deborah Douglass offers them "rules of the road," such as urging that they choose a wardrobe that conforms to men's "gray suit image." One of Connecticut General's two female vice-presidents, Kay Clark, advises younger women, but at times she confesses to feeling "over-used." Helen Haskins, a manager at Peabody Coal, says some female peers resent being mentors; they prefer to be, as Haskins put it, "left alone to do their jobs."

Father is usually the reason some women do not find the role of mentor a natural one. Margaret Hennig and Anne Jardim, the management consultants who studied twenty-five high-level female executives as part of their research for their best seller, *The Managerial Woman,* found that men—first fathers, then professional mentors—encouraged women to achieve, often in fields that had long been dominated by men. What the working woman seeks, particularly if, as is usually the case, her father was a big booster, is someone in the office with Daddy's character-istics. Transference is the psychiatric term for this phe-nomenon, and it also works in reverse: she may seek out a mirror image of father to be her mentor or, if she de-spised Dad, look for his diametric opposite.

The young female employee may be the last to realize this. As with male mentors and their male protégés, rela-tionships of this sort between men and women generally develop gradually. There is no magic moment at which a protégé comprehends that her career is being shaped by someone else. Geraldine Stutz had been a fashion model, copywriter, and editor and had worked only briefly in the wholesale end of the shoe business when the late W. Maxey Jarmyn, former board chairman of Genesco, asked her to take over the retailing operation of I. Miller's sixteen shoe stores in 1955.

Stutz was stunned. "I am not an experienced mer-chant," she told the retailing mogul.

"You have administrative and entrepreneurial skills," Jarmyn responded.

"What," she asked, "does that mean?"

Then began the series of questions that were the hallmark of Jarmyn's managerial style: Had she been the president of her class at college? Chief of the debating team? Editor of the school paper?

"The fact was that I had been considered a leader in my scholastic career," Stutz concedes. "It just never dawned on me that this was any kind of preparation for the business world. Like most young women of my background and education, I always performed on demand and never anything else."

And perform she did. In 1957 Jarmyn asked Stutz to become president of Genesco's financially troubled Henri Bendel. He gave her five years to turn the Manhattan department store around. Stutz did, and nineteen years later actually purchased Bendel's with the aid of foreign backers, becoming the nation's first female owner of a major department store. "Maxey was constructive, always," Stutz says. "He never countermanded my decision once he had agreed. He did not, however, easily agree. His method was to really make you lay out your decision to a problem and defend it."

On the surface, at least, Stutz and Jarmyn seemed to have little in common aside from protean energy. He was a Southern Baptist deacon who neither drank nor smoked and often opened stockholders' meetings with a prayer. Stutz, reared in the Midwest as a Roman Catholic, was a social drinker and chain-smoked cigarettes. His politics were conservative, hers liberal. It was not until she went through analysis in the mid-1970s that she saw the obvious parallels between Jarmyn and her own demanding, religious, teetotaling, nonsmoking father.

Like Stutz, almost all the women in the Hennig-Jardim study remained with the companies where they had first been groomed by a mentor. It was hard enough leaving Daddy the first time....

Trying to unravel the tangled allegiances, the inevitable pangs of guilt and remorse, is daunting enough. How much more complicated it all becomes when mentor is both father figure *and* lover. How common is this? Of the top female executives she studied, Jane Adams claims that "only a few women said that early in their careers they had slept with the boss. All found it a mistake—a personal mistake, because they truly cared for the men and they suffered professionally when the affair ended." Does Adams conclude that office sex is rare? Not at all: "Marlene Sanders, a correspondent and producer at CBS News, told me, 'Affairs happen all the time, I think people can handle it.' One 34-year-old said her rule of thumb was, 'Never say never, rarely say yes, and always say maybe.' No woman I talked to admitted using sex for professional advantage."

Uh-huh. Yet even the most naive observer cannot help but notice that affairs *do* happen between mentor and protégé, and that many a female employee's star has risen after she takes to the boss's bed. If he is ten or twenty years older than she, the prospective mentor offers his protégé the perfect opportunity to fulfill long-suppressed oedipal fantasies.

There are pitfalls aplenty in the protégé game. No one understands that better than Mary Cunningham. William Agee, then chairman and president of the multibillion-dollar Bendix Corporation, made himself her mentor and put her on the fast track. In 1980, at the age of 29 and after a scant fifteen months with the company, Cunningham was appointed corporate vice-president of strategic planning. Three weeks later, she quit amid rumors that a romantic relationship between the two had hastened her meteoric rise.

Feminists were outraged. If Mary had been a man, there would have been resentment from colleagues, but certainly no public scandal. Cunningham was soon snapped up by Seagram's for a similar high-level position there, and in the summer of 1982 Agee and Cunningham—claiming all the while they had fallen in love only after she was nudged out of Bendix—were wed. Not long after, Cunningham was quoted as advocating office romances as a way to increase productivity. As the theory, such as it is, goes, workers in love will pull together for the sake of the company. Aside from the obvious jealousies and Machiavellian intrigues that would result if Cunningham's scheme were to become business as usual, there would be another unpleasant side effect: Career women everywhere would be faced with having to reevaluate their fathers and the way their feelings toward him have influenced their relationship with office mentors.

Sexual liaisons notwithstanding, many experts feel that the role the mentor plays in the advancement of women in business is exaggerated. "It doesn't hurt to have friends," says Dr. Linda Keller Brown of Columbia University's Center for the Social Sciences. "But the notion that mentors are important to a woman's advancement is overblown." A study by social scientist J. J. Speizer indicates that the popularity of the mentor concept tends to reinforce the male-dominated organizational status quo. Dr. Carol L. Weiss, a Radcliffe teacher and research associate at the Wellesley College Center for Research on Women, and Wellesley professor Dr. Anne Harlen spent three years looking at one hundred female and male managers at two large concerns. The results of their study, released in late 1982, showed that the prevalence of the mentor was considerably less pervasive than supposed. "We discovered," said Dr. Weiss, "that most of the men and women didn't have one strong mentor figure to help them. They all said you need a mentor, but most of them didn't have one." And yet those men and women surveyed by Heidrick Struggles, a management consulting firm, responded two-to-one that a mentor or two had helped their careers along. Since the Wellesley study focused on women, the differences are strongly delineated.

If the Geraldine Stutzes are in the decided minority now, *The Wall Street Journal*'s Amanda Bennett says the mentor-protégé system is one that "could work very well to the advantage of women who, perhaps more than men, need the backing of high-ups to gain authority and experience." Concurs Herma Hill Kay, a professor of law at the University of California at Berkeley specializing in sex discrimination, "It's very hard for a woman to rise in an organization without depending on the protection of a male superior."

To avoid the Cunningham syndrome—i. e., the kind of uproar that led to Mary Cunningham's departure from Bendix—a male mentor might be advised, among other things, to minimize intimacy. Gail Neugarten, associate professor in the Graduate School of Public Affairs at the University of Colorado at Boulder, admits that "you can't prohibit natural attraction" between mentor and protégé. But while the organization may be willing to accept midnight planning sessions and weekend fishing trips when only male executives are involved, not so when women are involved. Dr. Robert M. James, professor of business policy at the University of Chicago's Graduate School of Business, believes that over the next decade a set of "highly useful taboos, customs and expectations" will develop around male-female business relationships just as they have around male-to-male dealings. "A depth of intimacy may have to be sacrificed," chimes in Harvard Business School assistant professor James G. Clawson, "for the integrity of the business relationship." And in the event a romance develops? "I'd get her out from under my wing right away," says Clawson. "Let it be seen that she can make it on her own."

There are examples of men whose mentors have guided their careers from thirty to fifty years. By the time the founder of a major corporation steps aside or dies in his late 70s or even his 80s, he may have one longstanding protégé who now takes the reigns of power in his 60s. Or perhaps he has gone through two or even more protégés.

Such instances are rare, but it is not at all unusual for

the mentor-protégé relationship to last twenty years—roughly the same amount of time a child spends at home under the tutelage of his or her father. How do we feel when we must move on to another job, another corporation, another mentor? The degree of our shame may vary, but it is there nonetheless. If we felt guilty about supplanting Father with a father figure who could promote our fortunes, then we are likely to harbor similar feelings when the time comes to jettison our mentor.

The son of a longshoreman, Douglas Bateman is now the treasurer of a major southern California land development firm. Less than six months after Bateman, age 40, was promoted to the $150,000-a-year position, the man who brought him into the company and groomed him died suddenly of a stroke at the age of 57. "I felt cheated by Bob's death," says Bateman, "and like a lot of people regretted that I never really had the chance to thank him. I was always going to ask him out to lunch, or over to the house for dinner. Of course I never did; don't we always feel that there's all the time in the world for that sort of thing? Most people I know don't hesitate to hug their mothers; with them there usually isn't this persistent thought that important things have gone unsaid. So right after Bob's funeral I called home and told my dad how grateful I was that he raised me and that I loved him. There was silence and then my mother came on the line. 'I don't know what you told your father,' she said, 'but he's sitting in the living room crying.' Bob had two sons and two daughters. I hope he lived long enough to hear it from them."

For most fathers, having to share a child's loyalty and even his or her affection with a surrogate or mentor must inevitably stir some feelings of jealousy. Father may not confess to these feelings; indeed, he may not be consciously aware of them. Even when the pain is palpable, there are mitigating factors. Dad must also concede that he is glad

that someone—often someone with the power and influence that he does not have—has become his child's champion. If, in the words of one father, "it hurts like hell" to
be supplanted in this fashion, then Dad has to admit that,
from his child's viewpoint at least, it also helps like hell to
have a mentor. As the airline executive who has been both
protégé and mentor put it: "This is reality."

The fundamental defect of fathers is that they want their children to be a credit to them.

—Bertrand Russell

CHAPTER VIII ————————

Breaking Away

I was never shy about being ambitious. When my ninth-grade social studies teacher asked us on the first day of class to scribble down what we wanted to achieve in life, I did not hesitate. He read through a number of answers aloud, then began glossing over them when it became clear that nearly all the responses sounded like speeches delivered by semifinalists in the Miss Universe Pageant ("I want to bring peace and understanding to the people of the world..."). Then he came to mine: "Wealth, fame, and power—though not necessarily in that order." He thanked me for supplying the day's only honest answer.

My father couldn't have been more delighted that at 14 I was—at least as he saw it—puncturing the illusions of my hypocritical peers. He often claimed that money was the only real measure of success. Since my family loves nothing more than a heated debate, he often made this claim for the sake of argument. Our genetic predisposition toward provocativeness prompted one fed-up family friend to brand us, all puns intended, "intellectual master-baiters."

Dad was baiting us on the subject of money, yes, but his reverence for it as a measure of success plainly derived from the poverty of those Depression days. In that he is surely not alone.

Leslie Fallon has not spoken to her father since 1975. He is the wealthy owner of a West Coast drugstore chain, and when his daughter chose to earn a Master's degree in art history, he was furious. "What money is there in that?" she says he demanded to know. "What a waste!" Fallon's younger sister had become a dentist—something they could understand, something *lucrative*—but a Master's in art history? Leslie taught for a time, but in the early 1970s she decided to turn to her second love: the arts. She began writing articles about Los Angeles's opera, ballet, and symphony scenes and soon landed with a by-line on the front page of the *Times*. Ecstatic, she phoned her father and told him the news. "How much did the paper pay you?" he asked. "Of course, it was next to nothing," says Leslie. "Newspapers don't pay free-lancers much. But I was just starting out and here I had a tremendous scoop and got a huge by-line on the front page! I was thrilled, but he couldn't have cared less."

Since then, Leslie has written hundreds of articles and published four books. She has not talked to her father since that day he asked her how much she got paid for the *Times* article, and she promises she never will. "He drags me down," she tries to explain. "It's taken me years to recover from what he did to my self-esteem, and I know he hasn't changed. Why should I go back and give him another chance to hurt me? I'm free of that now; I've got my own life."

How "free" of paternal influence any of us ever really gets is debatable. Convicted Watergate conspirator G. Gordon Liddy amazed and perplexed observers with his peculiar moral code and Spartan sense of duty. Wasn't it Liddy, the Fordham-educated lawyer turned burglar, who held his hand over a flame to prove his courage, and who offered to have himself assassinated if it would help get

President Nixon out of his Watergate scrape? Many of the answers are to be found in Liddy's Irish American father, Sylvester. Because his own father's hair-trigger temper (the old man apparently liked to deck his fellow workers and bosses) prevented him from keeping a job, Sylvester went to work on the loading docks in Hoboken, New Jersey, to support the family. He was 15. Liddy won a scholarship to a parochial prep school and was on his way to becoming a millionaire patent lawyer when he married the beautiful daughter of a socially prominent Washington family. "Nine months later almost to the day," G. Gordon Liddy writes revealingly in his autobiography, *Will*, "that extraordinary gene pool somehow produced a frail, sickly little crybaby they named George Gordon Battle Liddy.

"My father and I did the things other fathers and sons did too," Liddy goes on. "He took me to the big league baseball games and taught me that the best players are the smartest players. It is permissible, my father taught, to make an occasional physical error. It is never permissible to make a mental error, in baseball or anything else. To my father, the intellect was and must be supreme. From my earliest memory to the last day I saw him alive, if I made an error in his presence in English usage (or Latin or German, for that matter) he would correct me on the spot."

Rigid discipline had been Sylvester Liddy's passport out of poverty, and the nagging fear that those bleak days could always return kept father pushing son. The emotional toll was heavy. "Years after I became an adult," says Liddy, "my father told me that not once in his life had *his* father ever hugged him or shown him any similar sign of affection. Yet I knew my father had loved his father dearly, acting as his night nurse for more than a year as he died of cancer. As a consequence, my father tried to hug me often, but it always seemed to me that was just what he was doing; *trying* to hug me, wanting to but not knowing how, as if never having been the object of a fatherly embrace himself, he could not pass on what he had never received."

Liddy concedes that this is merely a subjective impression—"The fact of the matter is that he *did* hug me, often"—but G. Gordon's rationale for that impression is equally disturbing. "It may well have been that my self-loathing, born of contempt for my weakness in the face of fear, rendered me unable to recognize genuine fatherly affection and to receive it when offered." Liddy and his father would clash often over the years, but he insists they always "loved each other greatly" and that he "never respected any man more than I did my father. Nevertheless our relationship was, from its inception, almost formal." When 9-year-old G. Gordon told his father he really was not much of a ballplayer and didn't want to spend the summer of 1940 playing baseball with him, Dad wouldn't hear of it. He even drew up a written player's contract for his son (listing himself as "manager") and had G. Gordon's mother and 7-year-old sister solemnly sign as witnesses. "A deal is a deal," recalls Liddy, "and I reported to my father for spring training."

Liddy never broke away from his father's influence. He went to the schools his father wanted him to, became an attorney just as Dad had planned. All the while, Liddy seemed consumed by the need to prove to himself that he was not a coward, that he would not make those inexcusable "mental mistakes" his father had repeatedly chastised him for. In the long run, G. Gordon Liddy was not the only one to pay for Sylvester Liddy's "almost formal" attitude toward his son.

Young adulthood is usually the first time we pick up the heavy psychological baggage our parents have packed for us and take it on the road. In a son's case, the healthy aggressiveness generally instilled in him is reinforced in the scramble for grades, for acceptance by the right graduate school, for the best job, for swift career advancement and economic security.

That same aggressiveness may have also been instilled in a daughter, though more often than not, true success was still measured by both our parents in terms of marrying and raising a family. That double message again: Succeed on the job, Dear Daughter, but first see to it that you get a husband and give birth to a child. Still, for both sons and daughters, this breaking-away passage marks the first time that our fathers' fears and misgivings, their *aloneness*, at last comes into clear view. Or is it just that, as people striving for independence, we can at last see Father through the eyes of an adult and not the eyes of a child?

As with Fallon and Liddy, there are fathers who, by force of their own personalities, make that a difficult—sometimes impossible—task. No matter how much we achieve on our own, how distinct from our parents' lives we perceive our adult lives to be, Dad seems to hold the upper hand. If he wants to, and we let him, a domineering father can always make us feel that we have somehow disappointed him. We can waste our time feverishly trying to live up to his expectations and never achieve that distant point of perspective required to see Father for what he really is, ourselves for what we really are.

For all his tremendous success as a television talk show host, Michael Delaney Dowd, Jr.—better known as Mike Douglas—claims he loved his beer-drinking father dearly, but that he "never felt the same love in return." Dowd senior never put his arm around his son or showed any physical affection, and when Dad went fishing it was always with his friends, never with young Michael, even though the boy pleaded to go repeatedly. Once, Mike's father came home on Saturday afternoon after a few beers with the guys at the corner bar. He noticed a neighborhood kid flying a kite and asked Mike if he wanted a kite of his own. Mike was thrilled—it was one of the rare times that his father had ever offered to spend time with him. They went to the store and bought a kite, then returned home to fly it in the backyard. The other boy's kite was flying much higher and farther, so Mike's dad ordered his son to run back to the store and get more string. Later Mike discovered that his father disliked the neighbor and wanted to upstage his little boy. Buying Mike a kite had nothing to do with making his own son happy; he just wanted to one-up an enemy. "I never forgot that," said Mike.

On another occasion Mike came home with a report card that ranked him the second smartest kid in his class. Mike's father wanted to know why he wasn't number one (shades of Erica Jong). Next term the boy was twenty-second.

Long after he was a household name, Mike Douglas lived in the shadow of his older brother Bob. His father constantly praised Bob, and Douglas admits this "began to prey on my mind, so I was out to prove something." Calling Mike from Florida, his father asked if what he had read in the papers was true—was he earning $2 million a year? Once Mike verified the figure, his dad then asked if that was more than Johnny Carson's salary. At the time it was. All his father wanted to know, Mike realized, was if his son was number one.

The day before his father died, Mike visited him in the hospital. He leaned over the bed and whispered, "I love you and you're going to be fine." Then, for the first time, Mike Douglas heard his father say he loved him, too.

Mike Douglas' father was neither warm nor supportive toward his son, yet he set high standards that his son not only met but far exceeded. To acknowledge that he had been far outstripped by Mike's accomplishments would only have bruised the pride of a man like Mr. Dowd. So long as Mike felt he had disappointed his father, that he was being denied his father's love and respect because of something he had done or failed to do, father and son remained tethered by guilt. And because of his preoccupation with what he perceived to be his own shortcomings, Mike could not step back and see that the fault lay with his father, not himself.

To gain this necessary perspective, we must rebel. Attending a school other than our dad's alma mater, choosing a career other than the one he steered us toward, moving to another city, falling in love with someone who may not be his ideal—each is a step away from Father's control and often toward a better understanding of him.

We may well come full circle. The lawyer's son who eschews the business world to commune with nature after graduating with a Ph. D. in philosophy may often return to the fold; after the thrill of hang gliding wears off and he begins to chafe under the weight of his backpack, Sonny is frequently ready to suit up in Brooks Brothers' best.

California's iconoclastic former governor showed no signs of following in his father's footsteps as a youngster. Although Edmund G. "Pat" Brown had served two full terms as governor in Sacramento, young Edmund junior decided instead to enter the Jesuit Sacred Heart novitiate, rebelling against his father's plans for him. But after three and a half years he dropped out ("There wasn't anything left to learn from being a seminarian") and earned a degree in Latin and Greek at the University of California at Berkeley before attending Yale Law School. An antiwar activist and strong campaigner for Democratic candidate Eugene McCarthy in 1968, Brown decided to run in 1970 for the modest office of California secretary of state and won. Their relationship remains anything but stable, but at least in terms of Pat Brown's ambitions for his son, the one-time would-be monk had come full circle.

Alex Haley, author of the Pulitzer prize-winning *Roots*, is another example of someone who first distanced himself from the dreams of his father, a professor at Alabama A&M. Alex was not suited to the academic life and dropped out of college after two years to enlist in the Coast Guard. Retiring at the age of 37, he moved to New York and began writing. It had been his father's wish that Alex become an author.

My generation—the baby boomers born in the late 1940s and early 1950s—took this notion of rebellion against parental authority to ridiculous extremes. Drugs, the sexual revolution, the civil rights movement, and Vietnam all converged on the 1960s to make it a time of tremendous upheaval for the family. Yet, by the time the dust settled in the mid-1970s, these rebels—like their fathers before them—were in hot pursuit of the same tried-and-true middle-class dream: a well-paying job, a house, a car, a family. Yippie leader Jerry Rubin made the front pages every week by parading into congressional hearings in warpaint and telling his freaked-out followers not to trust anyone over 30. Rubin is now a pinstripe-clad stockbroker for a leading New York investment house.

Some of the things against which my contemporaries rebelled had nothing to do with war or poverty or the rights of minorities or the great political issues of the day. They were challenging the family, parental (i. e., paternal) authority. In this they were participating in a far greater and more enduring struggle than any conflict between nations. They were soldiers in the war of the generations, a series of skirmishes that spans centuries. Socrates complained emphatically about the declining morals and habits of the young, and it can safely be assumed that some Cro-Magnon patriarch bristled when his upstart son chose to paint pictures of beasts on the cave wall rather than hunt them.

The sons and daughters who fled to San Francisco's Haight-Ashbury district in the late 1960s were there because their parents gave them a message. It must be stressed that because Father was society's representative in the home—the setter of standards, the family's ultimate authority—defying one's parents more often than not meant defying one's *father*. A young M.B.A. who fled his more-than-affluent Grosse Point, Michigan, family in 1968 to join a commune in Massachusetts tells me he did it because he "did not want to make the same mistakes" as his father. His father, a Detroit auto executive, was, to hear the son tell it, "going around smiling and telling jokes, but he was miserable. Dad was a big success, and every day of his life he fought like hell to keep from being maneuvered out of his job by some other cutthroat. He was scared, but he only let us see it. His friends from work all thought he was the most relaxed man they'd ever met, the Perry Como of the Big Three. He was pathetic, really."

Why did he return after four years on the commune? "I discovered there is enough hypocrisy and backbiting on a commune to make Ford, IBM, and Exxon rolled up together look like a Sunday school picnic," explains the lapsed hippie. "I decided that if I was going to have to compete I might as well do it with the people my father used to call 'the big boys.' At 23, I enrolled at Northwestern and seven years later left Yale with an M.B.A." He now works for a Detroit-based management consulting firm and sees his father once a week for lunch. "He's still very wealthy and important and unhappy, but I'm not. Now that I know something of the world, I can understand why he has reacted the way he does to the pressures. Maybe the lesson is that we're not all meant to be happy. I just don't let the things that get to my father get to me."

Did this prodigal son return for the reasons he outlined? Perhaps. Another theory: Spoiled by his wealthy parents and yet afraid to endure what his father had to for material gain, the boy merely headed for the hills until the desire for luxuries like heat and reliable plumbing overtook him. Even this cynical assessment of the situation cannot dilute the fact that the child's perception of his father's unhappiness will influence the road he travels in his own life. Many sons consciously rebel against Dad if they believe him to be a failure when it comes to personal happiness.

Literature abounds in examples of sons confronted with the grim prospect of repeating their father's mistakes.

The focal point of Eugene O'Neill's *Long Day's Journey into Night* is no less the father, a faded matinee idol and peerless penny pincher, than it is the morphine addict mother. The characters were based on the Nobel prize-winning playwright's own parents, and O'Neill's widow, Carlotta, discussed with me how he sobbed as he poured his feelings of rage, pity, and remorse onto the page. O'Neill felt so strongly that he had betrayed his parents that he specified in his will that the play not be published or produced until twenty-five years after his death. (In fact, Carlotta waited only a few years to release *Long Day's Journey.*)

O'Neill's own father was a promising actor who squandered away his talent for financial security, touring the country for most of his professional life as the title character in *The Count of Monte Cristo.* He became wealthy from the part, but the memories of his poverty-stricken Irish childhood continued to haunt him. Eugene's birth was a difficult one, and to cope with the pain, his mother was given morphine and became hopelessly hooked. Eugene blamed himself to a certain degree, but he believed that his beautiful mother would never have become a junkie had it not been for the cheap quack his skinflint father had hired to treat her.

The Tyrones, as they are called in the play, spend as much time debating Father's miserliness and monumental ego as they do trying to figure out what can be done with Mother. At the play's end Eugene's character is packed off to a TB sanitarium. The play suggests that the father retreated in his decision to save money and send his tubercular son to the "state farm"; actually, Eugene was dispatched by his father to the Fairfield County State Tuberculosis Sanitarium in Shelton, Connecticut—a dilapidated farmhouse and two shacks that had been converted into an infirmary. O'Neill eventually persuaded his father to send him to a specialist. In the play we can only imagine that when he gets out—if he gets out—he will live up to his promise never to become a miserable tightwad like Pop.

In reality young Eugene accomplished that with a vengeance: A veritable spendthrift as a youth, he lived lavishly after his plays made him far richer than his father could have dreamed.

Ultimately, the meanness of spirit displayed by O'Neill's father toward Eugene and his elder brother was also visited on the playwright's own children. Eugene O'Neill never spoke to his only daughter, Oona, after she married Charlie Chaplin when she was 17 and Chaplin was over 50. Emotionally if not physically cut off from their father, O'Neill's two sons each eventually committed suicide—one by slashing his wrists and ankles in the bathtub, the other by jumping off the roof of a Brooklyn tenement.

Arthur Miller also wrote about his own father in *All My Sons* and *Death of a Salesman*. Both plays begin by depicting sons who worship their fathers. By the time the curtain falls, the fantasies about Dad have been demolished. Willie Loman, the character who has become synonymous with the kind of back-slapping hustler not uncommon in business, exhorts his son, Biff, to be the most popular guy in town. That, not values or ethics, is Willie's formula for success as imparted to his son. As Dad's career slips he becomes more of a double-dealer and conniver, until finally Biff's illusions are shattered when he finds his father in a hotel room with a hooker. To get back at Dad for cheating on Mom, Biff forsakes Loman's idea of the American Dream for the life of a penniless drifter.

Certainly Dustin Hoffman, for one, has recalled that the life of his father was similar to that of Willie Loman. The Hoffmans were never particularly affluent during his Los Angeles childhood. Dustin's dad was a prop man at Columbia Pictures before going into business as a furniture designer. There is little doubt that Harry Hoffman, coming home with loads of Hollywood stories to tell—stories about *other people's* success—fueled his son's desire to enter show business.

Even when it finally occurred to us that Father had

feet of clay, the smartest of us did not toss out the good with the bad. Martin Konigsberg of Flatbush had a light brush with show business—he once served as a waiter at Sammy's Bowery Follies—but spent most of his life driving a cab, working in a poolroom, tending bar, and dabbling in the jewelry business. The family was poor, but Martin Konigsberg brought a present home to his son, Allen Stewart, every day. "We couldn't afford a car," recalls young Konigsberg, "but my father plied me with money. Even today, I love to spend money." Nevertheless, puny Allen Stewart led a lonely, suffocating childhood. He was keenly aware of his father's Lomanesque foibles, but rather than deny or reject them, he chose another course by incorporating them into his angst-filled act. "My parents," he would crack, "believed equally in God and carpeting." This ability to merchandise his misery provided Allen Stewart Konigsberg—alias Woody Allen—his escape from the ghetto.

Whether or not he chooses the career his father wants for him, a young man will be influenced either directly or inversely by his father's attitudes toward work. The world's most industrious sanitation worker may raise a son who has chosen to dance with the American Ballet Theater. But if the son believes his father has benefited *personally*, i. e., derived satisfaction from hard work as well as tangible rewards, he is likely to pursue his own interests with equal vigor. Conversely, if Dad is lazy and doesn't seem to be suffering from it, then don't be surprised if his offspring becomes a champion slough-off artist.

The hitch comes when it is evident to the child that Father's hard work is getting him nowhere, or worse yet that it is making him desperately unhappy or adversely affecting his health. This may have always been known to us; Father may have complained incessantly or suffered in silence, but as children many of us knew all too well that work, for Dad at least, was not a happy place to be. If Dad was particularly adept at concealing his misery, or if we were merely too unsophisticated as children and teenagers to pick up on the many hints, then perhaps we did not detect his frustration until we left home. Then, from our new vantage point as young workers, his frustrations suddenly became blindingly evident.

How do we react? Of the men I interviewed who perceived their fathers to have been hardworking but unhappy in their jobs, some vowed never, as one put it, to be "a sucker like my dad." They made a concerted effort in their work not to be taken advantage of. They admitted that they did only what was required of them, nothing more. But just as many of these men who pledged not to repeat their father's mistakes were themselves exceedingly diligent at their jobs and admittedly miserable.

"My father worked himself into the ground for the railroad," said one man in his late 20s. "When I was 10 and he was 30, he looked 50. Once he got home he just ate dinner and passed out. He was always volunteering, as if that was going to get him somewhere. When it came time to retire, he got the proverbial gold watch and a pension that wouldn't keep a chipmunk alive. No way was I going to be screwed over like that." Now the son works for a computer company in California's Silicon Valley and is described by his co-workers and superiors as diligent beyond the call of duty. "I don't feel they pay me what I deserve to be paid, and yet here I am like Dad, killing myself."

Why? A father's impact on a son's approach to work runs far deeper than the example he sets on the job. Long before we were aware of his disappointments and frustrations—the unpleasant notion that Dad had been unfairly exploited—we were learning those concepts of responsibility and conscientiousness at his knee. When we were small, he usually had not yet had the opportunity to become bitter. So he taught us that if we did our homework, we would get good grades; if we mowed the lawn, we'd earn enough pocket money to go to the movies. Once ingrained, the work ethic is difficult to erase. "People have told me I'm nuts," says the computer company worker. "Even a couple of my supervisors have told me to slow down, and I want to. I just don't know how without feeling guilty." His diagnosis: "When it comes to work, my father and I have the same sickness. Maybe it's genetic."

Far more befuddling is the impact a father has on a daughter's behavior in the workplace. Because Father imparts a dual message to his daughter—be aggressive enough to succeed but passive enough not to scare away men— she can find herself effectively crippled once she breaks away and begins competing with these men for jobs.

Consider how far women have *not* come economically in the past quarter century. To be sure, women now make up 40.7 percent of the work force, compared to only 33 percent in 1960. But women's income averaged 63 percent of what a man earned back in 1956. That figure has dropped to under 60 percent today. According to the Department of Labor, 54 percent of working women earn less than $10,000 per year. Among women managers, the pay gap is wider. Women earned 54 percent of what men did in 1978, compared with 52 percent in 1968 (although the number of women managers more than doubled since 1969 to three million in 1981). Half the women employed outside the home work in jobs with no pensions, much less profit sharing or stock option plans. Sociologists have come to call the women stuck in these menial, semiskilled, dead-end jobs as "the 80 percent," for they account for an astounding 80 percent of all American females taking home a paycheck.

There are cultural pressures that have kept women at the bottom of the economic heap. Each year the American Council of Life Insurance sends out a questionnaire that asks its national sample for its definition of "masculinity." And each year eight out of ten respondents select the same answer: "Being a good provider." By making a decent amount of money, a woman jeopardizes her femininity in society's eyes. That is Radcliffe President Matina Hormer's thesis: that women fear their womanliness will be questioned if they are successful. Few men in this era of raised consciousness will admit it, but there can be no doubt that we are threatened by the prospect of our wife or lover earning more than we do. Women know this. Jane Adams discovered that even female managers are "concerned that their financial success might threaten potential mates." In fact, studies indicate that most women in the labor force are no happier than their household counterparts. No wonder. How rewarding can emptying out office wastebaskets and waiting on tables—the types of jobs in which the vast majority of women find themselves—be?

None of this explains, however, why those educated women who have made the decision to seriously pursue careers seldom get much further than their entry-level position. Although 36 percent of all corporate board members are women (often for decorative effect), only 2 percent of the nation's top executives are women, and without exception every company listed in the Fortune 500 directory is run by men. Colette Dowling writes, "Inwardly confused and anxious, women back off from living full out, at the frontier edges of their capabilities. A travel agent I met said, 'We're not yet able to stand on our own two feet and say, "Yes! I can *do* this. I'm competent."' Women are still afraid."

Again, women are co-conspirators against themselves. Employers have vociferously complained in recent years that the women working for them will not sign up for the advancement programs set up specifically for them by their companies. "We practically have to beg them to take part," claimed an Exxon executive. A writer friend of mine has for years turned down offers to promote her to editor. "I don't want the headaches," she shrugged. "I'm happy right where I am, in my little corner where nobody bothers me. Anyway, the whole idea scares me." Another acquaintance, a junior officer at a major metropolitan bank, also turned down a flat-out promotion to be the head of her department because she was convinced she would fail instantly and be fired. So long as she stayed right where she was, hidden by a phalanx of male superiors, she felt safe.

Fear. Anxiety. Most women have been taught since they were bouncing on Daddy's knee that they would be spared these things. Even if Daddy later turned out to be a world-class ogre, or if he pressed his little girl to achieve great things, it is this implicit promise that she will always be free from hurt that daughters remember. And live for.

Ambition is not a male trait. There are sufficient numbers of ambitious women to populate the highest echelons of all the Fortune 500 companies. They want to succeed, but often lack the ability or the finesse to do so. In the *Journal of the American Academy of Psychoanalysis*, Dr. Alexandra Symonds wrote that "it is not appropriate for an executive in a bank to break down in tears when her superior criticizes something she's done. It is not acceptable for a senior editor earning $30,000 a year to act cute and seductive when her plan is rejected; or for a college professor to sulk because she has been given a poor schedule, hoping the Dean will notice and change it. These are behavior patterns suitable for 'Daddy's little girl' rather than a liberated woman acting autonomously." She went on to explain that these were all women who had come to her for help.

If the number of managerial women seeking professional help of this kind is any indication, then job strains may bother them more than men. According to *The Wall Street Journal*, studies suggest that women with management posts are as mentally healthy as male colleagues, but show more signs of stress. Stanford researchers found that among a group of 123 M.B.A. graduates, mostly managers, four times as many women as men sought counseling. Women also reported more depression, nightmares, and stomach upsets.

Tests of 153 female executives by Chicago psychologist Kathleen Shea revealed that, overall, they are mentally healthier than men. But women scored lower on a key measure: "time competency," the ability to operate in the present tense on short-term tasks without unduly worrying about the long-range consequences. Women, she claimed, have more demands to "look sharp" in the long run; hence many fret about what even the smallest mistake might do to their reputations.

The father-daughter relationship is invariably at the base of a woman's desire to carve a niche of her own outside the role of wife and mother. Again, Margaret Hennig's Harvard doctoral thesis about twenty-five women managers showed that every one had had a strong attachment to and identification with her success-oriented father. That relationship is also at the base of her confusion in trying to achieve those goals. If, as a mentor, a boss is something of a father figure to a male, then he is even more so to a woman. The dilemma becomes even more complex if, as is not infrequently the case, a father fails to encourage his daughter to use her mind and talent to the fullest, preferring instead to see her automatically take a subordinate, "caretaker" role. The problem can only be remedied by stopping and considering what Daddy has done to his daughter. A woman stifled by her father as a girl need not wonder why she feels stymied in the office.

Because many women are first-generation workers, the daughters of housewives, they are more tentative than their brothers. They are not accustomed to criticism. A 1979 *Wall Street Journal* story revealed that most male managers were aware of this sensitivity and therefore reluctant to candidly criticize female subordinates the way they would their male counterparts. More than one male executive has told me of having female staffers choke back tears or, at the other extreme, fly into rages because they have been asked to do something differently. These men sometimes feel manipulated by what they perceive as "typical female behavior," while others chalk up such bouts with the petulance of some female subordinates as yet another sign of woman's inherent weakness. Either conclusion can have only one effect: to keep women in their lowly place.

There are obvious parallels between father and boss. To successfully cope with work, a woman must first consider how her relationship with Dad is distorting her behavior toward her superiors. Again this is part and parcel of Freudian transference, the unconscious association we make between a person we are dealing with in the present and someone from the past whom we loved or feared.

The protected daughter, therefore, may be perfectly content to remain in one undemanding position for her entire working life, cheerfully obeying orders, never facing a challenge, forever relying on an office "daddy" to shield her from all unpleasantness. Secure. Safe. Suffocating. A spoiled Daddy's Girl may look upon a reasonably demanding boss as a monster. His requests seem harsh, and he does not give her the constant praise and reinforcement to which she has become accustomed. Invariably, this kind of woman either quits in a snit or explodes at the boss and is canned. Explaining why she had quit five jobs in two years after friction with her superiors, an attractive office worker from Virginia made a classic and all-revealing Freudian slip: "My daddy," she shrugged, "told me not to put up with anything but the best treatment from *any* man." As one might suspect, this woman retreats to her father after every botched job and failed love affair.

The Adored Daughter syndrome may create its problems for the working women, but they can pale in comparison to the difficulties confronting the ignored or mistreated daughter. Accustomed to feeling inadequate in the eyes of her own father, her manner is almost an unspoken invitation to criticism. Yet she has never really recovered from the pain of rejection at the hands of her father, and when she fails to totally please someone above her, she may overreact. She becomes passive, defeatist. Or she becomes argumentative and quarrelsome, provoking the kind of battles with her boss that she waged against Father as an adolescent. Even though she is new to a job, she proclaims her independence from Father by constantly questioning her superior's instructions, asking his guidance and then rejecting it, rebelling against the rules of the organization. She may come into the office late or not at all to prove that she will not tolerate what she believes to be mistreatment from superiors—all the while demanding to know why she is not being given the choicest assignments and a hefty raise.

At the risk of being branded a misogynist, I must point out that such behavior is not uncommon. U. S. Labor Department statistics show absenteeism and illness to be 20 percent higher among women than men, and only a portion of that percentage can be accounted for by the working mother who is called home on occasion when the baby-sitter doesn't show or Jonathan fractures something falling off his bicycle.

Of course, when male managers concede that they consider female employees to be generally less reliable, chauvinism is the easy answer. Not so easily explained away are those women managers who claim they prefer to work with men.

One midlevel manager said that all seven of the women working under him required "special attention" on his part. One had frequent bouts with anxiety that caused her to remain home in bed an average of one day per week; another fled from business conferences in tears when her proposals were politely rejected, and yet another became enraged at the "plots" hatched by her co-workers to undercut her. Slowly he ascertained that each of the seven women still had unresolved conflicts with their fathers, ranging from the Daddy's Girl who fled in tears to the paranoid misfit never able to come to terms with her father's aloofness.

It must be reiterated that men, too, derive their work habits in large part from Father. But once his life apart from Father is on course, a son is far less likely to be so confused in reacting to male authority figures. Generally speaking, he has been told to be aggressive, but also how to play by the rules of the game. He has not received that damaging double message that fathers transmit to their little girls. In bed as well as the office, a son is aggressive, never passive. He would not know how to be both. Trouble is, neither do most women.

Dad had his reasons, certainly, for giving his daughter this impossible assignment. He did not want her to scare away lovers, and in this he was probably right. Much has been written in recent years about the sexual impact of the feminist movement. Much, too, has been written about the sexual harassment of women at work. But the erotic component of the father-daughter relationship makes a good deal of sexual game-playing at work inevitable. A woman in close contact with attractive peers and superiors is bound to experience erotic urges and to be given plenty of encouragement by some bosses to indulge those urges.

"In the old days, when a woman was usually just a secretary," writes Dr. William Appleton, "if she fell in love with her boss she left her job and married him. Now if she is an executive and falls in love with an attractive male above, equal to or below her in the hierarchy, she faces a much bigger problem because she does not want to abandon her career lightly. Consequently, controlling her sexual impulses at work is essential."

The woman still thrashing out her difficulties with Dad, still incapable of breaking away, is the least likely to control those desires. Like a restless teenager, her rebelliousness is coupled with impatience. Sleeping with the boss may look like one fast way to get ahead. It has happened. But even when love is involved, most office affairs do not end well. And when they are over, it is the exploited woman who is either fired or quits.

Again with 20-20 hindsight, it is easy for us to see how Father himself may have acted over the years to minimize the damage. The tyrannical dad could have loosened his grip, the indulgent dad might have tightened his. Recognizing what long-term damage he was inflicting by bottling up his own frustrations, or, conversely, airing them incessantly, he could have been more positive in front of the children. He could have taken the time to praise them for their achievements while being careful not to spoil them. Of course, had he made these maneuvers to correct the course of his and his children's lives, their breaking away would have been that much easier.

Trouble was, nobody bothered to tell Dad what the consequences could turn out to be *while all this was happening*. Predictably, most fathers I talked to were eager to take credit for their children's accomplishments. Few were willing to assume any of the blame for their children's shortcomings. Those who did offered much the same explanation for what went wrong. One, a major liquor distributor, admits that he was "too wrapped up" in his own career to see that he was demanding too much from his sons and not enough from his daughter. As a result, all four kids went through drug problems and two still have difficulty working with others.

"When you're starting a family," says this father, now in his late 50s, "all you're really interested in is staying afloat financially. By the time you're well enough off to think about how your kids are going to make it as adults, it's too late—the damage is done, and you're too set in your ways anyway." Confesses another dad whose daughter, a classic Daddy's Girl, has bounced from one sour affair and one botched job to another: "The easiest thing for me to do when she was little was to just say everything she did was right and perfect no matter what. It got me off the hook—how could she say I didn't love her? But I was just cheating both of us."

Unable to relive those formative early years, a father can still help us break the heavy psychological chains that bind us to him. He can, simply, admit to himself that he might be partly responsible for his child's inability to adjust to life as an independent adult and then point the way out. After she moved out of her boyfriend's apartment and quit her most recent job—all in the same week—Lee, a Daddy's Girl, was taken aside by Daddy. He told her what he finally acknowledged to be the truth—that he had spoiled her to the point where she had come to expect men and women to treat her like a princess. "I said that I had handicapped her, but that now she was an adult and had to start taking responsibility for her own actions," he recalls of their fateful conversation. "I told her she should be less volatile, less demanding, and a little more realistic about the men she dated and the people she worked with. I also said that she could always come home whenever she wanted, but that she should think it over very carefully before running home to Daddy every time she had a problem." Daddy's adored daughter did not speak to Daddy for two months, but when she finally called it was to thank him for the "shock treatment."

Another man in his 50s saw the results within weeks after confessing to his rebellious 22-year-old son that Dad's obsessive ambition at the office had been misguided. The boy, who had once tried to commit suicide because of poor grades and then dropped out of school altogether, returned to college. Without the pressure of having to live up to what he perceived to be his father's vaunted expectations, the son relaxed and ended up the semester with a respectable B average.

Independence is a loaded word. None of us will be, or for that matter want to be, totally free of Father's love and influence and even his (constructive) criticism. It is equally true that we sons and daughters will never be free to explore our full potential for happiness unless we seize the opportunity to fly away, to leave the nest intellectually as well as physically. For a working woman, that means divorcing oneself from the little girl of the past. It means keeping a tight rein on emotions and recognizing when a boss's criticisms are being heard as reprimands from Daddy. It means accepting the childlike state that accompanies an entry-level position, accepting the concept of paying dues and apprenticeship, and placing competence ahead of righteous indignation over imagined slights. It means not using sex as part of a career game plan. It means not being afraid to try and fail, and it means not being afraid to try and succeed. It means earning not only the affection of colleagues, but their *respect*. It means growing up.

We have gone through this ritual ever since I was 22. My mother and father are our guests for dinner. We all arrive at the restaurant—it does not matter if it's "21" or a roadside greasy spoon diner—and proceed to have a delightful meal. Someone asks for the check, and then the *real* fun begins. Water goblets fly and centerpieces topple as we both lunge for the bill, grasping in the air with one hand and whipping out wallets and credit cards with the other. That we asked *them* to dinner mattereth not to my father; it is a point of pride with him. He *always* picks up the tab.

This, of course, is particularly galling when birthdays, Father's Day, anniversaries, and the like are involved. The man has often insisted on paying for his own birthday dinner. On more than one occasion I've had to sneak off (under the guise of going to the men's room) to intercept the check before it reached the table. My father was furious. "We'll settle up later" provides him with yet another out. When it comes time after leaving the restaurant to even accounts, he is evasive. Money is pressed from my hand into his, only to be thrown back or allowed to fall to the ground. Cash I managed to surreptitiously slip into his jacket winds up mysteriously back in my coat pocket the next morning.

"When you're young," explains Dr. Joyce Brothers, "you're told—and you believe—that everything is under your control. As you get older, you discover that so much depends on just blind luck. You have less power over your life than you thought. A father gets older, weaker, but there is still one area in which he can maintain power and authority over his children. He has the means to pick up the tab. Let him pay the bill," she advises. "I do. It's one of my father's great pleasures. Why deprive him of it for my ego?" Why, indeed?

"The middle-aged father frequently finds himself in a painful situation," says Stanley Cath, M.D., a psychoanalyst and associate clinical professor at Tufts Medical School. "His adolescent children may be rebellious and challenging to him; he himself may be trying to separate from his own father, who may be aged or dying; and the grandfather himself may be looking for support" as he faces the debilitating effects of old age. "Of course, a man can be the father to his children, and also the father to his parents," says Dr. Cath. "We rediscover the father, and the definition of fathering, throughout our lifespan."

It could be a rerun of *The Waltons* or a scene from one of those thirty-second, three-hankie, shot-through-gauze Kodak commercials: An airport boarding area. The folks are seeing Junior off as he leaves home for the Big City. Junior is eager but also a little afraid. The camera glances over Pop as he gives Mom a little reassuring squeeze. Then the camera stays where we know it will—on Mother as she waves pathetically and bites her lower lip. Tears glisten in her eyes, and we see Pop's hand (only his hand, mind you) come around her shoulder to give another comforting hug. We understand, after all, how painful it is for the mother hen to see her chicks leave.

Conveniently coinciding with the years that most women experience menopause, the "empty nest syndrome" has long been the exclusive purview of Mom and her mid-life crisis. The kids leave home, and the sense of sorrow and loss send the menopausal mother into a tailspin of depression. What about Dad? "New evidence is emerging which suggests that men, too, in the role of husbands and fathers, can experience the empty nest syndrome which is like that experienced by women," says Dr. Michael E. McGill, author of the excellent *40- to 60-Year-Old Male.*

One-third of the managers polled in a 1980 survey stated that their children were their main worry—not their job, not the economy in general, not crime, not a nuclear holocaust. Their children. Perhaps this concern is a function of their career success; the father feels guilty because he has sacrificed time with them to pursue his personal goals. He missed too many recitals, too many parent-teacher nights. Will his children suffer because of it? he worries. Or maybe the children gave him a feeling of satisfaction that neither wife nor job could. With such intimacy comes worry, concern, *caring.* He basks in the glow of his children's affection, and as they grow he dreads the day he will lose it.

It is evident, though we have chosen to neglect the obvious fact, that many middle-aged men find their identity in the role of father. How many of our fathers gloried in this role above all others, even that of husband? And how many of us watched Dad join Mom on her downhill slide? Like their wives, most fathers passively accept their diminished self-image once the kids have flown and taken a large chunk of their parents' identities with them.

Depression is the first and most common reaction, experienced by mother and father both. It may be expressed in the same way: a significant mood change, withdrawal. "For most of these middle-aged men," writes McGill, "there is no fighting to forestall the loss or striking out against the source. There is instead a quiet, passive acceptance of a lesser self."

The course chosen by most, yes. But certainly not all. Men, as we have witnessed, are less accustomed than their wives to inaction. They have been taught their entire lives to take the initiative and face whatever challenges confront them.

There are those fathers who seek to continue influencing the lives of their offspring by thwarting their efforts at independence. They may deny us the financial backing needed to attend a college far from home, for example, or keep us tied to the family business. If they have made breaking away that difficult for us, then our later gropings for reconciliation are that much more painful. Yet these attempts at retaining control over our lives are obvious to us; like the redcoats marching out in formation onto the battlefield, these fathers have declared themselves to be enemies of our independence.

For that openness we are grateful. Father may twist our arm to keep us nearby; he may even use highly questionable tactics (one influential businessman tried to prevent his daughter from leaving the family firm and taking a better offer elsewhere by pleading with her prospective boss on the telephone to withdraw the job offer). Once we have taken the plunge, however, the game is essentially over. Dad may play on our guilt for having had the courage to call our lives our own, but he must concede defeat.

Far more insidious is the father who lets us delude ourselves that we run our lives and pulls the strings long distance. His tactics are right out of the Ho Chi Minh handbook. Many such fathers direct their Machiavellian maneuvers at their sons' and daughters' careers, attempting to manage them the way they would their own. Even more widespread is what I call the father-in-law phenomenon. Psychologists and stand-up comedians have long aimed squarely at mothers-in-law, and with plenty of justification. But Henny Youngman has no father-in-law jokes in his repertoire of one-liners. He should. I have heard countless stories of young couples suffering from father-in-law troubles. And when a father decides he is going to interfere in his child's marital life, he is often more dangerous than a meddlesome mom. This is for two reasons: (1) We do not usually expect it from him, so thoroughly brainwashed are we that this is exclusively a female trait, and (2) father-in-laws have the resolve and the clout to do considerably more damage should they choose to.

Fathers can and do make the kinds of cracks about a daughter-in-law's meager culinary skills and spendthrift ways, or a son-in-law's drinking and sloth, that are always attributed to moms. But fathers have also gone so far as to offer cash settlements for their daughters-in-law to leave their sons, conspire to have a son-in-law transferred thousands of miles away, whip up suspicion and jealousy by inventing stories of mistresses and lovers, and even make an untoward pass at a daughter-in-law to prove to a son that she's no good for him. With the possible exception of *The Graduate*'s lubricious Mrs. Robinson, rare is the mother who tries to pull that one off.

As we have noted, most of Father-in-law's transgressions tend to be of a more minor nature once we identify them. Dad may want to bust up the whole thing and have the kids under his roof and his thumb forever, but he usually settles for nagging. There are untold numbers of middle-aged Felix Ungers out there, instructing their sons' hapless wives on just the right way to load a Maytag dishwasher, just as there are countless Oscar Madisons out there broadly hinting to their daughters that they married a wimp or a loser.

In the age of narcissism we must be careful not to assume that the light goes out of our father's world the minute we have departed it. There are plenty of fathers for whom the childless house signals a return to more carefree times. "I never fully appreciated just how expensive the kids were," one 60-year-old father of twins told me, "until they left. Ever since, we've had enough money to pretty much do what we want."

The departure of Jonathan and Suzie may also have spelled a change for the better in Mom. Once they are no longer needed for the day-to-day feeding, clothing, and counseling of their children, many women return to school or pick up their careers or other interests where they left off. Dad often finds himself with a new, more exciting wife than the one he had become accustomed to. Most importantly, Dad can run around the house in his underwear or make love on the dining room table at high noon if that's what he and Mom feel like doing. Surprising how many feel like doing just that—frequently.

Eda LeShan's father is in his 80s. She has gone far beyond the battle-for-the-check routine and now faces the grim prospect of caring for Dad. "It's a terribly painful role reversal," says LeShan. "He is the head of the family. Once a man gives that up he's old and feeble and ready to die. My father was always my Rock of Gibraltar, but now he needs *me*. I don't want this to happen, but it's happening. And it's heartbreaking."

Long before we are haunted by the specter of warehousing our parents in nursing homes, we hear the clock ticking and attempt to forge a new, stronger link with Father. We can only do this because we are launched, and our dealings with our parents, superficially at least, are more cordial than they have ever been.

We are surprised to learn that the same struggles of childhood and adolescence have not been extinguished. The fires of rivalry and resentment are fanned again—this time over issues of pride (something seemingly as trivial as the long-running dispute over the check with my father signifies far more), jealousy (a father is almost never able to fully accept his daughter's sexual partners without at least a twinge of suspicion, loss, and/or feelings of betrayal), and guilt—the guilt both father and child feel for not having lived up to the other's expectations.

There is, however, a tremendous need, particularly as we enter our 30s and 40s, to at last reconcile with our fathers, to express the love we were never allowed to (or never allowed ourselves to) express.

To be sure, there are things about our fathers that we do not like. We are not about to say all is forgiven with a

Hallmark Father's Day card. If we do we are liars. We may try to smooth over the things about him we don't like—his selfishness, perhaps, his cruelty, indifference, or sexual reprehensiveness—by saying they aren't important. We "understand." We "forgive." All the while, we are stock-piling our resentment, incorporating into our personalities the very things about Father that we dislike.

Ironically, the very same is true if we go to the other extreme, seeing only the dark side of Father's nature and denying all that is good in him. During the six months between his father's first heart attack and his death, Dr. Richard Robertiello had the opportunity to assess his true feelings. "I never got on well with my father," conceded Robertiello, recalling that it was his grandfather who raised him while Papa pursued glory as a physician. "All my life I had denied I was like my father at all. And yet, during these last six months, I became aware that I was taking in aspects of my father I had always hated: his imperious nature, his hypochondria, all the rest. This was introjection, and I realized that if I didn't face my father squarely, the kind of man he was—good and bad—the guilt when he died would be too great. I knew only complete separation could stop the process. Otherwise, I would have continued to hate my father totally. I would never have seen the many good things I took over from him."

It is not a one-sided attempt at burying the demons of our past; our fathers often try to "recapture" the intimacy of early years—even if, as is so often the case, *it was an intimacy that never really existed.*

One father of a 24-year-old son and a 22-year-old daughter, both Ivy League graduate school students, turned his family on its collective ear one recent winter by demanding that the clan return to the Vermont ski resort where they used to vacation when the kids were little. He was upset to learn that neither son nor daughter had any particular desire to return to the ski lodge where they had romped in the snow as youngsters. Reason: While Mom and Dad both enjoyed schussing down the slopes and après-ski drinking by the fireside with friends, they had left the children in the hands of baby-sitters or to fend for themselves. While Dad remembered these as family outings full of warmth and parent-child togetherness, the children only recalled being shunted aside and ignored. This was, it turns out, the father's approach to his children on all family excursions. "We always took the kids with us, wherever we went," he says. "Sure, we put them in nurseries or with baby-sitters and did things on our own, too—adults and children aren't interested in the same things, after all. We were entitled to some fun, too. I don't know...these were the best times of my life, but my children don't see it that way—as a matter of fact, quite the opposite. Now I want to go back to those days, and they're telling me they weren't all that great for them."

There is an undeniable urge on a father's part to return to an earlier period of relative innocence—and of his children's dependence on him. Guilt may be one cause for this; by reaffirming a close personal tie with his adult offspring, Dad may succeed in assuaging doubts that perhaps he was not all that attentive and caring when they were growing up. Father may also be looking for a return to those days when he was in control, when the world of his children was in many ways the world he created. Or maybe when he blurts out "Do you remember when we used to play checkers?" it's all merely a ruse. He knows the intimacy was never there, but maybe you can be swayed. Even if you weren't close years ago, by convincing you that you were, Dad can forge or strengthen your adult parent–to–adult child relationship.

A common complaint of my contemporaries is that Dad "never took me fishing or hunting or any of the things fathers and sons are supposed to do." I had the same complaint, until I was quite properly reminded that I accompanied my father on hunting and fishing expeditions before I reached adolescence. The choice not to participate as a teenager was mine; Dad was constantly urging me to join him, but I found such pursuits boring. In trying to reconstruct the past, parents' memories often prove far more trustworthy than our own. Dr. Brothers: "We were blank slates when we came into their home, but father has no trouble remembering when we wet the bed." Clear knowledge of what transpired during our upbringing carries its own burdens. Every time my mother jokingly ascribes my behavior to the day Dad clumsily banged his newborn son's head into a wall, he becomes visibly upset (actually, she may have a case).

Parents can be held accountable for much. The danger is that we leave them to bear all the blame. Henry Fonda reconciled with Jane and Peter, but only after both sides took some responsibility for the rift between them. Henry certainly gave them cause for their initial rebellion, but from that point they were on their own. Fonda told me that in retrospect, he was immensely proud of his daughter's political stand and the courage his son displayed by bucking the moviemaking establishment with his hugely successful 1969 film, *Easy Rider*.

Watching Henry and Peter pose together for the 1976 *People* cover story I wrote about them, I could not comprehend how as a 10-year-old Peter was so desperately unhappy that he shot himself in the stomach and very nearly died. On that autumn day at the studio, they joked and kidded with each other as if they were at last enjoying the father-son intimacies that had never existed when Peter was a boy.

Reconciliations of this sort, if they come at all, often come too late. *Ordinary People* Oscar-winner Tim Hutton had little contact with his actor-father Jim Hutton, who divorced Tim's mother when the boy was barely 3. Tim was 14 by the time he overcame his ambivalent feelings and began to know—and love—his father. Less than four years after the two were reunited, Jim Hutton died of cancer at the age of 48. In Jim's hospital room, father and son had watched Tim's debut in TV's *Friendly Fire*. It was an emotional scene as Jim tearfully told his boy how proud he was of him. After he died, Tim says he "felt cheated. I was just getting to know my father."

The most moving account of a father-and-child re-union I have heard came from Sophia Loren as she sat barefooted and cross-legged across from me in the living room of her elegant suite at New York's Pierre Hotel. Sophia's father had not only abandoned his mistress—Loren's mother—and two daughters, but made it difficult for Sophia to collect the few dollars a month he was required to provide for his children's support. He even refused to give her his name—Scicolone—until she paid him one million lire for it, and then he tried to renege on the agreement in order to wring more money out of his daughter.

Still, she confessed during our talk, "I spent much of my life looking for substitutes for him; first Carlo, my husband, then my director, Vittorio De Sica, and so on. With all the grandiose gifts I had received in my life, the little blue auto my father gave me with my name on it stayed in my memory." In his last few months, when he felt well enough, Sophia's father would go to local theaters and sit for endless hours watching his daughter's image flicker on the screen. "I wondered what went through his mind as he sat alone in the dark observing me on the screen," she wrote in her autobiography. "Whether he ever recalled the early days of our existence when he had not only turned his back on us but in a curious way tried to punish us. Did he have any memory of, or guilt about, all the times my mother asked for his help when we were starving? I hated my father for what he had done. But as I got older and learned more about people, I came to realize that hate is an acid that eats away—not the person hated but the one who hates.

"I had also faced reality about my father; he was what

he was, and festering criminations about him was pointless. As my viewpoint about him changed, so did my emotions. I no longer had any hate or scorn for him—only pity. I felt sad for him...a self-defeatist. Destructive. I thank God I inherited none of that from him. I don't want to destroy myself or anyone else. So I pitied my father who couldn't give affection and love to his women and children. Perhaps toward the end he had a glimmer of this."

At her father's deathbed Sophia was introduced for the first time to her half-brother Giuseppe, the oldest of Scicolone's two sons by his first wife. Moments after her father's death, Sophia says she felt compelled to touch Papa's cheek with her fingertips: "'Ciao, Papa,' I said, and welcome into my heart forever." Giuseppe, who unlike Sophia had lived with his father as a child, began crying, and the two embraced tearfully. "How ironic that at his death, my father, who had given me so little in life, had left me a priceless legacy—a brother. I felt an eerie exultation, as if this young man had risen from the corpse of my father, his flesh and blood, to bring me the kind of kinship that I never had with my father."

The theme of rebirth explicit in Sophia's story is basic to every man's and woman's search for Father. We are free to truly know ourselves only when we finally come to see him as he really is, our vision not clouded by either total devotion or hate. Sophia the daughter accomplished this not by denying her father's true nature, nor by pretending to ignore his monumental transgressions. She fully comprehended that he was a ruthless schemer, and she pitied him for it. She also knew that she had only been exposed to him in a very limited way and had not adopted any of his negative characteristics.

Fortunately the majority of us do not have to cope with fathers who first abandon and then blackmail us. Our struggles are of a more subtle nature, but no less intense. The turnabout that comes as we approach the midpoint of our lives still has to do with the issue of dependence—

not ours this time, but his. Father may be living on a pension and finding it increasingly hard to make ends meet. But he must keep up appearances—witness the check wars. He must also, for his own self-esteem, hang on to his superior position as parent. Faced with even modest offers of assistance that he would have accepted had they come from someone else, a father may feel compromised if we try to help out. The result can be bruised feelings on both sides.

Jessica, 43, lives in New York with her husband and teenage daughter. She was raised in Los Angeles, and after she relocated to New York twenty years ago, she made a point of visiting her parents a minimum of once a year. After Jessica's mother died four years ago, she tripled the frequency of trips to California so she could "keep an eye on Dad." As it happened, Dad's only real problem was of a housekeeping nature. A formal, old-fashioned gentleman, he knew nothing of making beds or vacuuming; these had been his wife's duties, jobs Jessica insists her mother enjoyed. By the time Jessica made her usual Christmas visit, the dust had piled high enough for her to suggest that Dad hire a maid. Better yet, Jessica would take it upon herself to find him the best housekeeper-cook (Dad had been surviving on restaurant food and Swanson TV dinners) in the Los Angeles basin. Jessica interviewed a dozen women over a four-day period before hiring a pleasant woman, the daughter of Mexican immigrants.

Jessica was "thrilled" with her father's reaction to his new housekeeper. "She was a wonderful, warm person with a terrific sense of humor," says Jessica. "Dad joked around with her from the start, and you could see she liked him, too. It was a lot of hard work finding her, but I felt good because I had been able to do something to make Dad's life much easier." Jessica boarded the plane for New York without her usual anxieties about her father's welfare; she was leaving him in excellent hands, happier than he had been in years. The morning after she arrived home on Park Avenue, she phoned L.A. as she always did just to tell her father she had arrived safely. "I asked him how Maria was doing," recalls Jessica. "'She left,' he said. 'I really didn't need a housekeeper, so right after we drove you to the airport I let her go.' I called him stubborn and selfish; all that time I spent trying to find somebody, he never let on that he didn't want help. It took me a while to realize he was telling me something. That he didn't need me to watch over him. That he was still the father and I was still the kid. I still feel I owe him something." She does—Jessica owes it to her father to butt out.

Every June the pollen count soars where my parents now live east of Sacramento. The pollen problem lasts only six weeks or so, but it is so serious that my asthmatic mother has twice landed in intensive care as a result. They love it there the rest of the year, so we agreed that the best way to deal with the situation was to have my parents spend the perilous six weeks with us in New York.

During these visits, the most recent of which came just before his sixty-second birthday, my father has undergone a significant change in his attitude toward me. Instead of passively going along with whatever plans have been worked out by my mother or Valerie, my wife, he actively courts *me*. Where he once had to be dragged kicking to a movie or a restaurant, he now suggests stopping off at a pub or taking in a movie in the middle of the afternoon—so long as it's just the two of us. He has become particularly fond of impromptu late-night adventures, popping out for a drink at ten p.m. and not returning until we've hit every joint within a ten-block radius. Again, it was often just the two of us, and on the many occasions when I could not take Dad up on his offer to spend some time together, he could not conceal his disappointment.

These father-son sojourns are always enjoyable. We talk of politics and tax shelters and bitch about the rest of the family. Yet underlying it all is a disquieting sense of things unsaid. Perhaps he is searching for the way to say he loves and respects me without sounding insincere or like a simp. I know I am searching for a way to say the same to him.

But why now? I have lived a continent away ever since I was 21. Why, after years of dealing with his wife and children as a unit, does he suddenly express an interest in forging a one-on-one, man-to-man bond? The answer, I realized, lay not with anything I had said or done but with my sister. She had not lived home for years, but she was always within a two-hour drive of my parents. Dad's re-alignment of priorities coincided precisely with her marriage and flight to Florida. In the silence of his empty nest, he had clearly pondered our adult relationship and found it lacking.

So we talk once a week, though at times my mother must coax him to the phone. My sister and I joke that we call him to get the central California weather report, and that is invariably what he gives us, delivered in the modulated announcer's voice we hear when we tune in to the eleven o'clock news. Does he fear that the line is tapped, that someone is listening in on family secrets?

At frustrating times like these we feel the old angers rise once more. We are glad we are not bound up like him. Yet when we children are in this mood, everything that Dad does—and every trait we inherited from him—becomes negative. We are enraged when he tells us that the grand old captains' houses on Nantucket, where we have taken my parents to spend a week at our summer place, remind him of the rickety tenements of his Fall River childhood. But is this cruelty, or merely what we see, when it comes from us, as straightforwardness? If he, like so many of his contemporaries, repeatedly relives his World War II experiences, do we accuse him of being maudlin, or, worse yet, boring? We, who reminisce about the Beatles and Janis Joplin and have the nerve to call it "nostalgia"? Our knee-jerk response to his needling, to his goading, is part of what keeps us from recognizing that much of what is good in us comes from him.

It is three a.m. My father and I, both furiously jingling the coins in our pockets, are striding briskly up Third Avenue toward P. J. Clarke's. It is the classiest sawdust-on-the-floor bar in New York and, as at any time of the day or night, it is packed with bleary-eyed revelers. We try to look unimpressed as Jackie Onassis and Norman Mailer squeeze past each other in opposite directions. We sip our Jack Daniel's on the rocks and speak of...tax shelters, real estate, politics. The pauses are longer, the throat-clearing more intense, and still we are searching for those words. Maybe we are never meant to find them. The answer could be the search itself. In the meantime, I let him pick up the tab.

By profession I am a soldier and take pride in that fact. But I am prouder—infinitely prouder—to be a father.

—General Douglas MacArthur

Perhaps host and guest is really the happiest relation for father and son.

—Evelyn Waugh

CHAPTER IX _____

The Child Is Father— and Mother—of the Man

I am sitting alone in our darkened living room, drinking Moët and puffing on a Churchillian cigar. It is one a.m. and Katharine Haines Andersen, my first child, is already seven hours old; she and her mother are together not four blocks away in the maternity ward of New York Hospital. The calls to the grandparents and aunts and uncles and friends have all been made. I had been told to expect all newborns to resemble Yoda or E. T., but with more wrinkles. But from the moment of her birth, with eyes open wide, she was a dark-haired, pink-cheeked beauty.

Joy. I had anticipated that. Relief, too. Relief that, while the labor was long (twelve hours) and difficult, the delivery went well for both mother and child. What I had not expected was to feel so alone, so solitary. Stepping out onto our fourteenth-floor balcony and gazing out over the midtown Manhattan skyline, my thoughts went to that night in Japan twenty-one years before and the aura of aloneness that enveloped Dad as he awaited my sister's birth.

My becoming a parent constituted yet another giant step toward maturity. It also revealed to me a simple but all-important truth: *The more we as sons and daughters grow away from our fathers and define ourselves, the more clearly w*

*can see this other person who existed before he took on the burden
of parenthood.*

The irony is that while parenthood pushes us closer
to understanding our fathers, we must also look forward—
to the course we will steer in raising our own children. Am
I fated to be the other parent, the stranger in the house?
Much is written about the "New Father" that goes hand-
in-hand with the burgeoning literature on "parenting"—
a much overused and stilted word, but one that nonetheless
has wormed its way into everyday speech. Simply put, the
New Father is supposed to take on more of the "nurturing"
(another tiresome term) role in infancy and early childhood once thought to be exclusively maternal. The father
of today, as we have seen, nearly always gets started well
before the actual birth. He probably attends natural childbirth classes with his wife, "coaches" her breathing during
labor, talks her through childbirth, and snaps photos of
(or even videotapes) the new arrival. He is expected to
feed, bathe, and clothe the kid at every opportunity and
change Pampers or Huggies without complaint.

Whether the New Father has actually arrived en masse
in America—or for that matter whether he should—is
open to conjecture. He would not be unique in the world.
Margaret Mead's landmark 1930 study of the Manus tribe
of New Guinea reported that at the age of one year, children were handed over from the mother's care to the father's. He would feed, bathe, and play with the infant, even
take it to bed with him at night. Among Botswana's !Kung
tribesmen, fathers experience a considerable amount of
physical intimacy with infants; they are encouraged to fon-
dle and hold even newborns. And the Lesu people of Mel-
anesia provided that fathers care for the babies while their
wives were busy cooking or working in the fields.

To varying degrees, male figures are involved in child
care in nearly all cultures. Anthropologists still suggest that
even in nonindustrial societies, fathers tend to play a minor
part in the raising of small children. Researchers Melvin

J. Konner and Mary Maxwell West of Harvard found that distant fathers are associated with warrior and hunting cultures, particularly where men's military activities take precedence. Warfare of a different sort goes on in modern industrial cultures, where the males do battle in plants and offices. Toss in the Judeo-Christian ethic and you have the formula for fathering that has existed in this society until now.

Some seem convinced that fathers will now be willing to follow the example of the Manus and the Kung. But change of that magnitude seems doubtful. There is no doubting, however, that the reasons we are having children have changed. The Pill has provided the freedom to time pregnancy, and women have taken advantage of the reprieve. Rather than settling down to raise a family in their early 20s, they have followed the feminist lead and taken off after the same career goals men have always pursued. They merely ignored the biological clock until the ticking became so loud they had to make a decision.

Today economics plays a major factor—often *the* major factor—in a couple's reluctance to take the plunge into parenthood. More than 60 percent of all married women work because they feel they must to maintain their desired standard of living. Many of these women state that they simply can't afford to have a child.

Although my wife, Valerie, earned a handsome salary as an assistant vice-president of Manufacturers Hanover Trust, we decided we could forgo her salary so she could spend the first few years at home with our child. Our reasons for waiting were more esoteric; we liked our freedom, our life as a twosome. I suspect many couples reach the decision to have kids in the same cool, rational, non-mercenary manner we did. Toward the end of our seventh married year, Valerie spent two weeks in Paris conducting one of her seminars for the bank on international credit. On her return in December, I picked her up at Boston's Logan Airport and we drove to Hyannis, where we boarde the ferry for Nantucket. We started off the two-and-a-half-hour ferry ride reassuring each other that we were silly to be talking about children. After all, we were both only 30. When we drove off the ferry onto the wharf in Nantucket, we turned to each other and shrugged simultaneously. "What the hell?" Kate arrived nine months later. It was, needless to say, the best decision we ever backed into.

The baby boom among the baby boomers has been much discussed in recent years. The long-postponed entry into the parent ranks of people born between 1945 and 1953 was mirrored in the statistics. Even figuring in the disturbing rise of teenage pregnancies, the average age of a new mother in the United States jumped from 21 in 1970 to 25 in 1982.

Having become accustomed to their independence, not to mention the extra cash they bring into the household (sometimes needed, sometimes not), these women are anxious to return to work. By 1980, forty-four percent of the mothers of children under the age of 6 were working, with only 24 percent of existing families described as traditional nuclear families. The two-paycheck marriage became the norm for nearly half of all two-parent families in America. These statistics spelled radical shifts in the nature of the family that begged a redefinition.

To some extent society has altered its definitions of masculinity and hence somewhat legitimized the need for more involved fathers. "In a sense, fathers have come out of the closet," says E. Mavis Hetherington, a University of Virginia psychology professor who has studied family-related issues for thirty years. "They feel more comfortable about being parents, and are more actively fighting for their rights." However, it is James Levine's guess that women are pushing far harder for these changes than are the fathers themselves. Contends Levine, an associate at the Wellesley College Center for Research on Women and author of *Who Will Raise the Children?:* "I think it is becoming more of a question for women as more of them are working outside the home. Women make demands on men to parent in a way that fits in with their new concepts of how they will live their lives."

And Father is complying with Mother's wishes, right? No way. What we are witnessing is yet another monumental lie about Dad. "This is all part of a mythology that has been built up about the new father taking an active part at home," insists John Munder Ross. "Studies show that the average time father spends around his baby still varies greatly—from 8 hours to 37.5 seconds a day. Fathers are not all that involved, for the most part."

Trouble is, neither is the New Mom. "There is a tremendous supercareerism among the parents of young children today," worries Michael Maccoby. "This can do great damage to the emotional development of a child." Indeed, what we seem to be offering in place of the old one-and-a-half-parent family is a no-parent family, with both parents off at work while Jason or Jennifer is remanded to a succession of housekeepers or day care centers. A disturbing by-product of this trend: the three million "latchkey kids" who fend for themselves after school when Mother and Father are still at work.

The most glaring self-contradictions often occur at natural childbirth classes, where parents-to-be glory in the forthcoming blessed event. At our sixth and final Lamaze session before Kate's birth, an attractive woman of 28, who had conscientiously attended every class on time and with her equally eager-beaver husband in tow, at last opened her mouth to speak. She informed the instructor and the class with no small degree of pride that she had absolutely no intention of breast-feeding her baby. Not that she wasn't capable or willing, mind you. As it turned out, she was a designer of sheets, and there was an important sales convention she had to attend in Chicago scheduled for two weeks after her baby was due to arrive. The instructor politely suggested that she remember that there existed an avalanche of scientific literature proving that breast feed ing, even if only for a very brief time, is medically and psychologically beneficial for both mother and infant. The future mom would have none of it. Wamsutta (or whichever company it was) clearly came first. What seemed all the more remarkable and disconcerting was the response from our fellow expectant parents: No one, with the exception of the instructor and ourselves, saw anything wrong with the young woman's peculiar set of values. These other mothers also had jobs they planned to return to within months or weeks after delivery (the longest period any woman in the room was willing to spend exclusively caring for her newborn was six months). Thankfully, none of these other new mothers had sales conferences so soon afterward. *Sheets?*

The existence of parental instinct—paternal or maternal—is now open to debate. In her controversial 1981 book, *Mother Love,* Elisabeth Badinter, a professor at Paris's prestigious Ecole Polytechnique, argued that far from being innate, immutable, and biologically determined, mother love is a culturally conditioned phenomenon. Drawing on a fascinating range of sources, including religious and education tracts, family records, sociological surveys, and police reports, she chronicled four centuries of child care in France.

Badinter discovered that until Rousseau and the Romantics arrived in the late eighteenth century to create the concept of childhood, parental behavior oscillated between indifference and rejection. "On the eve of the Enlightenment," she writes, "mothers in cities and towns casually abandoned their newborn children to the care of wet-nurses. Deported to suburbs and the distant countryside where they would be boarded for an average of four years (often without ever seeing their mothers), these infants were confined to swaddling clothes and consigned to hovels that make Dickens' orphanages look like Montessori Schools. Half of these nurselings died before the age of two."

Badinter concludes that while the term "maternal instinct" has recently fallen out of favor, the feelings that underly it are as strong as ever. "If the 18th Century launched the idea of parental responsibility for a child's happiness, the 19th Century confirmed it, emphasizing the mother's role, while the 20th Century transformed it from maternal responsibility into maternal guilt." This emphasis on the mother's role, incidentally, is at the expense of Father's. Badinter adds that the economic and social pressures forcing Mother out of the house and into the workplace are also leading us to the inevitable conclusion that father love is as important for the socialization of children as mother love is. Yet the sad truth is that father is not giving that love, either.

Vinny Parisi was hailed as a pioneer, the embodiment of a "new phenomenon" in fathering, when he went on a six-month paternity leave in 1981. Parisi, a service representative for New Jersey Bell, was the first man to take part in a two-year, $350,000 international study by the Fatherhood Project of the Bank Street College of Education in Manhattan. The study, funded by the Ford Foundation, the Lèvi-Strauss Foundation, and the Rockefeller Family Fund, was a systematic attempt to determine practical ways the "New Fatherhood" might be made to work. "There's a convergence of thought in three different areas on the importance of fathering," said Joseph H. Pleck of the Wellesley College Center for Research, a co-director of the Bank Street project. "First, the father's impact on the child; second, the effects of fathering on women and on women's employment and third, the emergence of awareness among men that sex-role expectations have limited their participation in fathering."

The project's director, James A. Levine, noted that in the late 1970s "developmental psychologists have pointed repeatedly to the effects of a father's presence on children's cognitive, emotional, moral and sex-role development." And although there is a growing consensus about the importance of increasing the paternal role in child rearing, none of the current analyses pays serious attention to how it can be achieved.

"Clearly we're in a new stage," Levine adds. "The question is, how do you really change things? How do you get men involved? What are the supports that could make men more nurturant, for those men who want to be?"

Nuturant? Are we talking about people, or plants? Parisi, who in fact was the only man at New Jersey Bell to avail himself of the program, took the unpaid paternity leave for essentially economic reasons: His wife, a Bell supervisor, earned $9,000 more than he did.

Across the country, a number of corporations offer some sort of paternity leave for their employees. As with New Jersey Bell, the turnout is relatively small. The same situation exists in Sweden, where since 1974 the government's Parental Insurance System has offered Swedish fathers and mothers nine months of paid leave (at 90 percent of their previous salary), with a legally enforceable guarantee of reemployment at the same salary level. Less than 10 percent of eligible fathers took off one month or more. Swedish authorities figure that cultural conditioning plays a key role, and that some men feel they will be overlooked for future raises and promotions if they take the leave.

"I think we need to underscore that in this research," explained Michael E. Lamb, professor of psychology, psychiatry, and pediatrics at the University of Utah and another Fatherhood Project co-director. "We are not plugging father involvement. We're not saying it should be a goal for all fathers. But for those who may want greater involvement, what are the barriers to their participation?"

Do we have *any* indication that today's under-40 fathers want this "greater involvement"? In the face of feminism's New Woman, we dare not deny the need for a New Man, no matter that Vinny Parisi is the only one among thousands of New Jersey Bell employees interested enough to take paternity leave.

We have ample evidence that we may be pushing the pendulum back to the days of Badinter's indifferent parent. On weekends in Central Park, an army of uniformed nannies and denim-clad baby-sitters descends on the playgrounds, pushing their tiny charges in strollers and prams. New Mommy and New Daddy are concerned with more important matters, like prowling the housewares department of Bloomingdale's. Here we encounter the usual attitude: "It's the quality, not the quantity of time spent with the kid that counts." But studies have reinforced what common sense tells us: The person with the clout is the person who is *there*. A child encounters problems as they happen; there is no predicting when that might be. A parent is most effective when he or she is on hand to deal with them.

The soaring divorce rate has, as we noted earlier, added to the chaos surrounding Father in the 1980s. Awards of custody are now routinely contested by fathers not willing to separate themselves from their children's lives. Joint custody, by no means without its problems, nonetheless appears to be one logical way of ensuring that a child will receive the paternal exposure at last universally acknowledged to be of inestimable value. Even unmarried fathers have won legal custody of children in cases where the mother has put the child up for adoption.

Lucille Ball put it brilliantly: "Divorce is defeat." It leaves children feeling confused, uncertain. The best one can hope to do is minimize the damage. "One thing we know," says John Munder Ross. "Children suffer *terribly* if the father abandons them—either of his own volition or because of his wife—after divorce. A father's absence leads to heightened aggression, sexual identity confusion, classroom problems."

"Being a nurturing man makes you a wonderful father—but a very unhappy divorcé," said Dr. John W.

Jacobs, assistant clinical professor of psychiatry at the Albert Einstein College of Medicine. Dr. Jacobs is the author of a study described in the *American Journal of Psychiatry* that challenged a number of stereotypes about divorced fathers.

Not that all our notions about divorced dads are inaccurate. "Of course," conceded Jacobs, "there are many men who pack their bags and leave. I had simplistically thought that they were just happy-go-lucky playboys who didn't care about their children. But when they are interviewed, many say they just couldn't stand the pressures of separation.

"If his relationship with his children is threatened, a father can become wounded and panics," said Jacobs. It does not help matters for children to be used as a weapon in a divorce proceeding, either. When a wife's lawyers demand a hike in alimony or support payments in exchange for visiting privileges, for example, a father feels he is being victimized by a system geared to satisfying Mother. "His own lawyer tells him his wife has an eighty percent chance of getting custody, and that according to tradition, it is not presumed that he is a father once he's divorced," said Jacobs. "The result is stress and anxiety that can descend into panic."

Some fathers react by "fantasizing constantly about getting out, or becoming a beachcomber," Jacobs added. "Or they may actually disengage—they may move or start a new life, hoping to forget it all. Studies suggest that when they do this, it doesn't work in the long run."

So-called experts who are often consulted by troubled fathers in the midst of a divorce may aggravate the situation by recommending that a father completely disengage from his children. "Knowing what we know now," said Jacobs, "that would be tragedy. Fathers play an important role in the development of their children. Children deprived of their fathers due to divorce may suffer from a wide range of psychopathology. Similarly, divorced fathers often suffer from the loss of their children and, like their children, do better following divorce when there is a greater continuity of contact."

Again, we ask why a father's role in the child's psychological well-being has been dramatically downplayed by the psychiatric profession. "One of the reasons is the traditional stereotype of masculinity," explains Ross. "Psychiatrists, like everyone else, are prone to such stereotypes." Adds Dr. Ross: "There may be another factor. Many psychiatrists have been men who were fathers—and absent fathers. Especially the true analysts, who, during their long training, had given over much of the care of their children to mothers. Perhaps it has been difficult for them to address aspects of fatherhood."

The same people who are killing marriage are trying to do in Dad: the experts. Of their detrimental impact on man-woman relations, Maureen Green said, "Attempts to present all 'couple' problems as capable of solution, to encourage the notion that dissatisfaction in marriage can be solved by changing husbands and wives, or by transforming the partner we have, have brought marriage to the edge of ruin. The present high divorce rate is the work of the marriage perfectionists. The more we strive for an ideal marriage, the more certainly we shall finish marriage off."

This same principle applies to the way we are told to view fatherhood as a "skill," a technique to be honed and perfected like your golf swing. Actually, the parenting "skills" bear close resemblance to the teaching "skills" we have been saturated with, the how-to of it all. Hence the current glut on the market of how-to parenting books, each carrying the message that being a "good" parent is something you learn, being a "successful" parent is *something you work at.*

The rock-bottom assumption behind this avalanche of material is that our children have no minds of their own. They must be molded, shaped. It satisfies our own egos to know that we have total control over these short, pathetic creatures. But that is what the New Father wants to hear to assuage whatever feelings of guilt remain. He may not be around much, he may not know his child, but he has read all the books and gone to all the right parenting classes. He knows the how-to of it. He has the makings of a successful dad.

Explicit in all of this is the message that being a parent is rough stuff. "The enormous responsibility of fatherhood..." "The hardest job in the world..." "The most important and difficult job in society..." These are just a few of the phrases commonly used in parenting books and pamphlets. No one dare challenge the dictum that being a parent is, above all else, hard work. This plainly establishes today's fathers and mothers as noble, selfless beings. There is another purpose served, this in relation to Mother and Father's ongoing contest to decide who is the more deserving martyr. "This is the point," said William Reynolds, "where Mother's suffering with the kids meets Father's work agonies head-on in the Misery Derby. Mothers who openly admit the whole thing is fun are as rare as fathers who admit the same thing about working."

The mother of a 3-year-old son and a 1-year-old girl tells me she worries that her husband is not taking an active enough role in raising the kids. He works a standard 9 to 6 and is home on weekends, and, yes, he seems genuinely interested in the kids. But he hasn't gone to her parenting group, and he hasn't read any of the fathering books she bought for him. When I ask this woman what her relationship with her own father was like, she says "close, wonderful." And what fatherhood manual did he follow? "I guess he was just around," she replies, knowing for the first time that that is the same well-traveled road her husband has chosen as a father.

Being a father is not a job, and anyone who says it is or thinks it is communicates that to his child. Fatherhood is a state of being, and not only is it not that difficult, but the joys and rewards invariably outweigh all difficulties.

Home should not be a training camp. Approval or disapproval of our "success" at raising a child should not be sought from the outside world. A father lives with a woman, and he lives with his children. If there is ample opportunity for gentle symbiosis, for honest concern and warmth, then that is enough. Father does not *teach* his child to be creative, intelligent, humane. Creativity, intelligence, humanity, can only be allowed to develop. The contribution Father makes is one of subtle guidance.

Contrary to what is being widely preached by the high priests of pop psych, it is futile to try to get Mom and Dad to agree on every aspect of rearing the kids. Every household will have its pushover and its taskmaster, its grudge holder and its peacemaker, its brooder and its sprite. Parents are people too, and if they are forced to conform to some psychologist's idea of correct behavior, the child is quick to catch on.

Nothing is so crucial to the future of father and family, for that matter, than our ability to recognize the New Father for what he is: a fraud. Apart from taking a more active role in the delivery itself and a grudging willingness to take on a few chores during a baby's first couple of years, the American dad, like his wife, is spending less time with his own children, giving them less love. In a society that we claim is more child-oriented than ever, we have separated children from the fabric of our everyday lives. Instead of living and breathing the kids, as our parents did, we have placed little Michael in a bell jar where we can coldly observe and record everything about him. The thousands of minor decisions that our parents made to guide us through childhood were made with a minimum of fuss. Today we tend to reserve only the major decisions for ourselves, coldly deliberating ad nauseam in consultation with books and pediatricians and child psychologists. Those "minor" things—like whether Laura makes her bed or shares her candy bar with her brother, the niggling details that in fact mold our children's personalities and values, those we often leave to somebody else while Mommy and Daddy are away at work. Father is not forging brave new frontiers; he is backsliding. The answer lies with Old Dad.

How many times in this book have I talked about my anxious, fearful father, as if to deny that many of my best qualities came from him? How many times have I whined about his lack of involvement in his children's lives, of the emotional short shrift he and most of his contemporaries received from *frau und kinder* alike?

I can imagine that I invented myself, that whatever daring things I might have done in my life were done in spite of my father, not because of him. This is an impertinent thought. Wasn't he the one who left the Roman Catholic Church at 16 over issues of papal supremacy and confession and birth control, risking the wrath of his family? Didn't he take to the skies at 20, training in fabric-winged biplanes that had seen service in World War I? Didn't he fly dive-bombers in the Pacific during World War II, twice surviving a crackup on the deck of an aircraft carrier? And when that war and then the Korean conflict were over, didn't he test-fly the dangerous new double-prop helicopters that were the forerunner of the Hughies used in Vietnam twenty years later?

It is only now that I see, when somebody tells me I've "got guts" for pursuing a book or a story, that he is a main source of that courage.

The phantoms of fatherhood are elusive. If we consciously seek out the truth of our relationship, then our image of him is bound to change, sometimes from day to day. We try to divest Dad of the mystical properties that surround him in our memories. But his were the shoulders on which we perched to watch the parade, and there is no way of uprooting that from our subconscious. We continue to filter him through our emotions-of-the-moment. On Monday we are angry that he seems uncaring or aloof. On Thursday we rhapsodize about his courage and his humor.

My father keeps his medals and ribbons tucked away in a dresser drawer. On one wall of his den hang only a few mementos: his commission as an ensign, signed by then Navy Secretary James Forrestal and by Harry Truman, and a photograph of him at the controls of one of those deadly helicopters. I must dig through the rubble of a back closet to discover another photo, this one of my dad sitting in a cloth-winged biplane that looks as if it might have been flown by Orville and Wilbur at Kitty Hawk. Dad wears a leather jacket, leather flight cap, and the customary dashing white silk scarf. The year is 1937. "God!" he says in mock horror. "I look like the Red Baron." I keep a copy of the picture, which I had enlarged (more than one woman who saw the photo said he resembled Tyrone Power), at our apartment in New York.

Knowing that this Tyrone Power look-alike in the white scarf and the man made cautious by the Depression and by war are one in the same, I begin to realize that his personality was shaped by the great events of the century, events that transpired long before I ever appeared on the scene. Being a new father myself, the often cold reality of the father's lot is thrust upon me for the first time. And for the first time I am aware that, often regardless of how others in the family behave, a father will experience those moments when he feels emotionally quarantined, a stranger in his own house. Like his father before him, my father never voiced his bewilderment about why he felt this way. In that respect things haven't changed. My contemporaries still internalize their sorrow; today's New Father may read all the right magazine articles and attend the "parenting" classes with his wife, but he is nurturing the same old fears that haunted generations of his male forebears.

Before we can ever dispell those ghosts of the past, we must undertake to solve the psychological Rubik's Cube that is every person's relationship with his or her father. That is the magic: Not that we can ever make that Norman Rockwell painting come to life, but that in finally coming to terms with our real feelings for our fathers, we can truly make this generation—and maybe even the next—a generation of genuinely liberated men and women.

Finding Father is nothing less than an odyssey of self-discovery. We have learned to cast off the idealized image of Father as benevolent patriarch, but that is only a small first step toward understanding how much of Father survives in us. *He* did not make it easy; we have not made it easy for him. It was not part of Father Nature to communicate with the rest of the family, and indeed we did not invite him to share his hopes and fears, his dreams and doubts, with us. He was emotionally isolated, and the degree of that isolation had as much to do with the role Mother wished him to take as it did with the kind of father he might have wanted to be.

Within the carefully circumscribed boundaries that were set for him, Dad frequently had few choices. The course perhaps most frequently taken actually ran along two parallel tracks: Father as provider and Father as absentee disciplinarian. For too many families, he was judged largely on the basis of how comfortable he could make his wife and children. Beyond that, often all he had to do was exist as a strong authoritative figure so that Mom could occasionally unleash the familiar threat: "Wait till Daddy gets home."

Without trying, of course, Father was far, far more. He was our sexual, moral, and intellectual model—and often a model of neurotic and even psychotic behavior. He opened wide the window to the world that stretched before us, and his view of that world would forever color the way we came to see things. We would seek him, unknowingly, in surrogates and mentors. Friends and bosses and lovers would all be affected—for better or worse—by this first man in our lives.

Our search for Father, we discover, is unending. Plato said "the life which is unexamined is not worth living." The same is true of the father-child relationship. If we never bothered to analyze our father's impact on our lives, now is the time to start. If we thought we knew him and what impact he had—and still has—on our lives, it's time to look again. Father can be our most valuable partner in that endeavor. It is not enough for us to say we never really knew him, and let it go at that. For in fathoming him, we can at last fathom ourselves.

BIBLIOGRAPHY

Adams, Jane. *Women on Top*. New York: Hawthorn, 1980.

Appleton, William S. *Fathers and Daughters*. New York: Doubleday, 1981.

Badinter, Elisabeth. *Mother Love: Myth and Reality*. New York: Macmillan, 1981.

Bernstein, Stephen; Stern, Betty; Glaister, Joseph T.D. *Human Behavior*. April 1979, pp. 50–51.

Bettelheim, Bruno. *The Uses of Enchantment*. New York: Knopf, 1976.

Blos, P. "The Concept of Acting Out in Relation to the Adolescent Process," *Journal of American Academy of Child Psychiatry*. Vol. 2, (1963), pp. 118–43.

Brazelton, T. Berry; Yogman, M.W.; Als, H.; Tronick, E. *The Social Network of the Developing Child* (edited by M. Lewis and L. Rosenblum). New York: Plenum Press, 1978.

Brownmiller, Susan. *Against Our Will: Men, Women and Rape*. New York: Simon and Schuster, 1975.

Claiborne, Craig. *A Feast Made for Laughter*. New York: Doubleday, 1982.

Collins, Glenn. "A New Look at Life with Father," *The New York Times*. June 17, 1979.

———. "Paternity Leave: A New Role for Fathers," *The New York Times*. December 7, 1981.

———. "Daughters and Fathers," *Ms.* magazine, June 1979.

Cronkite, Kathy. *On the Edge of the Spotlight*. New York: Warner Books, 1980.

Dowling, Colette. *The Cinderella Complex: Women's Hidden Fear of Independence*. New York: Summit Books, 1981.

Erikson, Eric. *Childhood and Society* (second edition). New York: Norton, 1963.

———. "On the Generational Cycle," *International Journal of Psychoanalysis*. Vol. 61 (1980), pp. 213–223.

Fontaine, Joan. *No Bed of Roses*. New York: William Morrow, 1978.

Ford, Betty. *The Times of My Life*. New York: Harper & Row, 1978.

Ford, Gerald R. *A Time to Heal*. New York: Harper & Row, 1978.

Freud, Sigmund. *The Complete Psychological Works* (Standard Edition) (translated and edited by James Strachey). London: Hogarth Press, 1953–1974.

———. *The Origins of Psychoanalysis*. New York: Basic Books, 1954.

Fromm, Erich. *The Art of Loving*. New York: Bantam, 1972.

Green, Maureen. *Fathering*. New York: McGraw-Hill, 1976.

Gurwitt, Alan R. *Father and Child*. Boston: Little Brown, 1982.

Lenburg, Jeff. *Dustin Hoffman*. New York: St. Martin's Press, 1982.

Liddy. G. Gordon. *Will*. New York: St. Martin's Press, 1980.

Loren, Sophia. *Living and Loving*. New York: William Morrow, 1979.

Lorenz, Konrad. *On Aggression*. New York: Harcourt, Brace and World, 1966.

McGill, Michael E. *The 40- to 60-Year-Old Male*. New York: Simon and Schuster, 1982.

Merwin, W. S. *Unframed Originals*. New York: Atheneum, 1982.

Olivier, Laurence. *Confessions of an Actor*. New York: Simon and Schuster, 1982.

Ostrovsky, E. *Father to the Child*. New York: G. P. Putnam's Sons, 1959.

Paskowicz, Patricia. *Absentee Mothers*. Totowa, New Jersey: Allanheld, Osmund and Company, 1982.

Rather, Dan. *The Camera Never Blinks*. New York: William Morrow, 1977.

Reagan, Nancy. *Nancy*. New York: William Morrow, 1980.

Reagan, Ronald. *Where's the Rest of Me?* (1981 edition). New York: Karz Publishers, 1981.

Reynolds, William. *The American Father*. New York: Paddington Press, 1978.

Robertiello, Richard C. *A Man in the Making*. New York: Richard Marek, 1979.

Ross, John Munder. "The Development of Paternal Identity," *Journal of the American Psychoanalytical Association*. Vol. 23 (1975), pp. 783–817.

———. "A Review of Some Psychoanalytic Contributions on Paternity," *International Journal of Psychoanalysis*. Vol. 60 (1979), pp. 317–327.

———. *Father and Child* (with Stanley H. Cath and Alan Gurwitt). New York: Little Brown, 1982.

———. "Oedipus and the Laius Complex," *Psychoanalytic Study of the Child*. Vol. 37 (1982).

Salk, Lee. *My Father, My Son: Intimate Relationships*. New York: G. P. Putnam's Sons, 1982.

Saracheck, Bernard. *Journal of Economic History*. Vol. 38, No. 2.

Saroyan, Aram. *Last Rites*. New York: William Morrow, 1982.

Shepherd, Donald and Slatzer, Robert F. *Bing Crosby: The Hollow Man*. New York: Pinnacle Books, 1981.

Strasberg, Susan. *Bitter Sweet*. New York: G. P. Putnam's Son's, 1980.

Trudeau, Margaret. *Beyond Reason*. New York: Paddington Press, 1979.

Vonnegut, Mark. *The Eden Express*. New York: Praeger, 1975.

Weideger, Paula. "How Being a Daddy's Girl Helps Your Work Life, Hurts Your Love Life," *Mademoiselle*. September 1979.

White, Theodore H. *In Search of History*. New York: Harper & Row, 1978.

Yablonsky, Lewis. *Fathers and Sons*. New York: Simon and Schuster, 1982.